The Complete Idiot's Mixed Drink Reference: The Basics

Basic Highballs

The basic highballs are the most often requested mixed drinks. Mix them in a 9 oz. highball glass filled with ice. Start with the ice, add 1½ oz. of the spirit, and pour in the mixer. Do not stir carbonated mixers.

Bloody Mary: 1½ oz. vodka, tomato juice to ¾ full, splash lemon juice, dash Worcestershire sauce, dash Tabasco sauce, pinch salt and pepper, ¼ tsp. horseradish. Garnish with a celery stick and/or lime wedge.

Cape Codder: 1½ oz. vodka, cranberry juice to fill. Garnish with a lime wedge.

Cuba Libre: 1½ oz. rum, cola to fill. Garnish with a lime wedge.

Gin and Ginger Ale (also called **Gin Chiller**): 1½ oz. gin, ginger ale to fill. Garnish with a lime wedge.

Gin and Grapefruit Juice: 1½ oz. gin, grapefruit juice to fill.

Gin and Tonic: 1½ oz. gin, tonic water to fill. Garnish with a lime wedge.

John Collins: 1½ oz. whiskey, Collins mix to fill.

Orange Blossom: 1½ oz. gin, orange juice to fill.

Rum and Coke: 1½ oz. rum, cola to fill.

Rum and Ginger Ale (Rum Chiller): 1½ oz. rum, ginger ale to fill.

Rum and Tonic: 1½ oz. rum, tonic water to fill.

Rum Collins: 1½ oz. rum, Collins mix to fill. Garnish with a maraschino cherry and orange slice.

Rum Screwdriver: 1½ oz. rum, orange juice to fill.

Screwdriver: 1½ oz. vodka, orange juice to fill.

Sea Breeze: 1½ oz. vodka, grapefruit juice to ¾ full, cranberry juice to fill.

7 and 7: 1½ oz. blended whiskey, 7-Up to fill.

Tom Collins: 1½ oz. gin, Collins mix to fill. Garnish with a maraschino cherry and an orange slice.

Vodka and Ginger Ale (Vodka Chiller): 1½ oz. vodka, ginger ale to fill. Garnish with a lime wedge.

Vodka and Tonic: 1½ oz. vodka, tonic water to fill. Garnish with a lime wedge.

Whiskey and Ginger: 1½ oz. Bourbon, scotch, blended whiskey, or rye, ginger ale to fill.

alpha
books

Basic Cocktails

Serve cocktails on the rocks in a lowball glass. For straight-up drinks, use a cocktail glass.

Bacardi: Combine 1½ oz. light or gold Bacardi rum, ½ oz. lime juice, and ½ tsp. grenadine in a shaker with cracked ice. Shake vigorously, then pour into a chilled cocktail glass.

Daiquiri: Combine 2 oz. light rum, juice of ½ lime, and ½ tsp. sugar syrup in a shaker with ice. Shake vigorously, then strain into a chilled cocktail glass.

Gibson: Combine 2 oz. gin and ½ tsp. dry vermouth in a 12-ounce mixing glass at least half full of ice. Stir well, then strain into a chilled cocktail glass. Garnish with 2–3 pickled pearl onions.

Gimlet: Combine 2 oz. gin and ½ oz. fresh lime juice in a 12-ounce mixing glass. Stir well, then pour into the serving glass (serve on the rocks in a chilled lowball glass or straight-up in a cocktail glass). Garnish with a lime twist or lime slice.

Manhattan: Combine 2 oz. blended whiskey, ½ oz. sweet vermouth, and a dash Angostura bitters in a 12-ounce mixing glass. Stir well, then strain into a chilled cocktail glass and garnish with a maraschino cherry.

Manhattan (Dry): Combine 2 oz. blended whiskey, ½ oz. dry vermouth, and a dash Angostura bitters in a 12-ounce mixing glass. Stir well, then strain into a chilled cocktail glass and garnish with a maraschino cherry.

Margarita: Combine 1½ oz. tequila, ½ oz. triple sec, and juice of ½ large lime in a shaker with ice. Shake vigorously, then strain into a chilled cocktail glass that has been rimmed with coarse salt. Garnish with a lime slice.

Martini (Basic): Combine 2 oz. gin and ½ tsp. dry vermouth in a 12-ounce mixing glass at least half full of ice. Stir well, then strain into a chilled cocktail glass. Garnish with an olive or lemon twist.

Mint Julep: Put ½ teaspoon of sugar in the bottom of the serving glass (serve in an old-fashioned glass). Fill the glass one-third full with ice cubes. Add 2 ½ oz. bourbon. Stir. Add a splash of club soda. Garnish with the mint sprig.

Old-Fashioned: Combine 1½ oz. bourbon, splash of water, dash sugar syrup, and liberal dash Angostura bitters in the serving glass (serve on the rocks in an old-fashioned glass). Stir well.

Whiskey Sour: Combine 2 oz. bourbon or blended whiskey and 1 oz. sour mix in a shaker with cracked ice. Shake vigorously. Pour into a chilled cocktail or sour glass and garnish with a maraschino cherry and an orange slice.

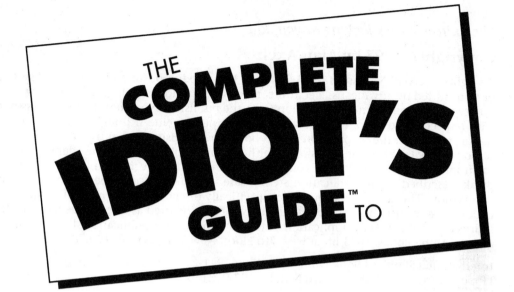

THE COMPLETE IDIOT'S GUIDE™ TO

Mixing Drinks

by The Players and Alan Axelrod

alpha books

A Division of Macmillan Reference USA
A Simon and Schuster Macmillan Company
1633 Broadway New York, NY 10019

For Anita—Here's looking at you, kid.

Copyright© 1997 by Alan Axelrod

International Standard Book Number: 0-02-861941-2
Library of Congress Catalog Card Number: 97-073154

02 01 00   8 7 6

Interpretation of the printing code: the rightmost number of the first series of numbers is the year of the book's printing; the rightmost number of the second series of numbers is the number of the book's printing. For example, a printing code of 97-1 shows that the first printing occurred in 1997.

Printed in the United States of America

Editorial Manager
Gretchen Henderson

Director of Editorial Services
Brian Phair

Development Editor
Jennifer Perillo

Production Editor
Phil Kitchel

Technical Editor
Andrew Gouldh

Illustrator
Judd Winick

Designer
Glenn Larsen

Cover Designer
Michael Freeland

Indexer
Chris Barrick

Production Team
*Tricia Flodder, Aleata Howard, Mary Hunt, Scott Tullis, Megan Wade,
Pamela Woolf*

Contents at a Glance

Contents

Foreword

A midnight martini suggested itself one snowy February at The Players. "Bombay, Felix," I said. Felix raised his eyebrows; my wife raised hell. Frank Sinatra laughed and said, "Me too."

A story goes with it, of course. Two stories, if you want to know the truth. I start with Elsa, my excellent wife, who hadn't heard me order one of those babies in 10 years.

My taste buds ran out on martinis, was why, and I never knew how come; all I did was swing to Johnnie Black. This satisfied my bride, who didn't think the juniper berry suited my life as a journalist.

"You don't mean it!" she cried, as Felix stirred the Bombay. "Just want to see if the bud is back," I said. I lifted the glass to my lips, closed my eyes, sipped and sipped, and said—"Marvelous."

"No no no," said Elsa. Sinatra beamed. Ol' Blue Eyes, who practically invented Jack Daniels, downed his Bombay and told us of the night he broke Lent with a martini in Palm Springs.

"I had a priest in for dinner," Sinatra said. "He had no idea I'd given up booze for Lent. I went behind the bar, mixed the martini, sipped it slowly—as you just did—and went 'Uhm uhm uhm.'" When I looked up, the priest's jaw was dropped so low he looked like he was ready for root canal. I think he figured I had the DTs."

What better place to deliver these anecdotes than in a book that features The Players. Where Charles Dana Gibson, the great illustrator, dropped in one twilight and asked Charley the bartender to mix him a "better martini." Charley dropped in an onion for an olive and the Gibson was born.

Which is not to say that the martini is the only mixed drink worthy of attention. This book reveals a society of cocktails and tells you how to mix 'em and enjoy 'em.

It comes at a propitious time. We are coming out of a politically correct world where the moralists and health fascists and prohibitionists would have us all drinking skim milk. But the children of the X Generation, bless them all, are thumbing their noses—drinking again, singing again, and having a helluva good time. I commend them as role models to their parents.

Of course, nobody says you have to drink. But if your liver says go, read on.

My Uncle Ben drank a quart of Johnnie Walker Black a day and lived into his late seventies. His brothers never took a sip and none of them made it to sixty.

"When I go, do me a favor," Ben said to me a couple of years before he met the Maker. "Put the Johnnie label on my stone and write under it, 'If it wasn't for him, I would've been here a whole lot earlier.'"

I told this story a couple of shots before Christmas at The Players. On Christmas morn a case of Johnnie Black showed up at my door. But there was no name on the card, just Somerset, the distributor. I called over there for the identity of the cheerful giver, but no dice. I panicked. If you don't acknowledge a gift like that, you make an enemy for life.

Late that afternoon, the phone rang. "I'm the public relations director for Somerset," a guy said. "I sent you the case of Black Label."

"I never met you," I said.

"I was a guest at The Players when you told that story about your uncle. You didn't see me, but I heard you, and it's the best booze story I ever heard. So drink up on us!"

The poor fellow died soon after, or I'd be in free flow forever. By the way, didja hear the one about...

Read this book, there's a million of 'em.

—Sidney Zion
NY Daily News columnist

Introduction

The very last person who should pick up a *Complete Idiot's Guide* is a complete idiot. These books are for people smart enough and sensitive enough to *feel* like complete idiots about certain subjects. Most people find quantum physics an intimidating subject, but even more are snowed by mixology: the art and science of creating alcoholic—we prefer the term *spiritous*—drinks. What liquor to buy, what drinks to mix, how to measure them, how to mix them, how to pour them, how to serve them, to whom to serve them, and how to plan a party—these are bewilderments sufficient to reduce Albert Einstein himself to a quivering mass of Jell-O. (By the way, you will find recipes for splendid Jell-O Shots in Appendix B.)

The Complete Idiot's Guide to Mixing Drinks is not just about buying, measuring, mixing, and pouring. It's about confidence and authority. It's about acquiring the expertise required to serve—and savor—spiritous drinks with maximum pleasure.

And while confidence, authority, and pleasure are the principal aims of this book, you'll also find what every adult needs to know about drinking and serving drinks responsibly. Included, too, are generous chapters for calorie counters and those who wish to enjoy adult beverages *without* alcohol.

How to Use This Book

The first part of this book gives you all the background you need to start mixing drinks and to enjoy—responsibly—the drinks you mix. Most of the rest of the book gives you the recipes for the most interesting and popular drinks, arranged by type of spirit. Special sections discuss dessert drinks, drinks for the calorie conscious, and drinks for non-drinkers. You'll also find advice on planning and managing a party and even what to do if you decide to pursue a part-time or full-time bartending career.

Part 1, "Belly Up to the Bar!," includes chapters on what you might like to drink and how you should drink it. You'll also find information on just what happens to you when you drink, how to prevent a hangover, and how to serve and enjoy liquor responsibly. For the truly curious, there is also a chapter on the chemistry and history of drinkable alcohol. Chapters 4 and 5 are a concise course on the basic equipment of bartending—including glassware, garnishes, mixers, and spirits—and on the secrets of measuring, mixing, and pouring like a pro.

Part 2, "Clear Choices," contains chapters on mixing drinks using the clear or so-called "white" spirits, gin and vodka. Included is a special chapter devoted to the martini in its many varieties.

Part 3, "Whiskey World," is about making drinks with bourbon, Tennessee Whiskey, American and Canadian blended whiskeys, rye, scotch, and Irish whiskey. Connoisseurship, including such key issues as straight versus blended bourbons and blended versus single-malt scotches, is thoroughly covered, together with the historical background of these great traditional spirits.

Part 4, "Almost Tropical," covers two of the most popular but least understood spirits: rum and tequila. In addition to the most popular tropical drinks, you'll find a discussion of the wide variety of rums available from New England to the Carribean islands and the nations of Central and South America. As for tequila, it emerges here from the murk of its undeservedly shady reputation and into the sunlight as one of the world's most delectable—and carefully crafted—spirits, the basis of many delicious drinks.

Part 5, "Just Desserts," presents a panoply of after-dinner and dessert drinks, made with brandy and with liqueurs. You'll also learn about creating comforting hot drinks and spectacular flaming drinks, as well as *pousse-cafés*, the multilayered masterpieces served in pony glasses to *oohs* and *ahhs* of appreciation.

Part 6, "A Fresh Round," contains a pair of chapters for those who want to create tempting drinks without losing count (or control) of their caloric intake, and for those who want to create and enjoy satisfying, alcohol-free adult beverages. But the section starts off with a new look at champagne, wine, and beer, and how you can combine them with "hard" liquor to create new and exciting drinks.

Part 7, "Putting It All Together," begins with a chapter on planning a party—including what spirits to buy and how much to buy. What follows is a chapter devoted to elevating punch from a dull substitute for individual drinks to the centerpiece of the party. This section concludes with advice for those who want to make the transition from amateur host to professional bartender, whether full- or part-time.

At the back of the book, you'll find **Appendix A: Buzzed Word Glossary**, a compendium of words either essential or helpful to choosing, serving, and enjoying liquor, and **Appendix B: Last Call**, a catalog of some new or out-of-the-ordinary drinks.

No one will be offended if you don't read this book cover to cover. Look at the chapters that interest you—or consult the Index for an alphabetical list of the drinks you want to make.

Extras

In addition to recipes, advice, guidance, and explanations, this book offers other types of information to help you mix drinks and enjoy the "pleasures of the spirit." These include definitions of key terms, tips from the world of professional bartending, a collection of popular toasts, choice barroom humor, and select drinking anecdotes from the annals of the Player's Club. Look for these easy-to-recognize signposts in boxes:

Buzzed Words
The vocabulary of bartending, **mixology**, and liquor.

Toast
Toasts—popular, unique, sincere, funny.

Quick One
Barroom humor.

Bar Tips
Expert advice on the finer points of mixology.

Players Script
Drinking anecdotes from The Players.

Special Thanks to the Technical Reviewer...

The Complete Idiot's Guide to Mixing Drinks was reviewed by a professional bartender who double-checked the technical accuracy of what you'll learn here, to help us ensure that this book gives you everything you need to know to become a confident bartender.

Special thanks are extended to Andrew Gouldn, self-proclaimed "King of the Random Job," from cooking to cleaning, acting to acting up, decorating sets to deconstructing them. Along the way he has found a need for a bartender in every port (pun intended), including an extended run at The Players.

Trademarks

All terms mentioned in this book that are known to be or are suspected of being trademarks or service marks have been appropriately capitalized. Alpha Books and Macmillan General Reference cannot attest to the accuracy of this information. Use of a term in this book should not be regarded as affecting the validity of any trademark or service mark. The following trademarks and service marks have been mentioned in this book:

7-Up, Absolut, Angostura, Appleton, Asbach-Uralt, Bacardi and Company, Bailey's Original Irish Cream, Benedictine, Bermudez, British Navy Pusser's, Cacique Ron Anejo, Captain Morgan, Chartreuse, Cherry Marnier, Coca-Cola, Cointreau, Dr. Pepper, Dubonnet, Finlandia, Glenfiddich, Glenmorangle, Grand Marnier, Hudson's Bay, Irish Mist, K.W.V., Knockando, Laphroaig, Lemon Hart & Sons, Macallan, Mandarine Napoleon Liqueur, Metaxa, Midori, Mount Gay, Myers's Rum, Old Overholt, Pernod, Peter Heering, Peychaud's , Pisco, Presidente, Rhum Barbancourt, Ron Medellin, Rose's Lime Juice, Seagram's 7-Crown, Smirnoff, Stolichnaya, The Glenlivet, Tia Maria, Wyborowa, Zubrowka.

Part 1
Belly Up to the Bar!

Okay, so maybe you don't need a book to tell you why, what, and how you should drink, but that's how this opening section begins: with some reasons for drinking, a descriptive inventory of the range of distilled spirits, and some guidelines for enhancing your enjoyment of liquor.

Handling, serving, and consuming alcoholic beverages are all adult activities, and this section discusses what happens when you drink, how you can prevent or minimize a hangover, and, most important, how to serve and enjoy liquor responsibly.

For those who like to poke around under the hood of their cars or take the cover off the computer to see what's inside, we've included a chapter on the chemistry and history of alcohol, starting on the molecular level and reaching back in time to prehistoric spit as an agent of fermentation.

Returning to the more practical present, you'll find a thorough discussion of everything the home bar and bartender needs, including the correct glassware, essential garnishes, requisite mixers, and choice spirits. Then you can find out how to use all these things—how to stir, shake, measure, and generally move like a pro.

Chapter 1

What to Drink and Why

In This Chapter

> ➤ Three reasons to drink (if you want to)

> ➤ Respecting the rights of non-drinkers

> ➤ Liquor: your basic choices

> ➤ How to taste, judge, and savor your drink

The great jazz trumpeter Louis Armstrong had a celebrated exchange with a society matron, who asked him to define *jazz*. "Lady," Satchmo is said to have replied, "if you gotta ask, you'll never know."

There are those who will tell you that something like this is also the appropriate reply to the question, "What should I drink?"

But we won't tell you this.

While this book is mostly about mixing drinks, before we get to the *how*, we think the *what* and the *why* are well worth talking about. Here goes.

Should You Have a Drink?

Going into the corner bar and ordering an aqua vitae will produce unpredictable results. If the bartender is sufficiently surly, at the very least your request will elicit a dirty look.

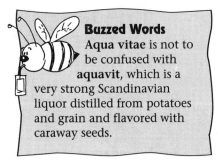

Buzzed Words

Aqua vitae is not to be confused with **aquavit**, which is a very strong Scandinavian liquor distilled from potatoes and grain and flavored with caraway seeds.

If, however, your neighborhood mixologist is up on his Medieval Latin, he will recognize *aqua vitae* as a term for strong distilled alcohol, such as whiskey or brandy. Perhaps he will go on to discuss the etymology of this phrase. *Aqua* is, of course, water, and *vitae* is a form of *vita*—life: Water of Life.

For untold centuries, *spirits* have been associated with vitality, conviviality (another word rooted in a Latin original, *vivere*, "to live"), life, or, more accurately, the enhancement of life's pleasures.

A Toast to Tradition!

To partake in alcoholic refreshment is to partake in tradition. Drinking is part and parcel of our culture. Alcohol, in the form of sacramental wine, plays a role in both the Jewish and Christian traditions, and other alcoholic beverages figure in the rites and rituals of numerous Native American and non-Western religions, both ancient and modern.

Buzzed Words

Spirits or **spirit** is a generic term for an alcoholic beverage based on distilled **liquor**.

In secular life, too, liquor plays a kind of sacramental role. Good friends traditionally cement their friendship with a drink. Business deals are "made official" with good-faith sips all around. Bride and groom are toasted with champagne or whatever else is handy. And on and on. Drinking is part of our social language.

Our Pleasure

As you will see in the next chapter, alcohol is a depressant. But first among the mind's faculties to be depressed are those that inhibit you, that say "No," that draw you back from the company of others, that check your speech and actions. The paradoxical result is that, taken in moderation, this depressant *seems* to invigorate, energize, and generally cheer you. In moderation, drink heightens your enjoyment of food, music, your surroundings, and the people you're with. Even though few drinkers enjoy every kind of liquor, so many varieties of spirits can be mixed with so many other flavorful things in so many ways that just about everyone can take pleasure in the drink itself—in its taste and in its glow.

Bar Tips

When it comes to alcohol, the operative word—you guessed it—is *moderation*. As is true of many adult pleasures, drinking can enhance your life or it can destroy it. Irresponsible drinking can reach well beyond your life to destroy other lives as well. Please read the next chapter carefully.

A Good Time Had by All

Conviviality—a fondness for good times among good company—can be enhanced by moderate drink. Most of us converse more freely (for better or worse) and are more emotionally generous basking in the glow of a drink. Alcohol has a long history as a social lubricant. Sharing spirits with friends can create social bonds and a sense of community.

The entrance to The Players in Gramercy Park, New York. The Players is famed for its history and celebrated clientele of actors, writers, and artists.

(Courtesy of Gurdon Howe, artist)

But It's Okay Not To

Despite the long lineage of alcoholic beverage, its firm position in our culture, and the pleasure it can afford, many choose not to drink. Some people make the choice for reasons of diet, health, religion, moral belief, or simply taste. As you would want others to respect your choice to drink, you must absolutely respect the choice not to drink. Never coax, cajole, or urge alcohol on anyone. Not even jokingly. If you are hosting a party or tending bar, always have a variety of appealing non-alcoholic beverages on hand. Offer these freely. (See Chapter 21.)

Bar Tips
Sophisticated hosts have always known that it is okay not to drink. These days, it's more okay than ever, as many people just feel better without alcohol in their lives. A professional bartender will not hesitate to honor a request for a non-alcoholic drink, and, certainly, no host should feel insulted if a guest chooses not imbibe.

What Should You Drink?

The short answer is you'll have a much better idea once you read this book, which offers a wide range of potables. But mixed drinks are to the drinker what compounds are to the chemist. Before you can appreciate them fully, you need to get acquainted with the elements from which they are made. Let's start by differentiating hard liquor from beer and wine, then explore the "elements."

Hard Liquor vs. Beer and Wine

An alcoholic beverage is *hard* if it contains a relatively high concentration of alcohol, as measured by its *proof.* An ounce of 100-proof bourbon (or other 100-proof hard liquor), for example, contains as much alcohol as 12 ounces of beer, five ounces of wine, or three ounces of sherry. Wow! Does that make bourbon *12 times* more potent than beer?

> **Buzzed Words**
>
> **Hard liquor** is a beverage with a high alcoholic content. Gin, vodka, bourbon, sour mash whiskey, scotch, blended whiskey, rye, rum, and tequila are the most common hard liquors.
>
> **Proof** is the alcoholic content of a spirit. It is determined by multiplying the percentage of alcoholic content by two, so for example, liquor that is 40 percent alcohol is 80 proof.

The answer is yes—and no. Yes, an ounce of bourbon is 12 times more alcoholic than an ounce of beer. But who drinks a single ounce of beer? A usual "serving" of bourbon is one ounce, whereas a usual serving of beer is 12 ounces: one bottle. So a "serving" of bourbon is roughly equivalent to a "serving" of beer in terms of alcoholic content.

Your choice of hard liquor versus beer or wine should be based on taste or occasion rather than on alcoholic content. For example, a bourbon or other hard liquor can make a pleasant prelude to a dinner, but you probably won't want to wash down the meal with spirits. Beer or wine, in contrast, go well with food.

Straight vs. Mixed

Another choice to make is whether you want your drink mixed or straight. You can mix hard liquor with a bewildering range of other fluids: water, carbonated water, fruit juices, soft drinks, other hard liquors, and even wine and beer. If you choose not to mix the liquor with anything, you are drinking it *straight* or *neat*. If you pour it over ice, you're drinking it *on the rocks*.

Why mix liquor with anything?

Well, why not? You may take your beef "straight"—let's say a plain, medium-rare New York Strip—or you may enjoy it "mixed"—with pâté de foie gras and served in a pastry shell as beef Wellington. As sauces and other ingredients add character to basic foods, mixers add a variety of flavors, textures, and sensations to basic liquor. Moreover, some people like to drink, but they really don't care for the taste of hard liquor. For these folks, mixers make the alcohol palatable.

Finally, while some mixed drinks combine two or more alcoholic beverages into a particularly potent blend, non-alcoholic mixers dilute the alcoholic content of the drink—an effect some people want. This, however, can be deceptive. Sugary mixers do dilute the alcohol, but the sugar also tends to accelerate the body's absorption of the alcohol, speeding its entry into the bloodstream. The result may be more of a "buzz" than you expected.

However, there's nothing wrong with an unadorned New York Strip. If you like the taste of alcohol, the best way for you to enjoy a drink may be straight, straight-up (poured over ice to chill, then poured into a glass, without the ice cubes), or on the rocks. That said, it's time to turn from the "compounds" and look at the "elements": the basic varieties of hard liquor.

Transparently Yours

Gin is a clear spirit, whose name is derived from the French *genièvre*, meaning juniper berry. There's a good reason for this: gin is produced from corn and rye (sometimes other grains as well) distilled into *neutral* (flavorless, odorless, and colorless) spirits, then flavored with juniper berries. Various gin distillers add other botanicals as well to produce a surprisingly wide variety of subtle flavors.

Some people love the taste of gin; others can't stand it. Spirits that evoke this kind of love-hate relationship are typically called "drinker's drinks." If you plan to drink gin in a martini or on the rocks (it is rarely consumed straight, though it may be drunk straight-up), you'd better like its taste. That's less important if you drink it with a strongly flavored mixer.

From Russia (and Poland, Finland, and Sweden) with Love

Another clear spirit, vodka is strongly associated with Russia, although it was probably invented in Poland and is now produced in several countries—most notably Sweden, Finland, and the United States—as well as Russia.

The word *vodka* is a "diminutive" form of the Russian *zhizennia voda*, which means *aqua vitae*, which (thanks to our classically educated barkeep) you know means "water of life."

Bar Tips
Should you buy expensive, premium-label liquors or cheaper "bar brands"? This is a matter of taste and budget. In general, the cheaper brands will taste just as good as the more expensive brands when mixed with fruit juices or soft drinks, whereas the premium brands are usually more enjoyable if you're drinking the liquor straight, on the rocks, or mixed with water, club soda, or certain other alcoholic beverages.

Buzzed Words
Distillation is a process of evaporating a liquid, then condensing the vapor to purify and concentrate the liquid, called the **distillate**. Manufacturers of spirits are called **distillers**. The distillate is a **neutral spirit**—flavorless, odorless, and colorless alcohol. **Aging** in wood and, sometimes, the addition of natural and artificial flavorings imparts color, aroma, and flavor to such spirits as whiskey and dark rum.

Buzzed Words
Malting is the practice of allowing the grain (usually barley) to sprout before fermentation. In whiskey production, this produces a variety of characteristic flavors in the finished product. **Fermenting** is the chemical process whereby complex organic substances are split into relatively simple compounds. In the manufacture of alcohol, special yeasts are used to ferment—convert—the starches and sugars of grain (or some other organic substance) into alcohol.

Russians use diminutives to name people and things they really like (for example, "Nikolai" is Nicholas, but "Kolya" is "Nicky"), and *vodka* may be translated as "dear little water" or "dear little water of life."

Like gin, vodka is distilled from grain—although almost any fermented carbohydrates can be used, including potatoes—to a very high proof (at least 190). The resulting *grain neutral spirits* are cut with distilled water to a strength of 80 to 100 proof and then charcoal filtered to remove taste.

Whereas gin is deliberately flavored with juniper berries and other botanicals, the distillation, dilution, and filtering process used to make vodka deliberately *removes* all aroma and taste. Almost. Dedicated vodka drinkers will tell you that different brands have distinctive characters, and this is certainly true, because the quality of the raw materials varies. Nevertheless, drinking vodka straight or on the rocks is not a very flavorful experience. This is precisely what appeals to may vodka drinkers, however, who enjoy the light, clean, refreshing "non-taste" of this spirit.

Whiskey

Whiskey comes in a wide range of varieties and variations in taste; however, all whiskey production involves the same four basic steps:

Buzzed Words
Whiskey versus **whisky:** American and Irish distillers spell the word with an *e*, while Scotch and Canadian distillers jump right from the *k* to the *y*.

1. Malting
2. Fermenting
3. Distilling
4. Aging

The last step, the aging process—in wooden barrels—turns the clear distillate tawny brown and imparts whiskey's characteristic flavor and aroma. Aging is a chemical reaction between the alcohol and the wood; while time marches on, the aging process stops as soon as the whiskey is bottled.

We will discuss the subject of whiskey varieties in much greater detail in Part 3, but here's a quick rundown on the range of whiskies available. Let's begin with the American varieties:

➤ *Bourbon* derives its name not directly from the French royal dynasty interrupted by the Revolution and Napoleon Bonaparte, but from Bourbon County, Kentucky, where this liquor originates. Only whiskey made in Kentucky can be called bourbon, just as only the sparkling wine originating in the Champagne region of France can properly be called champagne.

Bourbon is distilled from *mash*, a fermentable, starchy mixture, consisting of at least 51 percent corn, with the balance of the mash consisting of another grain (typically rye and barley). Bourbon is aged in oak barrels—the cheaper stuff for as little as two years, and the premium brands for up to 12. It is bottled at 80 to 90 proof, and no more than 160 proof. The typical flavor is dark and rich, with a distinct undertone of corn.

> **Buzzed Words**
> **Mash** is the starchy mixture—usually including grain and corn, or some other organic substance—that is subjected to fermentation to produce alcohol.

➤ *Corn whiskey* varies from bourbon in that the mash must contain at least 80 percent corn rather than 51 percent. It tends to taste sweeter and feel thicker than bourbon. Not surprisingly, the taste of corn is more recognizable.

➤ *Sour mash whiskey* comes from Tennessee (and thus may be termed "Tennessee Whiskey"). The mash from which it is distilled contains some portion of previously fermented yeast (fresh yeast produces *sweet mash*). The result is a liquor with a mellower, smoother taste and feel than bourbon. This is ideal "sippin'" whiskey.

➤ *Rye whiskey* (usually just called *rye*) is made from a mash that contains at least 51 percent rye grain. Its aggressive, sharp-toothed, somewhat musty flavor has appealed to fewer and fewer people over the years, and it has a reputation as a *real* drinker's drink.

➤ *Bottled-in-bond whiskey* is "straight" whiskey bottled at 100 proof and aged a minimum of four years in a warehouse that is bonded by the United States government.

➤ *Scotch* is—surprise, surprise—the whisky of Scotland and perhaps the most popular kind of whisky in the world. Based on barley (and sometimes corn), scotch acquires its characteristic smoky flavor as a result of the barley malt's having been roasted over fires fueled by peat. The smoked malt is then mixed with water to form the mash, which is then fermented, distilled, and aged for at least three years in uncharred oak barrels or in casks left over from sherry aging.

> **Buzzed Words**
> Don't confuse **straight whiskey** with ordering "whiskey, straight" (that is, "neat," with neither ice, water, nor a mixer). The mash for straight whiskey contains at least 51 percent of a certain grain: straight malt whiskey mash contains 51 percent barley; straight rye, 51 percent rye; and straight bourbon, 51 percent corn. However, straight corn whiskey is made from mash that contains 80 percent corn.

The better scotches are aged at least 12 years, and the premium brands, called *single malt*, contain only whisky distilled at one time and by a single distiller, as opposed to *blended scotch*, which consists of a blend of whiskies distilled at various times by more than one distiller. Scotch is usually bottled at 80 to 86 proof. The flavor of scotch—especially single-malt versus blends—varies so widely as to defy description. In general, though, it is at once sweeter and smokier than bourbon, and you should know that *most* scotch drinkers don't care much for bourbon and vice versa.

Buzzed Words
Single-malt scotch contains only whisky distilled at one time and by a single distiller. **Blended scotch** consists of a combination of whiskies distilled at various times by more than one distiller.

➤ *Irish whiskey* is becoming increasingly popular. Like scotch, it is based chiefly on barley and is produced by a similar roasting process; however, the malt is roasted in coal-fired kilns rather than over open peat fires, so it does not acquire the smoky flavor—although it tastes more like scotch than like bourbon. Aged five to ten years in used sherry casks, Irish whiskey is bottled at 86 proof. If you like scotch, you'll probably like Irish whiskey; it has a sweeter, sharper flavor.

➤ *Canadian whisky* is blended from a variety of straight whiskies *and* neutral, flavorless whiskies. You'd think the taste of such a blend would be more complex and richer than the taste of unblended whiskies. Not true. Canadian whisky has a simpler, lighter taste than either scotch or bourbon and is usually consumed in mixed drinks rather than straight.

Rum

Rum is produced chiefly in Puerto Rico, Barbados, and Jamaica, and the process varies from place to place, with Puerto Rican rums being the lightest and driest, Barbados rums darker and heavier, and Jamaican rum quite dark, heavy, and sweet. These differences will be discussed in greater detail in Chapter 13. All rum is based on sugarcane juice and molasses, which is fermented and distilled, and sometimes aged as well. It is bottled at anywhere from 80 proof to a throat-charring 150 proof.

Buzzed Words
Blended whiskey can be a confusing term. A blended whiskey may be a combination of **straight** whiskies and neutral, flavorless whiskies (this is true of Canadian whisky) or it may be a combination of similar whiskey products made by different distillers at different times (as in blended scotch).

Tequila

Tequila has a rather shady reputation, with suggestions that it is akin to the illicit hallucinogen mescaline.

Wrong.

To be called *tequila*, this liquor must meet strict standards set by the Mexican government, which means (among other things) that it must be made from blue agave plants (the blue variety of *Tequila weber*) grown in an officially designated area, centered on the town of Tequila. As you can't get blood from a turnip, neither can you get mescaline from agave. The Mexican government further decrees that the tequila mash must contain 51 percent blue agave juice (the balance may be as much as 49 percent sugarcane juice), must be fermented, then *twice* distilled, and, finally, charcoal filtered. It may then be bottled or aged from one to seven years in used oak barrels before bottling.

Aged tequila, which is called *anejo*, is golden rather than clear, and generally has a richer flavor that makes it more agreeable straight or on the rocks than unaged tequila, which is better consumed with a mixer. Tequila imported into the United States is 80 proof, while that sold domestically in Mexico is 96 proof.

Savor, Don't Swill

Like fine wines, good liquor, whether consumed straight or mixed with other things, is usually best enjoyed when it is sipped and savored. The exceptions are certain "shooter" drinks and other drinks served in a shot glass, which are meant to be downed in a single, eye-popping, table-banging swallow.

The Nose Knows

The art of wine tasting provides another guideline for savoring good liquor. *Nose* is the term wine connoisseurs use to describe the *aroma* (in younger, simpler wines) or *bouquet* (in older, more complex wines) of the beverage. Take time to enjoy the "nose" of a good glass of liquor. Scent should be very much a part of the drinking experience.

"Professional" Tasting

If you want to get more serious about enjoying liquor, here are some suggestions. Evaluate and compare unmixed spirits this way:

➤ Into a very clean, thoroughly rinsed sherry glass (called a *copita*; glassware is discussed in Chapter 4), mix equal portions of the liquor under consideration with demineralized, distilled water. Use a different glass for each liquor you evaluate.

➤ Look at the color. Is it appealing?

➤ Evaluate the aroma—the "nose."

➤ Savor the flavor—as well as the body and the aftertaste.

Bar Tips
We've all heard about "The Worm" in "real Mexican" tequila. Well, there *is* a worm, but not in tequila. It is often put in mescal, which is made from agave, but not necessarily in the Tequila region or under government control. The worm lives in the agave plant, and it is traditional to throw one into each bottle. Despite its name, mescal has nothing to do with mescaline, either.

Bar Tips
When taste-testing liquor, it is important to ensure that no soap or detergent residue left over from washing remains in the glass. Do not use ice, which may impart an unwanted flavor to the drink; the cold temperature will also dull the tastebuds.

The components of flavor, body, and aftertaste include:

➤ Intensity of flavor

➤ Smoothness; also called "finish"

➤ "Off-tastes"—suggesting chemical additives and including excessive woodiness (from the barrel), sweetness, acidity, astringency, musty flavor (unavoidable to some extent in rye), corkiness, or bitterness.

➤ "High notes"—pleasant characteristics, including overtones of spice, a nutty flavor, and so on. It is fun to try to identify overtones as specifically as possible.

In contrast to unmixed liquors, evaluating mixed drinks does not involve as great a need for a sophisticated palate. Pay attention to the following:

➤ Appearance: Does the drink *look* appealing?

➤ Aroma: Does it have an appealing, inviting smell?

➤ Flavor: Does it taste great?

➤ Refreshment value: Is it refreshing?

➤ Aftertaste: Is it pleasant or not?

➤ Staying power: Does the drink taste good sip after sip? Or does it quickly cloy?

Pacing

In the next chapter, we will discuss responsible drinking and responsible bartending. One key to responsible drinking—and to maximizing the enjoyment of liquor—is to *pace* yourself. Alcoholic beverages, even those mixed with sweet, refreshing, and delicious juices, are not meant to be guzzled or consumed in rapid succession, one after the other. The consequences of not pacing yourself range from making a fool of yourself, to getting sick, to getting dangerously drunk and becoming party to a potentially lethal accident. At the very least, poorly paced drinking greatly diminishes the pleasure to be derived from the liquor. Enjoy responsibly.

The Least You Need to Know

➤ In moderation, drinking is a traditional pleasure that can enhance your social life, but it should never be considered a prerequisite to a good time.

➤ Hard liquor has a greater percentage of alcohol by volume than wine or beer, but, in terms of the amount of wine, beer, or hard liquor that constitutes a "serving," is neither more nor less potent.

➤ The range of hard liquor choices is great. If you have any interest in drinking at all, you will almost certainly find more than one basic liquor to please you.

➤ With a few exceptions, hard liquor is best sipped and savored, rather than gulped down Wild West-style.

Chapter 2

Acting Like an Adult: Responsible Drinking and Responsible Bartending

In This Chapter

➤ What your body does with alcohol

➤ How to sober up

➤ Dealing with a hangover

➤ Drinking and your health

➤ Your responsibilities as a drinker and a host

➤ Drinking and driving

If you enjoy drinking, you are not alone. Two-thirds of adult Americans consume alcoholic beverages. Most of them do so responsibly enough to avoid ravaging their lives and the lives of others. However, more than 10 million suffer from alcoholism, and each year drunk drivers kill 20,000 people on the streets and highways of the United States.

Drinking should be a part of good times and civilized company. But the decision to drink—and to serve drinks—is one of the heaviest responsibilities an adult will ever take on.

A Physiology Lesson

Take a drink, and the alcohol is immediately absorbed into your bloodstream. Unlike most other substances you ingest, alcohol does not require digestion before it is absorbed and circulated. While it circulates throughout the body, alcohol is diffused in proportion to the water content of the various tissues and organs, appearing in greatest concentration in the blood and the brain.

> **Bar Tips**
> You've heard the advice before: Don't drink on an empty stomach. The presence of food in the stomach does delay the absorption of alcohol. However, mixing alcohol with carbonated beverages actually speeds absorption.

Just as it is quick to soak the alcohol up, your body wastes little time in starting to eliminate the substance. Some alcohol—very little—is exhaled, and a slightly larger amount is secreted in sweat. Even more is excreted by the kidneys and (as anyone who has anxiously queued up for the rest room at the local club knows) soon finds its way out in urine. Nevertheless, no more than 10 percent of the alcohol is eliminated through breathing, sweating, and urination.

The rest—at least 90 percent—is processed metabolically, chiefly by the liver. In the liver, enzymes convert the alcohol to *acetate*, which enters the bloodstream and is eventually transformed into carbon dioxide and water and then disposed of.

In a man of average size, about half an ounce of alcohol—the equivalent of an ounce of hard liquor, a 12-ounce bottle of beer, or a four-ounce glass of wine—can be *metabolized* (processed and eliminated) per hour. If you drink more than one drink per hour, unprocessed alcohol will accumulate in the bloodstream and continually affect the organs, particularly the brain.

> **Buzzed Words**
> **Blood-alcohol concentration** (abbreviated BAC and sometimes called blood-alcohol level or BAL) is the concentration of alcohol in the blood, expressed as the weight of alcohol in a fixed volume of blood. It is used as an objective measure of intoxication.

Let's go back to that average-size man and say he drinks four ounces of 100-proof bottled-in-bond whiskey within an hour. This will put 1 1/2 ounces of alcohol in his body, and, by the end of the hour, the concentration of alcohol in his blood will be 0.07 percent. If he continues to drink—another four ounces in the next hour—the blood-alcohol concentration will rise to 0.11 percent.

So what?

At 0.05 blood-alcohol concentration, inhibitions fade, and judgment becomes clouded. At 0.10, speech is slurred, and staggering is apparent. Behold! A drunk.

The following table shows you what you can expect at various blood alcohol levels.

Immediate Effects of Alcohol Consumption

BAC (percent)	Probable Effect
.05	Loss of inhibitions; clouded judgment
.10	Impairment of coordination; staggering; slurred speech; visual impairment
.20	Senses dulled; loss of control over emotions
.30	Blackout; possible loss of consciousness
.35–.45	Coma; possible death
.60	Death

The following table shows you how much drinking it takes to get to each level.

Alcohol Consumption, Gender, Weight, and BAC

Alcohol	Drinks/hour*	Female 100 lbs.	Female 150 lbs.	Male 150 lbs.	Male 200 lbs.
$^1/_2$ oz.	1	.045	.03	.025	.019
1 oz.	2	.09	.06	.05	.037
2 oz.	4	.18	.12	.10	.07
3 oz.	6	.27	.18	.15	.11
4 oz.	8	.36	.24	.20	.15
5 oz.	10	.45	.30	.25	.18

> ** Drink = 1 oz. 100 proof spirits*
> *12 oz. beer*
> *5 oz. wine*
> *3 oz. sherry*

Right to the Brain

Let's leave the blood now and enter the brain. What's happening here?

Alcohol, like barbiturates, minor tranquilizers, and general anesthetics, is a central nervous system depressant. However, in low concentrations, its effects are usually perceived as those of a stimulant because it tends first and foremost to depress inhibitions. However, as an increasing amount of alcohol is consumed, the depressant effect becomes more general and more apparent, leading to drowsiness, stupor, and coma. (Be grateful for the coma. If you're passed out, you can't drink any more and, therefore, may not end up ingesting a *lethal* dose of alcohol.)

Sobering Up

"Put on a pot of coffee—*black* coffee, *very black* coffee. Hot. Hot, *very, very black* coffee, and keep it coming! Hot, I tell you!"

A traditional cure. But not a very good idea. In the first place, the coffee will do nothing to sober you up. In the second place, the acids in the coffee will probably irritate your already precarious stomach. A better idea is to drink water, but only to help minimize the inevitable hangover. Water won't sober you up any more than coffee.

Sobering up is just a matter of time. The body metabolizes alcohol at the rate of a half ounce per hour. There's nothing you can do to speed that up.

Anatomy of a Hangover

Of course, even if you survive a hefty drinking bout—you didn't get into a fight, get into a car wreck, or insult your boss and lose your job—you may still find yourself *wishing* you were dead.

Throbbing head, pounding heart, cotton mouth, burning eyes, nausea, dizziness, stomach cramps, thirst, and a liberal shot of remorse. This is a hangover. And now you know why they call getting drunk *intoxication*. *Toxic* is in the middle of that word. You've been poisoned.

Many of the hangover symptoms are due to dehydration. Metabolizing alcohol uses up a lot of water. Alcohol is a diuretic: It makes you pee.

The nausea and stomach cramps are due in part to the irritating effects of the alcohol itself. It's hard on the stomach and intestinal linings. But the various flavorings and spices that find their way into liquor—and mixers—don't help the situation, and if the liquor you've been drinking is cheap, it's bound to have additives and out-and-out impurities that also upset your stomach.

First Aid for a Hangover

Your uncle knows how to cure a hangover. It's invariably some concoction involving tomato juice, Tabasco, and Worcestershire sauce. Not something easily downed if your stomach's awash on the high seas.

The sad fact is that no sovereign cure for a hangover exists—except for time. With the passage of some hours, you *will* feel better. If possible, take a nap.

This said, you can take some additional soothing—but not curative—steps:

1. Don't drink too much in the first place. (Okay! But we *had* to say it.)
2. When you drink, try to consume plenty of water as well.

3. If you go to bed realizing that you've overindulged, drink as much water as possible before retiring. Keep a glass of water beside your bed. If you wake up during the night, drink more of it. Minimize dehydration now, and you will almost certainly suffer less of a hangover later.

4. Avoid acidic fluids, including orange juice, tomato juice, and cola drinks.

5. In the morning, take a hot shower or (you should be so lucky) a sauna or steam bath. This will soothe and refresh by increasing your circulation.

6. Take a nonaspirin pain reliever. (Aspirin is great for headaches and other aches, but the alcohol and additives have already done a number on your digestive tract, and aspirin itself is hard on the stomach.)

> **Bar Tips**
> "To cure the bite of the dog, take a hair of the dog that bit you." For generations, misguided folk have recommended more alcohol to "cure" a hangover. While this may dull the immediate pain, it will only make your condition worse and may turn a temporary illness into a chronic one. If you've overindulged and are suffering, avoid alcohol (at least until you are feeling 100 percent better).

To Your Health!

Drinking in moderation has never been shown to have pathological—disease-causing—effects in "normal," healthy people. (The BIG exception: If you are pregnant, it is important that you avoid alcoholic beverages altogether.) And even getting a little tipsy *on occasion* will probably produce no long-term ill effects. However, frequent drinking to the point even of moderate intoxication can result in damage to the tissues of the mouth, esophagus, and stomach, and may increase your chances of developing cancer. The liver is alcohol's primary target, and it may be seriously damaged by its owner's chronic bouts of drunkenness. Heart muscle may also suffer.

> **Bar Tips**
> You're drunk. You can't stand the thought of how you'll feel come morning. Should you induce vomiting? While evacuating your stomach contents *will* reduce the aftereffects of the alcohol, inducing vomiting is almost never healthy. It can damage the throat and esophagus, it can make you choke, and it can harmfully change your body's pH balance. Don't do it.

Overindulgence over a prolonged period also creates nutritional problems, not the least of which is that, with its high calorie content, alcohol promotes weight gain without supplying nutritional value. (See Chapter 20 for information on low-calorie drinks.)

Alcoholism

People who drink hard enough and long enough to cause major organ damage are undoubtedly classifiable as alcoholics. There has been considerable debate as to just what *alcoholism* is, but the simplest generally accepted definition is the repetitive intake of alcoholic beverages to such an extent that repeated or continued harm to the drinker occurs.

> **Buzzed Words**
> The medical definition and the criteria for diagnosing **alcoholism** vary, but in general, this complex chronic psychological and nutritional disorder may be defined as continued excessive or compulsive use of alcoholic drinks.

Most experts believe that alcoholism is a disease, not some "moral weakness" on the part of the sufferer, though some also view it as a drug addiction, a learned response to crisis, a symptom of an underlying psychological or physical disorder, or a combination of these. There is evidence that alcoholism is, at least in part, a hereditary disorder. Certainly, the children of families in which alcohol abuse is present are most at risk for developing alcoholism.

The following list shows the warning signs of alcoholism. If you exhibit *any* of the signs, you have reason to suspect that you suffer from alcoholism. Consult a physician.

Warning Signs of Alcoholism

1. You indulge in binges—bouts of uncontrolled or clearly excessive drinking.
2. You drink for the purpose of getting drunk.
3. You are unable to stop drinking after one or two drinks.
4. You need to consume greater and greater quantities of alcohol to achieve the same effect.
5. You suffer problems caused by drinking: inability to concentrate on your job; lateness and absenteeism; arguments with colleagues, friends, and family.
6. You avoid family and friends when drinking.
7. You become irritated when your drinking is discussed by family and friends.
8. You are unable to keep promises made to yourself about curbing your drinking.
9. You feel guilty or remorseful about your drinking.
10. You black out frequently.
11. You eat irregularly during periods of drinking.
12. You use drinking to escape your problems.

What happens to alcoholics? Acute, immediate effects range from hangover to delirium tremens—the DTs—the symptoms of which resemble heroin withdrawal and involve shaking, fever, unspeakable panic, and terrifying hallucinations. *Polyneuropathy*, a degenerative disease of the nervous system, is likewise common, as are a host of other irreversible diseases of the central nervous system. The most familiar long-term effects attack the liver. They include diseases like *acute hepatitis*—inflammation of the liver—and *cirrhosis*, in effect scarring of the liver. If enough damage is inflicted, the diseases associated with alcoholism are fatal.

Alcoholics also suffer high accident rates and are more susceptible to infection. They readily lose jobs, friends, and spouses. They mess up the lives of their children, and they typically shorten their own lives by a decade or more.

> **Buzzed Words**
> A **blackout** is not a loss of consciousness. It is an inability to remember, even after you are sober, what you did and said while intoxicated.

Responsibilities and Obligations

As a drinker, your first responsibility and obligation is to know when to say enough. Your second responsibility and obligation is never to drive when you drink, even if you have been drinking in moderation. (We'll discuss drinking and driving later in the chapter.)

As a host who serves drinks, you also have responsibilities and obligations. (Key ethical and legal responsibilities of professional bartenders are discussed in Chapter 24.) Let's put it this way: You want to show your guests and friends a good time. You don't want to make them look foolish, you don't want to make them sick, you don't want to hurt their families, you don't want to see them injured or killed, and you don't want them to injure or kill anyone else. This being the case, you must serve alcohol responsibly:

> **Bar Tips**
> If you believe that you suffer from a drinking problem, seek help. Your best first resource is your physician, but you may also want to consult such organizations as Alcoholics Anonymous. Alcoholism is such a widespread problem that you will find it as a listing category in most Yellow Pages.

➤ Offer food with the drinks you serve.

➤ Offer a wide range of appealing non-alcoholic beverages.

➤ Never "push" drinks on any guest.

➤ Do not serve drinks to a guest who is intoxicated.

➤ Do not allow an intoxicated guest to drive. Provide the services of a "designated driver," who has not had alcohol to drink, or call a taxi.

Drinking and Driving

The statistics speak loudly. More than 20,000 people are killed each year in the United States in alcohol-related automobile accidents. Of this number, approximately 7,000 are nondrinking victims. The cost of alcohol-related accidents, in terms of legal, medical, and property expenses, is about $16 billion per year.

Not loud enough for you? Consider this: Given the present statistics and the trend they suggest, there is a 40 percent chance that *you* will be involved in an alcohol-related car wreck at some point in your life.

Most states have established standards for defining intoxication based on blood-alcohol concentration (BAC). In many states, you are deemed intoxicated—and therefore illegally driving under the influence (DUI)—if your BAC is .10 percent or higher; in a number of other states, the level is .08 percent (see the following table).

BAC and the Law

By law, .08% BAC is per-se (*conclusive*) evidence of DUI in:

California	New Hampshire	Utah
Florida	New Mexico	Vermont
Kansas	North Carolina	Virginia
Maine	Oregon	

By law, .10% BAC is per-se (*conclusive*) evidence of DUI in:

Alabama	Indiana	North Dakota
Alaska	Iowa	Ohio
Arizona	Kentucky	Oklahoma
Arkansas	Louisiana	Pennsylvania
Colorado	Michigan	Rhode Island
Connecticut	Minnesota	South Dakota
Delaware	Mississippi	Texas
District of Columbia	Missouri	Washington
Georgia	Montana	West Virginia
Hawaii	Nebraska	Wisconsin
Idaho	New Jersey	Wyoming
Illinois	New York	

By law, .08% BAC is evidence (but not per-se evidence) of DUI in:

Massachusetts

By law, .10% BAC is evidence (but not per-se evidence) of DUI in:

Maryland	South Carolina	Tennessee

All legislation is subject to change.

If you are an underage drinker, the BAC level at which you are judged DUI may be set *much* lower—from .07 percent to .00 percent (see the following table).

DUI BAC Levels for Underage Drinkers

State	BAC (percent)
Alaska*	.00(+)
Arizona*	.00(+)
Arkansas*	.02
California*	.05
District of Columbia*	.00(+)
Georgia***	.04
Idaho*	.02
Illinois*	.00(+)
Louisiana***	.04
Maine*	.02
Maryland*	.02
Massachusetts*	.02
Michigan*	.02
Minnesota*	.00(+)
Nebraska*	.02
New Hampshire*	.04
New Jersey*	.01
New Mexico*	.02
North Carolina***	.00(+)
Ohio*	.02
Oklahoma***	.02
Oregon*	.00(+)
Rhode Island*	.04
Tennessee*	.02
Texas*	.07
Utah*	.00(+)
Vermont***	.02
Virginia*	.02
Washington*	.02
West Virginia*	.02
Wisconsin**	.00(+)

*Underage = under 21
**Underage = under 19
***Underage = under 18
(+)Any evidence of alcohol consumption may be used as a basis for a charge of DUI, regardless of BAC. All legislation is subject to change.

Penalties for DUI vary widely, ranging from fines, license suspensions, and license revocations to serious jail time. And the trend is toward stricter laws and increasingly severe penalties.

As bad as getting caught is, the legal consequences of DUI are far less terrible than the potential human consequences: loss of life, injury, permanent disability, shattered families, and devastated finances.

And as strict as many DUI BAC standards are, they don't even kick in before your blood-alcohol concentration begins to impair your:

➤ Reaction time

➤ Judgment

➤ Coordination

➤ Reflexes

➤ General motor control

➤ Eyesight

At a mere .05 percent BAC, you are two to three times more likely to become involved in an automobile accident than you are at .00 percent BAC. At .08 percent—still below the legal DUI definition in most states—you are five to six times more likely to get into a wreck. At the legal definition point for most states—.10 percent—your risk jumps to seven to eight times the risk at .00 percent. Beyond this, if your BAC is higher than .10 percent, you are 20 to 50 times more likely to get into an accident.

> **Bar Tips**
> Chronic abusers of alcohol are seven times more likely to suffer a fatal accident as persons in the general population. They are 30 times more likely to suffer accidental poisoning, 16 times more likely to die from a fall, and 4.5 times more likely to die in a car accident.

If this isn't enough to make you think, consider that these figures represent the *lowest, most conservative* estimates of risk. They are the *best-case* scenario. Depending on your mood, your metabolism, the level of your fatigue, and your age, your risk can be much greater.

The bottom line? Driving drunk is incredibly stupid, criminal, immoral, selfish, self-destructive, destructive to others, suicidal, and homicidal. Do not do it. Do not let others do it.

See You in Court?

As if the human, humane, and moral motives for serving drinks responsibly weren't sufficient, you are, to a significant degree, legally liable for the actions of people to whom you serve alcohol.

Increasingly, lawmakers in every state have been shifting much of the responsibility for exercising good judgment from the consumers of alcohol to the servers of alcohol.

So-called *dram shop laws* make it legally possible to prosecute those who serve drunks. Such laws also open the gates to civil litigation: You could get sued. Criminal and civil penalties do not apply only to saloons and professional bartenders. The hosts of private parties have also been found liable for the mayhem inflicted by their drunk guests.

How can you protect yourself?

One sure way is to refuse to serve alcohol. Short of this extreme measure, take the steps outlined a little earlier in this chapter:

➤ Offer food with the drinks you serve.

➤ Offer a wide range of appealing non-alcoholic beverages.

➤ Never "push" drinks on any guest.

➤ Do not serve drinks to a guest who is intoxicated.

➤ Do not allow an intoxicated guest to drive. Provide the services of a "designated driver," who has not had alcohol to drink, or call a taxi.

You do not have to assume a morally superior tone to shut off the flow of alcohol to a drunk. While it is true that some people become hostile, even belligerent when they drink too much, most are pretty jolly—"feeling no pain"—and the best approach is a light and good-humored one. You see that Bill has had a bit too much. Approach him with a glass of water (*plain* water; seltzer or club soda—carbonated water—may accelerate the absorption of the alcohol already sloshing around inside him). Put your arm around his shoulder, hand him the glass, and say: "Bill, you'd better have some of this, or the furniture will begin to attack you."

Do *not* pose the classic rhetorical question—"Don't you think you've had enough?"—because the automatic answer is "No!" Tipsy folks need guidance and will usually accept it. Offer a glass of water and some good-humored attention and conversation.

The Least You Need to Know

➤ Your body processes alcohol at a specific rate (about a half-ounce an hour), and nothing you do can effectively accelerate this natural process.

➤ The only cure for intoxication—and, subsequently, for a hangover—is the passage of time.

➤ Drinking plenty of water after overindulging will not sober you up, but it should lessen the severity of a subsequent hangover.

➤ You have moral and legal responsibilities both as a drinker and as a host.

➤ Never drink and drive.

Chapter 3

Chemistry 101, History 101: A Short Course in Alcohol

In This Chapter

➤ Fermentation and distillation

➤ Potable and non-potable alcohols

➤ The earliest alcoholic beverages

➤ Early development of the major alcoholic beverages

You don't need to know any of the stuff in this chapter to enjoy, mix, or serve drinks—just like you don't need to know the history of the internal combustion engine to drive your car. But if you're interested, here's some more about the nature and composition of booze.

$CH_3 CH_2 OH$

Wines, beers, and spirits all contain $CH_3 CH_2 OH$—*ethyl alcohol*—also called *ethanol*. The alcohol is produced by *fermentation*, in which yeast enzymes decompose carbohydrates into carbon dioxide and ethanol. The carbohydrate source in wines is the sugars in fruits or berries (usually grapes); in beers, it's grains. In spirits, the carbohydrate source is also grains, but spirits differ in that they are put through an additional process, in which the alcoholic beverage is *distilled* from the fermented carbohydrate material.

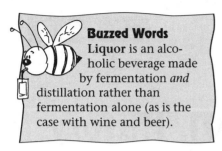

Buzzed Words
Liquor is an alcoholic beverage made by fermentation *and* distillation rather than fermentation alone (as is the case with wine and beer).

Although ethyl alcohol is the chief ingredient of all potable alcoholic beverages, very small amounts of amyl, butyl, propyl, and methyl alcohol also find their way into some beverages. You'll also find *congeners*—acids, aldehydes, esters, ketones, phenols, and tannins—along with occasional vitamins and minerals (but that doesn't make beer for breakfast a good idea). The various combinations of these substances—especially the congeners—produce the characteristic flavors, odors, and colors that differentiate one alcoholic beverage from another.

Fermentation

Fermentation has been known for at least 10,000 years, but not until the 19th century did the great French chemist Louis Pasteur describe the process in detail, defining it as chemical changes brought about by yeasts and other microorganisms growing *anaerobically* (that is, in the absence of air). Acting on carbohydrates, yeast fermentation produces alcohol, but by selecting various carbohydrates and other microorganisms, you can create a variety of products from fermentation, including glycerol, carbon dioxide, butyl alcohol, acetone, lactic acid, monosodium glutamate, citric acid, gluconic acid, and small amounts of antibiotics, vitamin B_{12}, and riboflavin (vitamin B).

Distillation

Okay. Fermentation is a *natural* process, in which organic materials containing carbohydrates are decomposed by yeasts. The process of fermentation produces a relatively low concentration of alcohol (no more than 14 percent by volume). Then, through an *artificial* process—*distillation*—it is possible to raise the concentration of ethyl alcohol above that of the original fermented mixture.

It works this way. Alcohol boils at 173.3 degrees Fahrenheit, while water boils at 212 degrees. If the product of fermentation—a liquid containing ethyl alcohol—is heated to a temperature above 173.3 degrees, but below 212 degrees, and the vapor coming off the liquid is condensed, the condensed vapor (the *condensate*) will have a higher alcohol concentration than the original liquid.

The process of distillation is old enough to have been mentioned by Aristotle—who lived from 384 to 322 B.C.—but Pliny the Elder (A.D. 23–79), a Roman, first described a *still*. At its most basic, a still consists of a *retort*, in which the liquid to be distilled is heated; a coil, called a *condenser*, at the top of the still, to cool and condense the vapor; and a

Buzzed Words
Ethyl alcohol is the potable alcohol obtained from fermentation. To produce hard liquor, ethyl alcohol is purified and concentrated by distillation. **Congeners** are acids, aldehydes, esters, ketones, phenols, and tannins that are byproducts of fermentation, distillation, and aging. These "impurities" may add character and flavor, but they can cause undesirable effects—notably, increasing the intensity of a hangover.

receiver, a vessel that collects the distillate. Over the years, various elaborate industrial stills have been created, but they all consist essentially of the same three parts.

Poison versus Potable

Ethyl alcohol, or ethanol, is the only type of alcohol that's safe to drink. The two other principal types—*methyl* (wood) *alcohol* and *isopropyl* (rubbing) *alcohol*—are highly toxic. Drinking wood or rubbing alcohol can result in blindness, severe gastric damage, or death.

In the Beginning, There Was Spit...

Although distillation was known to the ancients, it didn't become popular in the West as an adjunct to producing alcoholic beverages until the Middle Ages. As far as anyone can tell—or guess—the production and consumption of fermented (but not distilled) alcoholic beverages far predates recorded history. It is believed that, many thousands of years ago, certain folks chewed and spat out grain, then let the resulting "mash" ferment. There are plenty of yeasty enzymes in saliva, and the result was the conversion of the grain starch first into sugar and then into alcohol. Wouldn't you like to shake the hand of the first person with nerve enough to sample the brew produced by rotting grain and spit? Maybe not.

Babylonian Booze

The first evidence of the production of wine comes from Asia Minor about 4000 B.C., and the oldest known code of laws, promulgated about 1770 B.C. by King Hammurabi of Babylonia, contained statutes regulating drinking houses. Even earlier, about 2100 B.C., Sumerian physicians prescribed beer for what ailed (no pun intended) their patients. Egyptian doctors also prescribed wine and beer, circa 1500 B.C.

Quick One
Bartender to customer: "Bet I can make you do an impression of a train."

Customer: "Five bucks says you can't."

Bartender: "Knock-knock."

Customer: "Who's there?"

Bartender: "Chooch."

Customer: "Chooch who?'

Bartender: "You owe me five bucks."

Bar Tips
Ethyl alcohol is valuable as a solvent, but federal law requires costly tax stamps on all potable alcohol. To get around this, toxic solvents, such as acetone or methanol, may be added to ethyl alcohol to make it toxic and, therefore, unfit for consumption. This is called *denatured alcohol*.

Buzzed Words
Mash is the fermentable starchy mixture from which an alcoholic beverage is produced.

Early on, alcoholic beverages found their way into religious worship, doubtless inducing a state of ecstasy and trance in the celebrants. However, in ancient Mesopotamia as well as ancient Egypt, drinking as well as drunkenness spread beyond the temple and into common practice.

Land of Milk and Honey

Bar Tips
Alcohol is the oldest and most widely used drug.

The Jews of the Old Testament used alcoholic beverages for a host of sacramental purposes, from celebrating an eight-day-old boy's circumcision to toasting the soul of the recently deceased. Drinking also took place at weddings, and wine marked the arrival and departure of each Sabbath and festival. Like so much else in ancient Jewish life, drinking was strictly regulated. Drunkenness was frowned upon and condemned.

Greek Wine and Roman Orgies

The literature and art of the ancient Greeks and Romans is full of references to the copious consumption of wine by gods and people alike. The cult of *Dionysus*, or *Bacchus*, god of wine, was the most popular of Greek as well as Roman religious cults.

The Greeks and Hebrews enjoyed their wine cut 50/50 with water, but a minority took it straight. Whether diluted or not, wine was far more popular than water—not surprising in an age when the communal water source was also the communal sewer.

The Middle East, Africa, and Asia

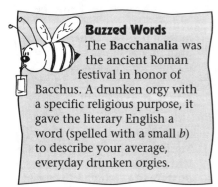

Buzzed Words
The **Bacchanalia** was the ancient Roman festival in honor of Bacchus. A drunken orgy with a specific religious purpose, it gave the literary English a word (spelled with a small *b*) to describe your average, everyday drunken orgies.

The Middle East gave rise to the first religion to actively condemn wine, Islam, though pre-Islamic Arabs developed a distillation method that was used to produce a distilled beverage from wine. In Africa, maize, millet, bananas, honey, palm and bamboo saps, and many fruits were used to ferment thick, rich beers and wines—including Kaffir beer and the highly potent palm wines that are still enjoyed today.

The people of Asia produced wines in prehistoric times, using barley and rice as raw materials. By 800 B.C., the Chinese produced the earliest recorded *distilled* liquor, a strong beverage from rice beer.

In the New World

While the Old World was busy imbibing, many of the peoples of the New World—the pre-Columbian Indians of North America—were without booze. When Europeans introduced them to it, the results were usually tragic, and alcoholism remains a serious problem among Native Americans.

Toast
May the grass grow long on the road to hell for the want of use.

In the American Southwest, the Papago Indians fermented wine from cactus, and the Tarahumara of northern Mexico made beers from corn and from the agave, the plant that would eventually be used to produce tequila. Farther south, in Central and South America, people made *chicha* and other alcoholic beverages from maize, tubers, fruits, flowers, and saps.

Spiritual Origins

Where did the spirits we enjoy come from? The ancient Greeks and Romans knew about distilling, but distilled liquor doesn't seem to have been very popular with them. The Romans have no written references to distilled beverages before A.D. 100. In Britain, distilled spirits were produced before the Roman conquest, and Spain, France, and western Europe also produced distilled spirits, but these didn't become popular until the early Middle Ages—about the eighth century.

The venerable bar at The Players continues to boast a classic variety of liquors and mixers.

(Photo courtesy of the Walter Hampden Memorial Library, at The Players)

Whence Whiskey?

The Middle Ages also saw the production of the first distilled spirits made from starchy grains, as opposed to sugar-based materials such as grapes and honey (the bases of grape brandy and distilled mead, which is fermented honey and water). Distilling liquor from grains is the origin of whiskey. By the 17th century, various European governments were beginning to regulate the distilled spirits industry, which soon became a rich source of tax revenue.

The first whiskeys seem to have come from Ireland and Scotland. Indeed, the word *whiskey* is derived from the Celtic *usquebaugh*, similar to the Irish Gaelic (*uisce beathadh*) and the Scots Gaelic (*uisge beatha*), all of which came from—guess what?—the Latin phrase *aqua vitae,* "water of life." The earliest account of whiskey making is found in Scottish writings dating from 1494.

Commercial whiskey production hit America by the early 18th century and soon became an industry associated with what was then the western frontier: Kentucky, Pennsylvania, and Indiana. Canada joined the party in the early 19th century, producing characteristically blended products.

Quick One

A rope decided to drop into a bar. "Hey," the bartender growled. "We don't serve *ropes* here. Get lost!"

The rope tried a second saloon and was again tossed out. Looking down the street, he saw yet another bar. He tied himself in a knot, then rubbed himself ragged on the sidewalk. Entering the bar, he called to the barkeep: "Whiskey, please!"

"Whoa there. Aren't you a *rope?*"

"Frayed knot." And he got his whiskey.

Genesis of Gin

As mentioned in Chapter 1, the name *gin* comes from the French name for the juniper berry, *genièvre*. It is the only spirit whose origin can be traced to a single inventor: one Franciscus Sylvius, a 17th-century professor of medicine at the University of Leiden in Holland (where, incidentally, *genièvre* is called *genever* or *jenever*). Sylvius distilled the juniper berry with spirits in order to create a cheap medicine with the diuretic properties of much more costly juniper-berry oil.

Soon the medicine became popular as a beverage, and English soldiers marching through Holland during the wars of the later 17th and early 18th centuries took a liking to the drink and brought it back to England, where its name was contracted to *gin*. (The soldiers called it "Dutch courage.") While all classes enjoyed the beverage, the cheap spirit was especially popular with the less privileged, and its widespread use gave rise to an epidemic of alcoholism.

Vodka's Unveiling

Vodka was first distilled sometime in 14th-century Poland, and soon spread throughout Poland, Russia, and the Balkans. It became popular in the United States and Western Europe after World War II.

Rum's Reign

Rum originated in the West Indies and is first mentioned in records from Barbados dating from about 1650. At first, it was called "kill-devil" and "rumbullion," but, by 1667, it appeared in written records as simply "rum."

Rum was an enormously popular commodity and was soon exported to the North American mainland. In Puritan New England, a rum-distilling industry developed, becoming one of the three legs of the infamous "triangle trade": slaves were brought from Africa and traded to the West Indies for molasses; the molasses was sold in New England, where it was made into rum; and the rum was in turn traded to Africa for more slaves. The industry received a major boost in the 18th century, when the British Royal Navy instituted a policy of issuing a rum ration to all sailors.

A Tale of Tequila

The native peoples of Mexico had been fermenting the juice of the *agave* for many years before the Spanish invasion of the 16th century. Among the many cultural innovations the Spanish introduced to the Indians was distillation, and soon the Mexicans put distillation to work on the fermented juice of the *blue agave*. The result was a liquor named for the town of Tequila in the Mexican state of Jalisco, where the beverage is still produced under strict government control.

The Bona Fides of Brandy

The word *brandy* is of Dutch origin; *brandewijn* means "burnt wine," a reference to the application of heat in distilling the beverage from wine. Brandy was first distilled commercially in the 16th century. It is said that a particularly enterprising Dutch sea captain, seeking to reduce cargo costs, hit upon the idea of distilling wine in order to concentrate it. His plan was then to reconstitute the wine by the addition of water when he reached port. However, somebody sampled the concentrated beverage, liked it, spread the good news, and brandy was born. It was immediately successful.

Soon, most wine-producing countries began making brandy. Best known and most prized are the great French brandies, and outstanding among these are cognac—from the Charente and Charente-Maritime *départements* (administrative districts)—and Armagnac, from the Gers region. Spain and Portugal also produce distinctive brandies, as does Greece: *Metaxa* is sweetened and usually darkened with caramel, and *ouzo* is colorless, flavored with anise or licorice.

Liqueur Lineage

The source of the word *liqueur*, in Church Latin, *liquefacere* ("to make liquid"), betrays its origin in the world of the medieval monks and alchemists, who first produced these beverages commercially in the Dark Ages. Originally, they were used as medicines, balms, elixirs, tonics, and—above all—aphrodisiacs. The range of available liqueurs will be described in detail in Chapter 16; however, you should know that the formulas of the great proprietary liqueur brands are closely guarded secrets, dating to the Renaissance in some cases. French Bénédictine, for example, was first produced in 1510; its formula has remained a closed book since that year. Chartreuse debuted in 1607, and other famous liqueurs followed, including Cointreau, Grand Marnier, and Vieille Cure. Drambuie, derived from scotch, is made in Scotland from a French formula obtained in 1745.

No News?

Will the coming years see the evolution of new spirits? Probably not soon. But even though the basic spirits may remain the same, the possibilities of new mixed drinks remain virtually without limit, and, each year, enterprising mixologists develop novelties of temptation.

The Least You Need to Know

➤ Alcohol is produced by the action of yeasts on carbohydrates—a process called fermentation.

➤ Spirits are alcoholic beverages in which the alcohol content has been concentrated by distilling alcohol-bearing liquid produced by fermentation.

➤ Alcoholic beverages predate recorded history and are certainly as old as civilization.

➤ Fermented beverages have ancient lineage. Distilled spirits did not come into wide use in the West until the Middle Ages.

Chapter 4

Of Ponies, Garbage, and Garnishes: The Basic Equipment of Bartending

In This Chapter

➤ Stocking a basic liquor cabinet

➤ What you need for an advanced bar

➤ The basic and advanced mixers

➤ Glassware and other equipment

There is no "right" way to stock your bar. The liquor and the equipment you select depend on your personal needs, your taste, what you and your friends enjoy, and your budget. This chapter gives you suggestions ranging from the bare minimum to the truly well-stocked bar.

As for quantities, you may want to weigh the savings of buying large bottles against the opportunity to sample more brands and kinds of liquor if you buy smaller bottles.

A Portfolio of Potables: Price vs. Value

We're not going to say much about specific brands here, except to point out that the price of liquor varies substantially from brand to brand. You should base your buying decisions on two factors:

1. **Are you mixing it with something?** It makes no sense to spring for a premium rum if you're going to mix it with Coke. If you intend to drink liquor straight, on the rocks, with water, with seltzer or club soda, with mildly flavored mixers, or in such mixed drinks as martinis and Manhattans, then your enjoyment will be enhanced by investing in the better, more expensive brands. But see #2.

2. **What's more important to you, price or value?** Old Rotgut whiskey may have the lowest price, but if it tastes like Sterno squeezed through a dirty sock, it's not a good value. At a higher, but still moderate price level, you may find a whiskey to your liking. For you, *that* may represent good value. If, however, you enjoy the flavor and feel of a fine sippin' whiskey, a premium price may be an even *better* value, since (as far as you're concerned) it delivers more of what you want than the moderately priced brand.

Bar Tips
Each chapter in Parts 2 through 5 is devoted to a major type of liquor, including advice on what qualities to look for in that type of liquor.

You must decide whether price or value is more important to you. Our suggestion: First decide what you want from a drink. If you're after an unalloyed pleasurable experience, "value" means spending enough to make drinking worth your time, and we suggest trying some of the premium or near-premium brands in an effort to decide on the ones you like best.

The Basics: Liquor

At its most basic, the home bar can be a kitchen-cabinet collection of the two or three kinds of mixers and spirits you and your friends enjoy. Only a little less basic is this "starter bar" selection:

- ❏ 1 750-ml bottle of bourbon
- ❏ 1 750-ml bottle of Canadian whisky
- ❏ 1 750-ml bottle of blended scotch
- ❏ 1 1.75-liter bottle of gin
- ❏ 1 1.75-liter bottle of light rum
- ❏ 1 1.75-liter bottle of white tequila
- ❏ 1 1.75-liter bottle of vodka
- ❏ 1 750-ml bottle of brandy

The Basics: Liqueurs

Even a basic bar should stock small bottles of the most popular liqueurs. Include the following:

- ❑ triple sec
- ❑ crème de menthe
- ❑ crème de cacao
- ❑ amaretto
- ❑ Kahlúa
- ❑ Drambuie
- ❑ Bénédictine
- ❑ Cointreau
- ❑ Grand Marnier

The Basics: Wine and Beer

The subjects of wine and of beer are vast, and you'll find *Complete Idiot's Guides* devoted to both. For the purposes of mixing drinks, you will need wine and beer, so we'll give them the merest mention here. For the "starter bar," stock at least the following:

- ❑ 1 small bottle of dry vermouth
- ❑ 1 small bottle of sweet vermouth
- ❑ 2 bottles of white wine
- ❑ 2 bottles of red wine
- ❑ 1 bottle of champagne or sparkling wine
- ❑ 2 six-packs of beer
- ❑ 1 six-pack of lite beer

The Basics: Mixers

You will want to stock at least five carbonated mixers:

- ❑ 2 1-liter bottles of cola
- ❑ 2 1-liter bottles of diet cola
- ❑ 2 1-liter bottles of tonic water

These mix well with light alcohols, such as gin, vodka, and rum.

For the dark spirits—such as scotch and bourbon—have on hand the following:

- ❑ 3 1-liter bottles of club soda
- ❑ 2 1-liter bottles of ginger ale
- ❑ 2 1-liter bottle of 7-Up (or the equivalent)

You may substitute seltzer, soda water, or sparkling spring water (such as Perrier) for plain soda water. And please note carefully: This basic stock of five carbonated beverages is what you need for mixing drinks. In addition to these, be certain to have plenty of cola, ginger ale, 7-Up (or the equivalent), and other soft drinks to offer guests as an alternative to alcoholic beverages.

You'll also need five basic juices. If possible, purchase them just before use, so that they'll be fresh:

❏ 3 quarts of orange juice

❏ 2 quarts of grapefruit juice

❏ 1 large can of pineapple juice

❏ 1 large bottle of cranberry juice

❏ 3 large bottles of tomato juice

(You'll need the tomato juice for Bloody Marys, but that's not all. See Chapter 7 for more on the ingredients that make for a great Bloody Mary.)

A number of drinks call for *sour mix* or *bar mix* (which is the same thing). You can buy this bottled or in ready-to-mix powdered form at liquor stores or grocery stores, or, if you prefer, you can prepare it yourself. There are two basic recipes.

Sour Mix Recipe #1

Juice of $1/2$ lemon per drink

1 tsp. sugar per drink

Simply combine these with other drink ingredients in a shaker with ice. Shake vigorously.

Commercial powdered sour mix adds powdered egg white to the product to make the drink foam up. Shaking the cocktail vigorously should provide plenty of foam, even without the egg white, but if you want to ensure a foamy sour, use the following recipe:

Sour Mix Recipe #2

12 oz. lemon juice (the juice of 6 lemons) $^1/_4$ cup refined sugar

18 oz. distilled water   1 egg white

Blend all ingredients in a blender. Refrigerate.

Note: The mix will keep for about a week under refrigeration. You must shake or blend before each use.

Round out the "starter bar" basic mixer arsenal with:

- ❏ 1 small bottle of Rose's lime juice
- ❏ Superfine granulated sugar
- ❏ Coarse (not table) salt (for margaritas and Salty Dogs)
- ❏ Grenadine
- ❏ Sugar syrup (also known as simple syrup)

Finally, don't neglect water and ice. If the water that comes from your tap tastes great, use it. If not, buy a couple of half-gallon bottles of good spring water. Don't foul good liquor with bad water.

Even if the ice that comes from your freezer tastes okay—that is, has no flavor whatsoever—you will want to buy a couple of large bags for any party. Commercial ice is more reliable, as far as flavorlessness, and you'll probably need more than you can produce in your freezer (unless you really plan ahead).

One Step Beyond

If "basic" isn't enough for you, here's the next logical step. To the "starter bar," add the following spirits:

- ❏ 1 bottle of Dutch (Genever) gin
- ❏ 1 bottle of premium English gin
- ❏ 2 bottles of premium Scandinavian or Russian vodka

Bar Tips

Raw eggs may be a source of **salmonella**, a type of bacteria that causes food poisoning. The only way to avoid the risk of salmonella infection is to cook the egg. For this reason, you may wish to avoid all drinks made with raw egg white, raw egg yolk, or raw whole egg. You may wish to use commercially prepared sour mix, which uses powdered egg white (not associated with salmonella).

Bar Tips

You can buy sugar syrup ready-made or prepare it at home. In a saucepan, gradually dissolve 2 cups of sugar in a cup of water. Simmer for 10 minutes, stirring frequently. Refrigerate until needed.

- ❏ 1 bottle of rye
- ❏ 1 bottle of Irish whiskey
- ❏ 1 bottle of single-malt scotch
- ❏ 1 bottle of bourbon or Tennessee whiskey
- ❏ 1 bottle of gold rum
- ❏ 1 bottle of dark (Jamaican) rum
- ❏ 1 bottle of gold tequila (*tequila anejo*)

There is a wide range of exotic liqueurs available. Consider the following additions to the basic roster:

- ❏ framboise
- ❏ kirschwasser
- ❏ slivovitz
- ❏ crème de cassis
- ❏ sambuca
- ❏ peppermint schnapps
- ❏ peach schnapps
- ❏ Galliano
- ❏ Frangelico

You can add any number of great wines and beers to your collection. Do consider:

- ❏ aperitif wines (Dubonnet, Lillet, and Campari are the most popular)
- ❏ 1 bottle of cream sherry
- ❏ 1 bottle of port
- ❏ 1 bottle of madeira
- ❏ 1 bottle of amontillado

Get at least two or three flavored brandies:

- ❏ 1 bottle Calvados or applejack (apple brandy)
- ❏ 1 bottle apricot brandy
- ❏ 1 bottle peach brandy

In addition to the most-requested mixers, you might also keep on hand the following:

- ❏ coffee
- ❏ cream (heavy and light)
- ❏ cream of coconut
- ❏ Falernum (a spicy, lime-flavored sweetener)
- ❏ orgeat syrup (almond syrup)
- ❏ passion fruit nectar
- ❏ bitters

> **Bar Tips**
> **Bitters** is an *alcoholic* mixer (Angostura bitters is the best known) that gives a special piquance to Manhattans, old-fashioneds, and even Bloody Marys. Be careful *not* to use it to flavor non-alcoholic drinks for non-drinkers.

While Angostura Aromatic Bitters are the most famous and popular bitters, you might want to stock Abbott's and Bokers as well. Campari is an aperitif wine that many people class with the bitters. You will also want to know about Jaegermeister, another aperitif that is often deemed a bitters. For drinks with a Cajun accent, invest in a bottle of New Orleans's classic Peychaud's Bitters.

Garnishes and Garbage

Many mixed drinks have solid as well as liquid components. If a piece of fruit or vegetable added to a drink changes the way it tastes, then it is a *garnish*. If it's just for decoration, it's *garbage*.

The basic bar should have the following garnishes and garbage available:

> **Buzzed Words**
> A **garnish** is a bit of fruit or vegetable added to a drink principally to enhance its flavor. **Garbage** is a bit of fruit or vegetable added to a drink primarily for the sake of appearance. It does not significantly enhance the flavor of the drink.

Lemon twists　All you use is the peel. The way to get the most peel from each lemon is to slice off the ends, then use a spoon to force the fruit out one end. Now you have an empty lemon peel. Slice it lengthwise into strips one-quarter inch wide. When a drink calls for a "twist," take one of the strips, twist it over the drink, rub the inside of the peel around the edge of the glass, plunk it in, then stir. It is best to have some strips prepared and ready to go.

Lime wedges　Lime is rarely cut into twist strips; you use it in wedges. Think of the two bumps at either end as its poles, then cut the lime at the equator. Quarter each hemisphere. The result is eight wedges. Use one per drink, squeezing the lime over the drink, rubbing it around the rim of the glass, then dropping it in. Because lime wedges are such a popular garnish, you should have several limes cut and on hand.

Orange slices Oranges are typically sliced. Create as many $1/4$-inch-thick semi-circles as possible from each orange. Cut the orange in half, starting at the stem. Put each half flat-side down, then cut widthwise to make your semicircles. Notch a small cut in the fruit side of each slice so that you can slide it onto the rim of the glass. Do not squeeze the orange into the drink.

Maraschino cherries These super-sweet, surrealistically red (-dyed) little numbers are garbage; that is, they add no flavor to the drink. However, drinkers like to pull them out of the drink and eat them, so make certain you leave the stems on. Have at least two jars of maraschino cherries on hand.

Olives Most martini drinkers like their libation with an olive or three. Use medium-size green pitted olives—and hold the pimento (it will discolor the drink). Usually, the olive(s) are skewered on a toothpick or little plastic sword and placed in the drink. Some even like their martini "dirty," meaning they like some olive juice splashed in.

Pearl onions A martini harboring a pearl onion (or two or three) rather than an olive or olives is a Gibson. Have a little jar of these handy. Stored under refrigeration in their own juice, they'll keep indefinitely. The pearls may be skewered on a toothpick.

Celery stalks These add the finishing touch to a Bloody Mary. The width and length of the stalk should suit the glass you use. To add some flair, leave the stalk's leafy end on.

Cucumber peel A curlicue peel is used to decorate a few specialty drinks.

Inedible Additions

Don't forget cocktail toothpicks or, if you yearn for a touch of kitsch, little plastic cocktail swords. You'll also need swizzle sticks or cocktail straws. And, for tropical drinks, paper parasols. The little touches will make you the consummate host.

Tools of the Trade

There's a load of gadgets and glassware a bartender can buy. Some of them are even useful.

Cocktail shaker   *Speedpourer*   *Strainer*   *Jigger-pony measure*

Shaker Upper

The trademark of the pro is the cocktail shaker. You'll need one to make sours, daiquiris, margaritas, and a straight-up martini á la James Bond. ("Shaken, not stirred.") Buy one with a stainless steel shell—the bigger, outer part—and glass, the smaller, inner part. A 12-ounce shaker should be ample.

You'll also need a cocktail strainer that fits over the shaker so you can pour the chilled drink without disgorging the ice cubes. This is called pouring a drink "straight-up."

Other Essentials

If you're going for that pro look, you'll also want a number of *speedpourers*—the plastic gadgets that fit into the mouth of a liquor bottle, allowing you to pour the liquor at an even, measured rate without spilling.

While you're at it, why not buy a genuine *bar spoon*? This has a small paddle spoon at one end of long handle that is twisted in the middle. The spoon is the bartender's Swiss army knife: drinks can be stirred with the handle, garnishes can be manipulated with the spoon (if you don't want to use your fingers), and the swirled part can be used to pour the ingredients of layered drinks—such as pousse-cafés—in which it is important to not mix the layers.

Speaking of Swiss army knife-type things, you might pick up a combination corkscrew/ bottle opener/can opener, commonly called a *captain's knife*. You're bound to need all three.

Finally, there is the *jigger-pony* combination measure. The larger cone is a jigger (1$\frac{1}{2}$-ounce measure), and the smaller is the pony (1 ounce).

Other equipment you are likely to already have in your kitchen:

- ❏ A paring knife for cutting fruit garnishes
- ❏ An electric blender
- ❏ An ice bucket with ice tongs (for the fastidious and hygienic)
- ❏ A juice squeezer

A Glass Act

True, you could get by with a collection of jelly jars, but a wide range of glassware has evolved to accommodate a wide range of drinks.

Glassware is far less critical in serving liquor than it is in serving fine wine. However, glass size and shape can enhance or detract from the experience of enjoying straight liquor as well as mixed drinks. Let's go over the basics.

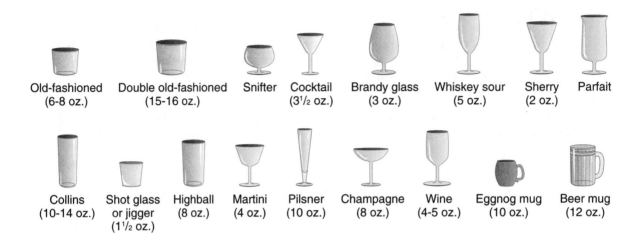

Old-fashioned (6-8 oz.)   Double old-fashioned (15-16 oz.)   Snifter   Cocktail (3½ oz.)   Brandy glass (3 oz.)   Whiskey sour (5 oz.)   Sherry (2 oz.)   Parfait

Collins (10-14 oz.)   Shot glass or jigger (1½ oz.)   Highball (8 oz.)   Martini (4 oz.)   Pilsner (10 oz.)   Champagne (8 oz.)   Wine (4-5 oz.)   Eggnog mug (10 oz.)   Beer mug (12 oz.)

Highball and Low

The *highball glass* is the one you'll use most. Highball glasses are used for scotch and soda, scotch and water, bourbon and water, gin and tonic, vodka and tonic... you get the picture. The orthodox highball glass is a tall 8 ounces; however, some hold 12 ounces.

Only slightly less popular is the *lowball glass*, which some bartenders call a *rocks glass*, since it is used for many drinks served on the rocks. Ranging from four to nine ounces, this short, clear glass is used for martinis on the rocks, various whiskey-rocks combinations, Manhattans on the rocks, and so on.

Both the highball and lowball glasses should be clear, not frosted. How many of both you purchase depends on your hosting plans, but a dozen of each is a good minimum number for the committed host.

Collins and Old-Fashioned

The *Collins glass* is not just for the Tom Collins, but for any of the larger mixed drinks that benefit from a cooling, refreshing image. This includes the various fizzes and a wealth of tropical drinks. The 10- to 14-ounce Collins glass is frosted (sometimes with an icy pebble effect as well) to about ³/₄" from the top. This portion is left clear, partly, perhaps, to caress the drinker's lips, but mainly to remind the bartender to add soda water to the top of the Tom Collins.

Old-fashioned glasses come in two sizes, large (seven-ounce) and small (four-ounce), and are similar to the lowball glass, except for the bump at the base of the glass. Presumably, this is to remind the bartender to prepare the fixings for the old-fashioned.

While the Collins glass is not an ideal substitute for the highball glass, the old-fashioned glass can certainly do double duty as a lowball or "rocks glass." The frugal host will, in fact, choose one or the other. As for the Collins glass, it's a good idea to have at least a half-dozen of these in addition to your highball glassware.

> **Bar Tips**
> The Collins glass would be the same as a large (12-ounce) highball glass, except that the highball glass is entirely clear, whereas the Collins glass is partially frosted.

Cocktail and Sour

The classic *cocktail glass* is so classic—an inverted cone perched on a long stem—that it is, quite literally, *the* icon of the cocktail lounge, often immortalized in neon signs. The four-ounce glass is used for any cocktail ordered straight-up. Its stem is more than decorative: since drinks served in cocktail glasses have no ice in them, the stem enables you to hold the glass without warming the contents with your hands. Six to twelve of these should be adequate for the moderately serious host.

You might add a few four- or five-ounce *sour glasses* to your collection. These are stemmed glasses with elongated bowls that make whiskey sours (and other foamy sour drinks) more inviting.

Wine and Sherry

The subject of wine glasses is complex. If you enjoy fine wines, read *The Complete Idiot's Guide to Wine*, which includes a discussion of glassware. For the basic bar, however, the sturdy, stemmed, globe-bowled glasses of a Parisian-style bistro are adequate.

You may also stock some *sherry glasses*. These $2^1/_2$- to $3^1/_2$-ounce stemmed glasses can be used for aperitifs and port as well as sherry. The best kind of sherry glass is the *copita*, which features a narrow taper that captures the wine's aroma. If you prefer, however, you might serve these drinks in the smaller *pony* or *cordial* glasses.

Champagne: American Style and in the European Mood

Like wine, the subject of champagne lies beyond the scope of this book; however, basic bar equipment should include a minimum of a dozen champagne glasses. The question is, which style?

Americans tend to favor a stemmed glass that looks like a shorter, wider, shallower version of the cocktail glass. It holds four to six ounces of bubbly. Europeans, however, prefer a very different glass, the champagne flute, which is tall and fluted—bulging gracefully at the bottom and tapering toward the rim.

> **Bar Tips**
> Using champagne flutes results in less spillage than American-style champagne glasses.

We recommend the European flute over the American champagne glass. Not only does it hold more of a good thing (capacities vary from 7 to 11 ounces), but, more important, its tapered profile reduces the surface area and slows the dissipation of the bubbles.

Small Stuff: The Cordial Pony and Your Best Shot

Buzzed Words
A **jigger** is the glass or the metal measuring cup used to measure drinks. It is also what you call the amount the jigger measures: 1¹/₂ ounces. Strictly speaking, a **pony** is a 1-ounce measure; however, pony glasses range in capacity from 1 to 2 ounces.

Every bar should have a supply of shot glasses, which you can use not only to serve shots, but also to measure drinks. Shot glasses come in one- to two-ounce sizes, and your wisest choice is 1¹/₂ ounces—a *jigger*—because this is the ideal size for measuring most drinks.

If you enjoy bitters, cordials, or sherry, stock either sherry glasses or some of the smaller pony glasses.

Snifter Story

The *brandy snifter* is a particularly elegant piece of glassware. It ranges anywhere from about 5 to 25 ounces; however, no snifter is meant to hold so vast an amount of brandy. Opt for about a 16-ounce snifter, in which you serve no more than 1 or 2 ounces of brandy. The idea is that the oversized balloon shape will waft and funnel the aroma of the wine into the drinker's nose. If you use a snifter smaller than 16 ounces, reduce the amount of brandy proportionately. Snifters larger than 16 ounces are unwieldy, tend to be fragile, and add nothing special to the drinking experience.

Unless you have a lot of brandy- or cognac-drinking friends, you shouldn't need many snifters. Fine brandy or cognac is best enjoyed in an intimate group, anyway.

Mugs and Pilsner Glasses

As with wine, the subject of beer is too vast for this book; fortunately, a *Complete Idiot's Guide to Beer* is available. But while we're on the subject of glassware, be sure to have a dozen 10-ounce beer glasses on hand.

Should you choose mugs, Pilsner glasses, or both? Mugs won't break as easily, but if you are serving really wonderful premium beer, the tall, elegant *Pilsner glass* can enhance the drinking experience. It's your call. In either case, drinking beer from a mug or glass is far more enjoyable than sucking on a bottle or slurping from a can.

Other Specialized Glassware

Now that you've had a rundown of the basic bar glassware, you should also know about the following specialized glasses.

❏ **Pousse-café glass**   A three- to four-ounce stemmed glass with little or no flare or tapering of the bowl. It is handy for layered dessert drinks.

❏ **Parfait glass**   A slightly larger version of the pousse-café glass, the parfait glass usually has a flared lip. It is also used for layered dessert drinks.

❏ **Fizz glass**   This five-ounce stemmed glass is shorter but wider than a five-ounce sour glass. It is useful if you want to serve fizz drinks in something smaller than a Collins glass.

❏ **Martini glass**   Some people prefer their martini in this modified version of a cocktail glass rather than in a cocktail glass. Typically four ounces, the martini glass tapers to a very shallow point at the stem, unlike the cocktail glass, which tapers to an acute point.

❏ **Eggnog mug**   This large, barrel-shaped mug is a fun way to enjoy eggnog drinks.

Do you really need any of these? Base your decisions on your taste, on what you and your guests like to drink, and on just how "complete" a host/bartender you want (and can afford) to be.

The Least You Need to Know

➤ The basic bar stock recommended here should be sufficient for most casual hosts.

➤ Err on the side of stocking more soft-drink mixers than you think you need. Ensure that you always provide alternatives to alcohol.

➤ Ice is the most frequently neglected ingredient in drinks. Too many hosts have too little of it, and what they do use too often tastes of nasty things in the freezer.

➤ If you must reduce glassware to a *sub* minimum, make sure you at least have high-ball and lowball glasses.

Chapter 5

Mixology Demystified: Secrets of Measuring, Mixing, and Pouring

In This Chapter

- ➤ The three basic kinds of drinks
- ➤ Methods of measuring
- ➤ When (and how) to stir, when (and how) to shake
- ➤ Pouring like a pro
- ➤ Preparing your glassware

If you've comparison-shopped before buying this book—or if you've been disloyal and mistrustful enough to consult another book after purchasing this one—you may have been overwhelmed by the sheer number of drinks it is possible to mix.

Don't panic. The fact is, almost all of those hundreds, even thousands of "different" drinks are variations on three basic themes: the highball, the stirred cocktail ("lowball"), and the shaken cocktail. Master the themes, and you'll have no trouble with the variations. This chapter will show you how.

Your First Highball: A Seminar in Measurement

Most of your guests who order mixed drinks will ask for a highball. They won't *call* it that. They'll ask for a rum and Coke, a gin and tonic, a scotch and soda, a screwdriver—something like that—but they're all highballs.

So what's your primary piece of equipment? The highball glass, obviously. Grab one and proceed.

A Firm Foundation

Fill the highball glass about two-thirds with ice. Ice: This is the foundation of most mixed drinks. Anyone thinking about buying a house has at least some awareness of the impor-

Bar Tips
Almost all the drinks you'll mix will be highballs.

tance of a sound foundation. Yet the foundation, below ground and out of sight, probably gets the least attention from the prospective buyer. Similarly, drinkers as well as bartenders give little thought to ice—yet it is probably the most critical component of any drink poured over or chilled by ice.

Ice for mixed drinks is subject to two problems:

Bar Tips
Buy one pound of ice per each guest at a four-hour party, unless you know it's primarily a beer-and-wine crowd.

➤ Bad taste

➤ Insufficient supply

Both problems can be solved by a single solution. Buy commercial *cocktail* (small-cube) ice. It's flavorless, as it should be, whereas most home freezer ice takes on slight but nevertheless disagreeable odors or tastes. Bagged ice is also available in virtually *unlimited* quantities!

If you absolutely must mix a drink with refrigerator freezer ice, it is a good idea to rinse the cubes under cold tap water. This gets rid of any freezer burn and superficial tastes or odors that may cling to the surface of the ice.

The Jigger Method

Having laid your two-thirds-ice foundation, pour in one jigger (that is, $1^1/_2$ ounces) of liquor. Either use a jigger measure or a jigger-size shot glass. Then pour in the mixer—right to the top. Not only will this give you the proper liquor-to-mixer proportion for taste, it *looks* generous. Most important, it will keep you from mixing your drinks too strong. Your object is to dispense enjoyment, not intoxication.

If the mixer is carbonated, your work is done (unless the drink calls for the addition of a garnish) because the bubbles, not you, do the mixing. Indeed, resist the temptation to stir. Doing so will only accelerate the dissipation of the bubbles, and the drink will taste flat.

If the mixer is noncarbonated, either give the drink a few quick stirs with your bar spoon or just put a straw in the glass and let the drinker stir to his or her heart's content.

The Two-Finger Method

There is nothing *wrong* with measuring out liquor with a jigger, and the method certainly ensures a high degree of accuracy. However, it has four drawbacks:

➤ It's slow. This is not a problem if your guests are few, but it can cause a backup at the bar (and monopolize too much of your time) if you are hosting a large party. For *professional* bartending, the jigger method is almost always unacceptably slow.

➤ It's messier; you dirty more barware, and you can drip all over the place.

➤ Measuring out each drink jigger by jigger may be perceived as amateurish.

➤ Worse, it may be perceived as cheap—as if you're rationing out the liquor guest by guest.

One alternative to jigger measurement is the "two-finger method." Just wrap your two fingers together around the bottom of the glass and pour the liquor until it reaches the top of your fingers. If you have especially slender digits, leave a little air between them when you wrap them around the glass. If you're fat-fingered, stop pouring *before* the liquor tops off at the horizon of your fingers.

Toast
May you live as long as you want to, and want to as long as you live.

The two-finger method is fast and at least roughly accurate. It's also inconspicuous and looks thoroughly professional.

The Three-Count Technique

If you use a speedpourer (see the previous chapter), which provides a steady, controllable, even flow of liquor, you might want to use the Three-Count Technique. Of the three measuring techniques, it's the only one that calls for practice. Here's how to do it:

1. After filling a highball glass two-thirds with ice, grab the liquor bottle firmly by the neck. The bottle *must* have a speedpourer inserted!

2. In a single, quick motion, invert the bottle—*completely upside down*—over the glass.

3. Count three. (Not out loud. And don't move your lips.)

The object is to practice to the point that a three count ("one-thousand one, one-thousand two, one-thousand three…") will dispense $1^1/_2$ ounces. You'll probably want to practice with water in a shot glass until you've got the cadence matched with the pour rate.

Why bother?

Bar Tips

It pays to practice the Three-Count Technique. Once you match three counts with a 1$\frac{1}{2}$-ounce pour, you can match one count to one half ounce—and four counts will give you two ounces—should you ever need to deviate from the standard jigger.

Quick One

There was a college that had the reputation of being a fountain of knowledge. Everyone went there to drink.

This is a virtuoso method that makes you look like a pro. Moreover, once you've got it down, you won't have to think about counting. Your sense of timing will kick in automatically. The result will be effortless and rapid drink preparation.

Shaken, or Stirred?

So what's the big deal when Agent 007 suavely orders his martini, specifying that it be "shaken, not stirred"? It's unorthodox, that's what. It's bold and daring—as befits a secret agent who has license to kill.

For the classic martini is stirred, not shaken. Arguably, shaking rather than stirring the martini "improves" its taste by aerating the drink. Maybe. But it also may cloud the martini with tiny air bubbles—not aesthetically pleasing. Here's the accepted rule of thumb: If a drink consists of clear, relatively thin ingredients (such as the gin and vermouth of a martini), use the "least invasive" blending method—that is, stirring. If, however, a drink contains thicker fluids, such as fruit juice, shaking is required to blend the drink properly.

The Stirred Cocktail

Stirred drinks may be prepared on the rocks or straight-up. Let's walk through the mixing of a vodka gimlet as an example of a stirred cocktail prepared and served on the rocks:

1. Fill a lowball glass almost to the rim with ice.
2. Pour in 2 ounces of vodka.
3. Add $\frac{1}{4}$ ounce of Rose's lime juice.
4. Stir *well*.
5. Garnish with a lime wedge; drop it in.

That's one way to do it. You can also prepare on-the-rocks, stirred cocktails in a two-step process. Another vodka gimlet, please:

1. Fill a shaker glass (the small, inner part of a cocktail shaker) two-thirds with ice.
2. Add 1 ounce of Rose's lime juice.
3. Pour in 5 ounces of vodka.
4. Stir vigorously. The objective is to let the ice thoroughly chill the drink.

5. Strain the gimlet into a lowball glass large enough to accommodate it—or divide the drink between two smaller lowball glasses. (You'll learn how to use a cocktail strainer just a little later in this chapter.)

6. Garnish with a lime wedge.

Bar Tips
Tips on preparing lemon twists, lime wedges, orange slices, and other garnishes and "garbage" are found in Chapter four.

The process of making a drink straight-up is identical to the two-step method of preparing a drink on the rocks except that, instead of straining the chilled drink into a glass filled with ice, you just pour it into an empty, preferably chilled, glass. (See "Glassware Prep," later in this chapter.) The key step is stirring vigorously and for a generous span of time—perhaps a count of 10 or 15. The drink really has to chill.

Great Shakes

Serious bartenders have always taken great pride in the panache with which they wield the cocktail shaker. And, despite the risk of catastrophic spillage, the secret is to be bold, vigorous, aggressive, even. Shake *hard*.

The following is the procedure for shaking a classic shaken drink, the whiskey sour:

Bar Tips
See Chapter 4 for sour mix recipes.

1. Into a shaker glass two-thirds full of ice, pour 2 ounces of Canadian whisky.

2. Add 1^1/$_2$ ounces of sour mix.

3. Take the stainless steel shell of the cocktail shaker and put it on top of the glass. Press down *firmly* in order to create a leakproof seal. The beauty of the steel shell is that it will contract during shaking, because the icy fluid lowers its temperature.

4. Use both hands. Put one hand on top of the shaker, and the other on the bottom. Grasp firmly. Shake hard for at least six counts.

5. If you've done everything right, the laws of physics will have created a stout seal between the stainless steel top and the glass bottom of the shaker. To break the seal, so that you can get at the drink, look for the frost line on the steel shell. That's where the top and bottom are sealed. Firmly tap this line with the heel of your hand. You should hear a snap—that's the seal breaking.

6. The shell will now come off very easily. *But don't take it off yet.* First turn the shaker over, so that the steel shell is on the bottom. This will prevent spillage. *Now* take the glass out.

7. Strain the drink from the steel shell into a lowball glass or into a whiskey-sour glass, if you have one. The advantage of the whiskey-sour glass is that, if the drinker handles it by the stem, the straight-up drink will stay colder longer.

CLINK ∘ Toast
Here's to wives and sweethearts—may they never meet!

8. Garnish. The classic finishing touches are a maraschino cherry inside the glass and an orange or lemon slice perched on the lip of the glass.

There is a downside to shaken drinks: the clean-up. Unless you are making one right after the other of the same drink, you'll need to clean the shaker immediately. It will get gummy and nasty if you don't. Rinse it with water, then wipe it out.

Mix, Blend, and Puree!

Given a shaker and sufficient elbow grease on the part of the bartender, shaking is sufficient to blend most drinks. However, if you want to prepare frozen drinks, such as a frozen margarita, a frozen daiquiri, or a frozen piña colada, you'll need an electric blender.

First, make sure that your blender is up to the task of handling ice. A heavy-duty model is best. Then:

1. Make sure the motor is off. Pour the liquor into the blender. Next come the mixers, then the fruit. Last: Add ice—enough to fill the blender to three-quarters full.

2. Make sure you put the lid on properly. Hold it down with one hand and start the machine at low speed. Once the initial mixing is complete, switch to high until everything is thoroughly blended.

3. Pour the drink directly into glasses. No straining is necessary because the ice has been crushed and blended with the drink.

Popping Your Cork

To open wine, begin by completely removing the foil "capsule" from the top of the bottle. If you are using the popular waiter's corkscrew, insert the point of the helical screw (called a "worm") into the cork slightly off center. Bore deeply into the cork, then pull straight up, twisting slightly to loosen the cork. An easier alternative is to use either a twin-lever corkscrew or a screwpull-type corkscrew. These are available in most stores that sell food-preparation utensils.

Buzzed Words
Frozen drinks are also called **freezes**.

Opening champagne is at once easier and more challenging than opening a bottle of wine. It's easier, because you don't have to use a corkscrew. It's more challenging because the contents of the bottle are under great pressure.

➤ Inspect the bottle before opening it. Look for deep scratches or nicks. Deep imperfections in the glass may cause the bottle to explode.

➤ Do not chill champagne below 45 degrees. Chilling below this temperature increases the potential for an explosion.

➤ During the uncorking process, point the bottle away from you and others.

To remove the cork, point the bottle away from you and others, and remove the foil "capsule" covering the top. Next, untwist the wire cage that is over the cork. While doing this, place your palm over the cork to keep it from shooting out of the bottle. Now, still pointing the bottle away from all living beings, gently twist the cork, cupping your palm over it. As the cork works free, it will press against your palm. Do not release the cork. Do not let it pop. It should clear the bottle with a barely audible hiss or very muffled pop.

Pouring

Pouring is easy. If you aren't using a speedpourer, prevent spillage by turning the bottle slightly as you come to the end of the pour and bring the bottle upright. For the sake of an appearance that is both professional and generous-looking, try to accomplish the pour in one motion rather than with tentative dribs and drabs.

Using the Speedpourer

We've already discussed the speedpourer as absolutely required for bartenders using the Three-Count Method. Even if you don't use that method, however, speedpourers make your job quicker and neater. Do take time to put the speedpourer in the bottle so that the slant of the mouth is at a right angle to the label. This will put more speed into your pour by allowing you to grab the bottle without having to check which way the stream of liquor will emerge. Moreover, your guests will be able to see the label as your pour—a nice touch, especially if you are serving premium liquor.

Using a Cocktail Strainer

You've seen that little paddle-like metal gadget with the Slinky-style spring running around it. It's a cocktail strainer, and its function is to hold back the ice as you pour a finished drink from the shaker. The strainer is intended to fit neatly over the mouth of the shaker, so that you can hold it in place with one finger.

Developing a Multiple Personality

If you've admired the speed of the super-fast bartender who can prepare multiples of the same drink simultaneously, now is your chance to admire yourself. *You* can do it!

Just line up X number of glasses in a row. They should be filled with ice, and they should be standing rim to rim. Make sure a speedpourer is in the bottle of booze. Grab the bottle by the neck. Do a smooth inversion over the first glass, count three, move the still-inverted bottle smoothly to the next glass, count three, go on and on and on.

Unfortunately, because you can't put a speedpourer into most mixer bottles, you'll have to pour this ingredient in one glass at a time. Same goes for dispensing the garnish.

Pouring the Pousse-Café

The delicately layered pousse-café presents the ultimate pouring challenge. We'll discuss the actual creation of these dessert drinks in Chapter 18, but here's a glimpse of the pouring technique.

You have to pour each ingredient in the drink slowly and carefully, so that the layers don't combine. Always start with the heaviest or thickest liquid (bottom layer), proceed to the next heaviest (middle), then on to the lightest (top). Use a twisted bar spoon to guide the liquor into the pousse-café glass. Hold one end of the handle against the bottle containing the ingredient, and place the tip of the handle against the edge of the pousse-café glass. Now let the fluid gently slide from the bottle, down the twisted bar spoon, and into the glass. Take care, but have confidence. This works. Your skill will be a subject of wonder and praise.

Glassware Prep

The most important item of glassware preparation is cleanliness. Ensure that your bar glassware is spotless and, equally important, thoroughly rinsed, so that no soap or detergent taste or aroma lingers in the glass.

Certain drinks call for additional preparation.

Chilling

If you want to chill a glass before pouring a drink into it, refrigerate the dry glass for an hour or longer, then fill the glass with ice water. Prepare the drink. When you are ready to pour the drink, dump out the ice water.

Frosting

Frosting is a step beyond chilling. Dip the glass in water, then put it in the freezer for half an hour. This will give it a frosty white appearance. If the glass has a stem, hold it by the stem to avoid melting any of the frost.

Salting

Salting means rimming the glass with salt—something you may want to do for a Salty Dog or a margarita. It's easy if you remember to use rock salt rather than table salt.

Pour rock salt on a plate. Take a lime wedge and rub it around the rim of the glass. Roll the glass rim around in the salt.

Flavoring the Rim

Aside from salting, you can flavor the rim of any glass with the fruit used to garnish the drink. Just run the orange, lime, or lemon peel on the rim. It will impart a subtle flavor and aroma to the drink.

The Least You Need to Know

➤ Most drinks are variations on three basic types: the highball, the stirred cocktail ("lowball"), and the shaken cocktail.

➤ Mastering either the Two-Finger Method or the Three-Count Method of measuring makes you look like a pro and speeds the mixing process.

➤ Practice using your cocktail shaker before you use it. Prevent embarrassing accidents.

➤ Ensure that glassware is clean and free from soap or detergent residue.

Part 2
Clear Choices

Gin and vodka are the crystalline spirits—colorless, but hardly without character. They vie with one another for first place as the most popular of all mixed-drink ingredients. This section provides guidance in choosing the right gin as well as making great gin-based drinks. From there, you launch into the "world of vodka," a spirit even subtler in character than gin. Here you'll find the history of this Polish-born and Russian-raised liquor, which, after gaining popularity in the United States after World War II, has become the sales champion among all spirits. The catalog of vodka-based drinks is extensive.

Perhaps no mixed drink is more discussed and debated than the martini—the "Silver Bullet." Controversial ever since it developed from the 19th-century Martinez, the martini simply cannot be dry enough for some, while others painstakingly search for the magic perfect ratio of vermouth to gin. We try to represent the claims of all sides in the great martini controversy, and we include gin as well as vodka recipes.

Chapter 6

Brother Juniper: The Joys of Gin

In This Chapter

➤ How gin is made

➤ The difference between London dry and Dutch (genever) gin

➤ The range of flavorfulness of gin

➤ Gin recipes

A deeply aromatic spirit, gin doesn't appeal to everybody, but those who admire it cherish its bracing, refreshing qualities, redolent of juniper berries and a host of other *botanicals*—an often exotic collection of extracts from roots, barks, seeds, and leaves—that give gin its character. Unlike vodka, which is (or should be) flavorless, the character of gin varies greatly from brand to brand and invites a lot of "comparison shopping."

Distiller's Secrets

The creation of a fine gin almost has more in common with the creation of a great perfume than other alcoholic beverages. And, as with the formula used to create Chanel No. 5, the recipes behind the world's great gins are closely guarded.

British and American Varieties

The gins made in England and the United States start with fermented malt, which yields a beer that is distilled into a *malt wine*. This is purified to produce an almost neutral spirit that, like vodka, is without flavor or aroma. Next, the distillate is diluted with distilled water. At this point, it may be combined with flavoring agents, which we will discuss in a moment. The concoction is distilled again, and once again reduced with water, to yield a final product of 40 to 47 percent alcoholic content: 80 to 94 proof. Although most gins are not aged, some American producers do age their product, which gives it a pale golden coloring. Some British distillers create this effect with the addition of a small amount of caramel coloring.

> **Buzzed Words**
> Gins are often designated **dry gin** or **London dry gin**. These originated when "sweet" (called **Old Tom**) as well as "dry" gin was available. Today, the distinction is mainly superfluous, because almost all English and American gin is now dry. Also note that London dry gin doesn't have to be made in London or even England. This describes a manufacturing style, not a place of origin.

There's more than one way to get the flavoring agents into the gin. If they are not added prior to the second distillation, they may be suspended from special racks *during* the second distillation, so that the flavors are percolated by the distillate as it condenses. In this way, the flavor of the botanicals permeates the spirit. Makers of some less-expensive American gins mix the spirits with essential oils and do not redistill. Others add the flavorings to the mash from which the malt wine is fermented. In this case also, the gin is distilled only once.

All gins share a base flavoring of juniper berries, but they diverge widely in combining such other botanicals as orris, angelica and licorice roots, lemon and orange peels, cassia, cinnamon bark, caraway, coriander, cardamom, anise, bergamot, cocoa, and fennel.

We don't like recommending one brand over another; the choice is highly subjective. If you like gin, you'll almost certainly enjoy all of the premium brands as well as many of the less-expensive brands—especially when combined with tonic or other mixers.

That said, it may help you choose your favorites to know that of the three most popular *premium* brands—Beefeater, Tanqueray, and Bombay—Beefeater is the least distinctively flavored and Bombay the most highly and complexly flavored, with Tanqueray somewhere in between. This is not a judgment of quality. Many people prefer the relatively "clean" taste of Beefeater to the more complex, "spicy" quality of Bombay, while others prefer to straddle the fence with Tanqueray. Sampling all three gives you a good idea of the range of flavoring possible in fine gin.

Dutch Varieties

Dutch gin—called Hollands, genever, geneva, jenever gin, or Shiedam gin (after the distilling center just outside of Rotterdam)—is widely consumed in the Netherlands, but is less popular in the United States. In smaller U.S. cities, you may have trouble finding a liquor store that stocks it.

In contrast to the bracing, crisp, clean taste and feel of American and English gins, genever is thick, full-bodied, and, barley-born, savors of malt. Something of an acquired taste, devotees find it delicious, and it is well worth looking for.

Genever gin is also worth a try because it is your opportunity to taste what the "original" gin must have been like. Invented by Franciscus de la Boe—better known as Dr. Franciscus Sylvius—as a diuretic medicine, it was carried back to England by British soldiers, who called it "Dutch courage."

Gin and...

Although not everyone likes the taste of gin by itself, it vies with vodka as the most mixable of spirits. It can be combined with just about anything.

Also called Pink Gin, Gin and Bitters is a singularly bracing and sophisticated combination.

Bar Tips
Unlike American and English gins, genever does *not* go well with mixers. It is meant to be enjoyed neat or, if you wish, on the rocks. All the gin recipes in this book are meant to be mixed with American or English dry gin.

Bar Tips
Don't look for a martini here. It gets its own chapter: Chapter 8, "The Silver Bullet."

Gin and Bitters

Serve straight-up, strained into an old-fashioned or lowball glass.

2 oz. gin

$^1/_2$ tsp. Angostura bitters

Stir the gin and bitters in a glass with ice cubes until well chilled. Strain into the serving glass.

Another refreshingly astringent drink combines gin with Campari. If you enjoy Campari, you'll love this. Unlike Gin and Bitters, it is meant to be served on the rocks.

Gin and Campari

Serve in a lowball glass.

$1^1/_2$ oz. gin

$1^1/_2$ oz. Campari

Orange slice or twist of orange

Combine gin and Campari in a cocktail shaker with ice. Shake vigorously, then strain into the serving glass filled with ice. Garnish with an orange slice or a twist of orange.

Yet another piquant drink with gin is served straight-up in a cocktail glass. It's seductively dubbed Gin and Sin.

Gin and Sin

Serve straight-up, strained into a cocktail glass.

2 oz. gin

1 tbs. Cinzano

Combine gin and Cinzano in a glass with ice, stir until well chilled, then strain into the serving glass.

Probably the most frequently requested "bitter" gin drink is the provocatively puckering Negroni.

Negroni

Serve straight-up in a chilled cocktail glass.

2 oz. gin   Splash of club soda (optional)

1/2 oz. sweet vermouth   Orange peel

3/4 oz. Campari

Combine all ingredients, except the orange peel, in a shaker with ice. Shake vigorously, then strain into the serving glass. Twist the orange peel and drop into the glass.

Ginger ale is just sweet enough to leaven the bitterness of gin, but not so sweet that it entirely overpowers or clashes with the spirit. This is a favorite drink with many.

Gin and Ginger

Serve on the rocks in a chilled highball glass.

1 1/2 oz. gin

Ginger ale to fill

Lemon twist

Combine gin and ginger ale in the serving glass filled with ice. Drop in the lemon twist.

Players Script

John Barrymore's legendary reputation as a great actor was all but eclipsed by his renown as a great drinker. A man of extraordinary wit and charm, "The Profile" (as Barrymore was dubbed) was a fixture of the Broadway stage as well as The Players bar. In his cups, the sophisticate's veneer inevitably dissolved, as Barrymore yielded to some primal impulse. He would regularly stagger into the club's sitting room, address the great fireplace, and, with a few preliminary gestures, relieve himself copiously and at length into its warming and welcoming blaze. Club regulars became accustomed to this, though, doubtless, many of their guests felt they had seen more of the Profile than they cared to.

John Barrymore, famed actor and member of The Players. (Photo courtesy of Photofest.)

A lot of folks confuse tonic water with soda water. The two are quite different. Tonic is carbonated sugar water flavored with a bit of lemon and quinine, which gives this mixer a provocatively bitter taste. Soda water, in contrast, is nothing but unflavored carbonated water.

No great disaster will result if you mix gin with soda water. What you get is a—guess what?—Gin and Soda.

Bar Tips

An open bottle of tonic water or club soda is only good for about a day. To make sure they're always crisp, consider buying them in six packs of small bottles, which you can finish before they get flat. For a big party, go for the larger bottles.

Gin and Soda

Serve on the rocks in a highball glass.

1¹/₂-2 oz. gin

Club soda to fill

Lemon twist

Pour the gin into the serving glass filled with ice. Add club soda, and garnish with the lemon twist.

But the *real* thing is Gin and Tonic—next to the martini, the most popular gin-bearing drink. The key to a successful Gin and Tonic is *fresh* tonic water. Carbonated mixers quickly go flat, and none goes flatter more quickly than tonic water. To a sun-parched drinker eagerly anticipating the refreshment of a sparkling G&T, few things are more disappointing than a flat, bitter drink. Make certain you use freshly opened tonic water. Once you open a bottle, keep it refrigerated; this will retard the dissipation of the bubbles.

Gin and Tonic

Serve on the rocks in a highball glass.

2-2¹/₂ oz. gin

Tonic water to fill

Lime wedge or lemon twist

Pour the gin into the serving glass filled with ice. Add tonic, and garnish with a lime wedge (traditional) or, if you prefer, a lemon twist.

Gimlet Eye

Gimlet is a word that goes back to Middle English and has to do with sharpness and the quality of penetration. A gimlet is a sharp little hand tool for boring holes, and a "gimlet-eyed" individual possesses a piercing gaze. Take your cue from the history of this word: A gimlet should meet the taste buds with an eye-opening sharpness.

The best gimlets are made from freshly squeezed lime or, for a delicious variation, freshly squeezed *limon* (the offspring of a lime-lemon cross).

If you don't have fresh limes or don't want to exert the effort to squeeze them, use Rose's lime juice.

Gimlet with Fresh Lime

Serve in a chilled old-fashioned or lowball glass.

2 oz. gin

$^1/_2$ oz. Fresh lime (or limon) juice

Lime twist or lime slice

Stir gin and juice very vigorously in a mixing (shaker) glass with cracked ice; pour into the serving glass. Garnish with a lime twist or lime slice. May also be served straight-up: Stir with ice cubes, then strain into the serving glass.

Gimlet with Rose's Lime Juice

Serve in a chilled old-fashioned or lowball glass.

2 oz. gin

$^1/_2$ oz. Rose's lime juice

Lime slice

Use a shaker or blender to mix the gin and Rose's with cracked ice; pour into the serving glass. The best garnish is a lime slice, which gets more of the natural juice into the drink. May also be served straight-up: Strain the shaken or blended ingredients into the serving glass.

Once popular enough to deserve its own glass, the appeal of this drink has waned over the years, but it remains a part of the standard repertoire nevertheless.

Tom Collins

Serve on the rocks in a Collins or highball glass.

2-3 oz. gin	Club soda to fill
$1^1/_2$ oz. lemon juice	Maraschino cherry
$1^1/_2$ oz. sugar syrup	

Combine all ingredients except club soda and cherry in the serving glass with ice. Stir well. Fill with club soda, and garnish with the cherry.

Juices (Mostly)

Most of us are familiar with vodka and orange juice (the screwdriver) and with vodka and grapefruit juice. No law says you can't substitute gin for vodka in these faithful standbys.

Gin Screwdriver

Serve on the rocks in a highball glass.

1$\frac{1}{2}$ oz. gin

2-3 oz. orange juice

Stir well. If you like, add a dash or two of Angostura bitters.

The cocktail variation on the Gin Screwdriver is called the Orange Blossom.

Orange Blossom

Serve in a chilled cocktail glass.

1$\frac{1}{2}$ oz. gin   Orange slice

1 oz. orange juice

Combine all ingredients, except the orange slice, in a shaker with ice. Shake vigorously, then strain into the serving glass. Garnish with the orange slice.

Gin and Grapefruit Juice

Serve on the rocks in a highball glass.

1$\frac{1}{2}$ oz. gin

2-3 oz. grapefruit juice

Combine all ingredients in a serving glass filled with ice. Stir well.

Pretty easy, huh? The following are only a little more challenging—and a lot more interesting. Begin with the Abbey, which adds an extra dimension to the Gin Screwdriver.

Abbey

Serve on the rocks in a lowball glass.

1$\frac{1}{2}$ oz. gin   Dash or 2 of orange bitters

1$\frac{1}{2}$ oz. orange juice   Maraschino cherry

Combine all ingredients, except for the cherry, in a shaker with ice. Shake vigorously, then strain into the ice-filled serving glass. Garnish with the cherry.

There is also a cocktail version of the Abbey.

Abbey Cocktail

Serve straight-up in a chilled cocktail glass.

1¹/₂ oz. gin

³/₄ oz. orange juice

¹/₄ oz. sweet vermouth

Dash or 2 of Angostura bitters

Maraschino cherry

Combine all ingredients, except for the cherry, in a shaker with ice. Shake vigorously, then strain into the serving glass. Garnish with the cherry.

Its name notwithstanding, the Bronx Cocktail is a product of upscale Manhattan. Johnnie Solon, legendary bartender at the old Waldorf-Astoria Hotel, invented it. It's simple and delicious.

Bronx Cocktail

Serve straight-up in a chilled cocktail glass.

1¹/₂ oz. gin

¹/₂ oz. orange juice

Dash of dry vermouth

Dash of sweet vermouth

Combine all ingredients, with ice, in a shaker. Shake vigorously. Strain into the serving glass. Some drinkers prefer more of the vermouths—¹/₂ ounce each—and a full ounce of orange juice. If you want a dry cocktail, skip the sweet vermouth.

A variation on the Bronx Cocktail is the Lone Tree, which omits the orange juice and adds orange bitters. If you like martinis, you'll want to try this.

Lone Tree

Serve straight-up in a chilled cocktail glass.

³/₄ oz. gin

³/₄ oz. dry vermouth (optional)

³/₄ oz. sweet vermouth

Several dashes of orange bitters (optional)

Olive (optional)

To a shaker filled with cracked ice add all ingredients except for the olive. Shake vigorously. Strain into the serving glass and garnish with the olive.

Sours aren't just made with whiskey. Gin makes a great sour, too.

Gin Sour

Serve straight-up in a whiskey sour glass or lowball glass.

2-3 oz. gin	Orange or lemon slice
1 oz. lemon juice	Maraschino cherry
1 tsp. sugar syrup	

In a shaker, with ice, combine all ingredients except the garnishes. Shake vigorously. Strain into the serving glass. Garnish with an orange slice and maraschino cherry.

A Fizz and a Rickey

A "fizz" is cousin to the Collins. It is made with sour mix, sugar, and club soda. Everybody's heard of the Sloe Gin Fizz. Well, you won't find it in this chapter, because sloe gin isn't gin, but a liqueur (check out Chapter 16). Nevertheless, the Gin Fizz—with *real* gin—is a classic, which you *should* know how to make.

Gin Fizz

Serve on the rocks in a Collins or tall highball glass.

1$\frac{1}{2}$ oz. gin	Club soda to fill
1 tbs. powdered sugar	Maraschino cherry
3 oz. sour mix	Orange slice

To a shaker filled with ice add the gin, sugar, and sour mix. Shake vigorously. Pour into the ice-filled serving glass, then add club soda. Garnish with a maraschino cherry and an orange slice.

A near relation to the Gin Fizz is the Gin Daisy—as in "fresh as a." This is a thoroughly delightful drink.

The Gin Rickey is a must for any mixologist's repertoire. Fortunately, it's quick and simple to make.

A Gin Sidecar is a variation on the simple Rickey.

Gin Daisy

Serve in a chilled highball glass.

2-3 oz. gin

1 oz. lemon juice

1/4 oz. raspberry syrup or grenadine

1/2 tsp. sugar syrup

Club soda to fill

Orange slice

To a shaker filled with cracked ice add all ingredients except for the club soda and orange slice. Shake vigorously. Pour into the serving glass. Add club soda to fill, then garnish with the orange slice.

Gin Rickey

Serve on the rocks in a highball glass.

1 1/2 oz. gin

Club soda to fill

Juice of 1/2 fresh lime

Fill a highball glass half full of ice cubes; pour in the gin, then the club soda to fill. Add the lime juice.

Gin Sidecar

Serve in a chilled old-fashioned or lowball glass.

1 1/2 oz. gin

3/4 oz. triple sec

1 oz. lemon juice

Pour all ingredients into a shaker with cracked ice. Shake vigorously. Pour into the serving glass.

Surprising Gin

"Bracing," "astringent," "clean," and "bitter" are words you've already heard to describe the taste of gin. But this sharp-toothed libation has some softer surprises in store. What follows is not your father's "gin and…"

Buzzed Words
A **rickey** is any drink with soda water and lime—and sometimes sugar.

The Admirals

The Admiral Benbow is a hybrid cross between a gimlet and a martini.

Admiral Benbow

Serve straight-up in an old-fashioned or lowball glass.

2 oz. gin

1 oz. dry vermouth

$^1/_2$ oz. lime juice

Maraschino cherry

Stir gin, vermouth, and lime juice vigorously with ice, strain into the serving glass, and garnish with a Maraschino cherry.

Bet you didn't know gin can go very nicely with cherry liqueurs such as Peter Heering or Cherry Marnier. Try the Admiral Cocktail.

Admiral Cocktail

Serve straight-up in a chilled cocktail glass.

2 oz. gin

$^3/_4$ oz. lime juice

$^1/_2$ oz. Peter Heering or Cherry Marnier

Shake all ingredients vigorously with ice in a shaker or use a blender; strain into the serving glass.

Bar Tips

If you use a blender, be careful not to over-blend this and all the recipes that follow.

Liqueur Refreshed, Brandy Rebranded—and a Dash of Dubonnet

Liqueur: heavy, sweet, and ideal for dessert drinks. That's a true assessment as far as it goes, but, if you know how to combine gin and liqueur, you'll see that this truism just doesn't go far enough. Neither liqueur nor flavored brandy need be reserved just for desserts.

A gin and liqueur combination that deserves wider recognition is the Cornell Cocktail. Since you'll need an egg white, it's easiest to make two of these at a time.

Slings are sweet drinks made with brandy, whiskey, or gin. Here's the gin version.

> **Bar Tips**
> Most drinks that call for egg white require half an egg white. But it's almost impossible to get *half* an egg white; therefore, all recipes in this book calling for egg white make *two* drinks. (You really shouldn't drink alone.)

Cornell Cocktail

Serve straight-up in a chilled cocktail glass.

4 oz. gin

1 oz. Maraschino liqueur

1 egg white *

Vigorously shake all ingredients with ice in a shaker or blend; strain into the serving glasses. *Recipe makes two drinks.*

* *Raw egg may be a source of salmonella bacteria. You may wish to avoid drinks calling for raw egg yolk or white.*

Gin Sling

Serve in an old-fashioned or lowball glass.

2-3 oz. gin $^1/_2$ oz. orgeat or sugar syrup

1 oz. lemon juice   Club soda to fill

Fill serving glass half full with cracked ice. Add all ingredients except club soda. Stir. Add club soda to fill. If you don't want a fizzy drink, substitute plain water for the club soda.

Tropical Heritage

Back when the sun never set on the British Empire, Royal Navy physicians mixed gin with quinine (tonic) water, mixed gin with bitters, mixed gin with a lot of things in the belief that it would stave off a host of

> **Buzzed Words**
> A **sling** is any brandy, whiskey, or gin drink that is sweetened and flavored with lemon.

71

terrible tropical diseases that felled sailors, soldiers, and colonial administrators alike. Gin bombed out as a medicine, but it has had tropical connections ever since. Here are some exotic temptations.

Bermuda Cocktail

Serve in a chilled old-fashioned or lowball glass.

$1^{1}/_{2}$ oz. gin

1 oz. apricot brandy

$^{1}/_{2}$ oz. lime juice (fresh or Rose's)

1 tsp. Falernum or sugar syrup

Dash of grenadine

Orange peel

$^{1}/_{2}$ tsp. curaçao

To a shaker filled with cracked ice add all ingredients except the orange peel and curaçao. Shake vigorously. Pour into the serving glass. Garnish with the orange peel twist, then carefully top with curaçao so that it floats.

By far the best-known "tropical" gin drink is the Singapore Sling. It's sweet, fun, and it's your big chance to deploy some of those little paper parasols.

Singapore Sling

Serve on the rocks in a chilled Collins or highball glass.

2 oz. gin

1 oz. cherry brandy or Peter Heering

Juice of $^{1}/_{2}$ lemon

Dash of Benedictine

Club soda to fill

Lemon slice

Mint sprig

In a shaker with cracked ice combine all ingredients except for the lemon slice and mint sprig, but including a splash of club soda. Shake vigorously. Strain into the serving glass. Add ice cubes and club soda to fill. Garnish with lemon slice and mint sprig.

People love "retro" drinks, and nothing's more retro than the Pink Lady.

Pink Lady

Serve straight-up in a chilled cocktail glass.

3 oz. gin	2 tsp. sugar syrup
3 oz. applejack or Calvados	2 tsp. grenadine
2 oz. lemon juice	1 egg white *

Combine all ingredients, with ice, in a shaker. Shake vigorously. Strain into serving glasses. Recipe makes two drinks.

* *Raw egg may be a source of salmonella bacteria. You may wish to avoid drinks calling for raw egg yolk or white.*

The Least You Need to Know

➤ The premium gins are distilled twice, with the special flavoring added in the second distillation process.

➤ Use premium gins with subtle mixers and the less expensive gins with sweet or strongly flavored mixers.

➤ Dutch (genever) gin is well worth trying, but, in contrast to British or American gin, it does not make a good mixer.

➤ Every bartender should know how to make a gin Gimlet, a Gin Rickey, a good Gin Fizz, and a Tom Collins.

Na Zdorovye!: The World of Vodka

Colorless, tasteless, and aromaless, vodka outsells any other category of spirits in the United States. This may strike you as surprising when you consider that vodka was rarely consumed here before World War II.

It would make for exciting reading if we could tell you that American soldiers brought the stuff home from war-torn Russia, but that's not the case. World War II saw the American people subjected to rigorous rationing of almost every product they had previously taken for granted. Alcoholic beverages were no exception. With peace came an end to rationing, but, after four years of war, liquor dealers had precious little product to offer.

Smirnoff Takes Off

That's when serious drinkers—and dealers in spirits—discovered a small distillery with a Russian name, which had been making vodka in the United States since shortly after the end of Prohibition. The label on their bottles proudly proclaimed that the Smirnoff family had been distilling vodka for the czars since the 19th century. (The label did not explain that the Smirnoffs and their product had fled the Bolshevik Revolution.)

The Smirnoffs plied their trade on this side of the Atlantic, purveying vodka to what was then the relatively small Russian community in the United States. Little of the product broke through the ethnic barriers and into the mainstream—until 1946.

Once discovered, the Smirnoffs promoted their spirit with one of the most memorable slogans ever to appear in liquor advertising: *"It leaves you breathless."* The double-entendre was unmistakable. Not only did the product deliver a buzz, it left no aftertaste—nor any telltale after-odor. The Smirnoffs also came up with the Moscow Mule, a drink you, too, can make (we'll show you how later in this chapter).

Vodka today is more popular than ever, and dozens of brands have followed Smirnoff into the fray. There are now a number of American brands, and enthusiasts can choose from such premium imported labels as Russia's Stolichnaya, Poland's Wyborowa, Sweden's Absolut, and Finland's Finlandia.

While sales of vodka have risen steadily since 1946, they exploded in the 1980s, despite a general decline in liquor consumption. While many professionals were opting for bottled waters instead of scotch with lunch, others refused to forsake alcohol, but did retreat from the more flavorful spirits to the cleaner, lighter taste of vodka.

Vodka can also be had in flavors. In the United States, vodkas flavored with peppercorns, lemon peel, raisins, anise, basil, berries (especially black currants), and caraway are popular.

Straight, No Chaser

By U.S. law, all non-flavored vodka consumed here must be filtered after distillation to remove all distinctive character, aroma, taste, and color. However, even the flavorless vodkas—especially the premium brands—do have a certain character, an undertone of flavor, that partisans of particular brands prize.

> **Bar Tips**
> Vodka is becoming increasingly popular as an alternative to gin in martinis, but don't look for your vodka martini here. You'll find it, with its gin-based brethren, in Chapter 8.

It's worth sampling the premium brands to discover what you like best. Serve the vodka in a lowball glass on the rocks—or, better yet, put the vodka in the freezer to get it *very* cold, and enjoy it straight.

Remember, for most mixing purposes, any decent vodka will do. Don't waste a premium brand on a cocktail: the flavor undertone is so subtle that almost any flavored mixer will overpower it.

Bloody Mary

Mary I ruled England from 1553 to 1558. Mary was determined to undo the Protestant Reformation her father, Henry VIII, had begun, and, during her reign, she ordered the execution—by public burning at the stake—of some 300 Protestants.

Bar Tips
Most shaker drinks should be shaken vigorously, but not the Bloody Mary. Shake *too* hard, and the tomato juice may separate. Go gently.

Thus the name "Bloody Mary" was bequeathed to history, and was snatched to describe one of the most popular drinks ever invented. The drink is usually credited to Fernand Petiot, a bartender at Harry's New York Bar in Paris, the 1920s gathering place of F. Scott Fitzgerald, Ernest Hemingway, e.e. cummings, and others.

Now, some folks just throw a little vodka and a little tomato juice together and hand you what they call a Bloody Mary. But that's, at best, a vodka and tomato juice, not a Bloody Mary. The classic recipe, evolved and elaborated upon from Harry's original, follows.

Bloody Mary

Serve in a chilled Collins glass.

2 oz. vodka

4-6 oz. tomato juice

1 tsp. lemon juice

$1/4$ tsp. Worcestershire sauce

Few dashes Tabasco sauce

Pinch white pepper

Pinch or two of celery salt

$1/2$ tsp. dried or fresh chopped dill

Celery stalk

Combine all ingredients (except for the celery stalk) with cracked ice in a shaker. Shake gently. Pour into the serving glass. Garnish with the celery stalk and, if you wish, add two or three ice cubes.

Robert Benchley (right): Writer, Algonquin wit, and member of The Players. (Photo courtesy of Photofest.)

Variations on a Bloody Theme

The Algonquin Bloody Mary is the creation of a bartender at the Blue Bar in New York City's celebrated Algonquin Hotel, once a favored watering hole of the literati, most notably the so-called "Algonquin Wits," which included Dorothy Parker, Robert Benchley, and James Thurber, among others.

Algonquin Bloody Mary

Serve straight up in a Collins glass.

1½ oz. vodka	1 tsp. Worcestershire sauce
4 oz. tomato juice	4-6 dashes of Tabasco sauce
Salt and ground pepper (to taste)	Lime wedge
Juice of half a lime	

In a shaker, combine all ingredients except the lime wedge. Shake gently. Strain into the serving glass, and garnish with the lime wedge.

The Bloody Blossom adds orange juice.

Bloody Blossom

Serve in a Collins glass.

1½ oz. vodka	3 oz. tomato juice
3 oz. orange juice	Mint sprig

In a shaker, combine all ingredients except the mint sprig with cracked ice. Shake gently. Pour into the serving glass, and garnish with the mint.

Don't limit yourself to the variations listed here. If you like, try substituting other spirits for vodka. People have enjoyed the O Sole Maria (made with Galliano), the Shamrock Mary (made with Irish whiskey), the Sake Mary (with sake), the Bonnie Mary (with scotch), the Bloody Maria (with tequila), and La Bonne Marie (with cognac).

Russians Black and White

Two frequently requested vodka drinks are the Black Russian and the White Russian. They are simple to make.

Black Russian

Serve in a chilled old-fashioned glass.

1^1/$_2$ oz. vodka

^{3}/$_4$ oz. Kahlúa

Combine the two ingredients with cracked ice in a shaker. Shake vigorously, then pour into the serving glass. Optionally, add a few dashes of lemon juice for a "Black Magic." Garnish with a lemon twist, if desired.

White Russian

Serve in a chilled cocktail glass.

1^1/$_2$ oz. vodka ^{3}/$_4$ oz. heavy cream

1 oz. white crème de cacao

Combine the ingredients with cracked ice in a shaker. Shake vigorously, then strain into the serving glass.

Citrus Productions

Vodka mixes beautifully with citrus juices. Don't invest in premium-label vodka for citrus drinks; instead, spend a little extra to buy freshly-squeezed juices or spend a little extra time to squeeze the juice fresh yourself. You'll taste the difference.

Moscow Mule and Other Mostly Lime Juice Drinks

The Moscow Mule is the drink that kicked vodka into the American drinking mainstream. The classic recipe that follows originated in Los Angeles, at the Cock 'n' Bull Restaurant.

Ever since the Ocean Spray company became closely associated with cranberry juice, drinks made with that juice have been given names savoring of the sea and seashore. The Cape Codder starts out with vodka and a dash of lime juice.

Moscow Mule

Serve in a chilled highball glass or a chilled coffee mug.

3 oz. vodka

1 tsp. lime juice

Ginger beer to fill

Lime wedge

Combine the vodka and lime juice in the serving glass one-third filled with ice cubes. Add ginger beer to fill, and garnish with the lime.

Cape Codder

Serve in a large (double) chilled old-fashioned glass.

1½ oz. vodka

Dash lime juice

4 oz. cranberry juice

1 tsp. sugar syrup

Combine all ingredients in a shaker with cracked ice. Shake vigorously, and pour into the serving glass.

The gimlet is among the most popular of vodka vehicles. If at all possible, squeeze a fresh lime directly into the drink. The taste is irresistibly refreshing.

Vodka Gimlet with Fresh Lime

Serve on the rocks in a lowball glass.

2 oz. vodka

1 oz. fresh lime juice

Combine all ingredients in a shaker. Shake vigorously. Pour into the serving glass. *Or,* combine both ingredients in the serving glass and stir.

If you must use concentrated lime juice, try the following:

Vodka Gimlet with Rose's Lime Juice

Serve in a chilled cocktail glass.

2 oz. vodka

$1/2$ oz. Rose's lime juice

Combine both ingredients with ice in a mixing glass. Stir. Strain into the serving glass.

Salty Dog and Other Mostly Grapefruit Juice Drinks

Vodka and grapefruit juice are a natural combination; the puckery acidity of the grapefruit juice makes a perfect complement to the alcohol. You can keep it simple and just fill a highball glass with ice, pour in two fingers of vodka, add grapefruit juice to fill, and down the hatch. Or you can be more ambitious. The best-known vodka and grapefruit juice drink adds a bit of salt and sugar.

Salty Dog

Serve in an old-fashioned glass with a salted-sugared rim.

Salt

Granulated sugar

Lime wedge

2 oz. vodka

Grapefruit juice to fill

Prepare the glass by rubbing the lime wedge on the rim and salting the glass (see Chapter 5 for more information about salting). Fill glass one-third with ice cubes. Pour in vodka, sugar, and grapefruit juice, stir, and garnish with the lime wedge used for rimming.

Once again, the addition of cranberry evokes salt air and high seas.

Sea Breeze with Juice

Serve in a chilled highball glass.

2 oz. vodka

3 oz. grapefruit juice

3 oz. cranberry juice

Combine all ingredients in a shaker with cracked ice. Shake vigorously. Pour into the serving glass.

Screwdrivers, Wallbangers, and Other Mostly Orange Juice Drinks

To think of vodka and orange juice is to think of a screwdriver, a very basic drink named for a very basic tool. It's best if the orange juice is freshly squeezed!

Screwdriver

Serve on the rocks in a chilled highball glass or in a large (double) chilled old-fashioned glass.

$1^1/_2$ oz. vodka

4 oz. orange juice

Orange slice

Fill serving glass one-third with ice cubes. Pour in vodka and orange juice, stir, and garnish with the orange slice.

The Harvey Wallbanger is a screwdriver with the addition of Galliano, the popular Italian liqueur that comes in a ridiculously tall bottle.

Harvey Wallbanger

Serve on the rocks in a chilled Collins glass.

$1^1/_2$ oz. vodka

4 oz. orange juice

$^1/_2$ oz. Galliano

Fill serving glass one-third with ice cubes. Pour in vodka and orange juice, and stir. Carefully add the Galliano so that it floats. Do not stir!

A little thought will tell you where the name of the next drink comes from, a combination of a fruit that sports a "belly button" and a fruit covered with fuzz.

Fuzzy Navel

Serve on the rocks in a highball glass.

$^3/_4$ oz. peach schnapps

$^3/_4$ oz. vodka

Orange juice to fill

Combine all ingredients in the serving glass and stir.

Sex on the Beach

This certainly sounds more inviting than vodka and pineapple juice, which is what it is. You won't find a *Kama Sutra*-full of versions of this drink, but there are a few. We'll begin with what most authorities agree is the original.

Original Sex on the Beach

Serve in a chilled highball glass.

1 oz. vodka

$^1/_2$ oz. Midori melon liqueur

$^1/_2$ oz. Chambord (substitute other raspberry liqueur if necessary)

$1^1/_2$ oz. pineapple juice

$1^1/_2$ oz. cranberry juice cocktail

Combine all ingredients in a shaker with ice. Shake vigorously and pour into the serving glass.

Some people prefer their Sex on the Beach as a *shooter* (a drink served as a single shot). To make one, use the "original" recipe, but reduce the juices by a half-ounce each. *Strain* into three shot glasses.

Alternative Sex on the Beach

Serve on the rocks in a highball glass.

$^3/_4$ oz. peach schnapps

$^3/_4$ oz. vodka

3 oz. pineapple or grapefruit juice

3 oz. cranberry juice cocktail

Combine all ingredients in the serving glass with ice and stir.

Another popular shooter is the Kamikaze. Banzai!

Kamikaze

Serve in a shot glass.

1 oz. vodka   1 oz. lime juice

1 oz. triple sec

Shake with ice; strain into *three* shot glasses.

Coffee Combo

Here's a coffee and vodka drink you'll enjoy.

Russian Coffee

Serve in a chilled brandy snifter.

$^1/_2$ oz. vodka   1 oz. heavy cream

$1^1/_2$ oz. coffee liqueur

Combine all ingredients in a blender with ice. Blend until smooth, then pour into the snifter.

Russian Winter in the Tropics

The spirit associated with the frozen North is also an apt vehicle for tropical libations.

Melonball

Serve in a cocktail glass.

$^3/_4$ oz. vodka   2 oz. orange juice

$^1/_2$ oz. melon liqueur

Mix ingredients in a shaker with ice. Pour into a cocktail glass. Garnish with an orange slice.

With Brandy, Liqueur, or an Aperitif

A neutral spirit, vodka mates beautifully with more flavorful alcoholic beverages and gives an added kick to brandies, liqueurs, and aperitifs.

Alexander Nevsky was a 13th-century Russian hero who halted an invasion of Germans and Swedes. For this, the Eastern Orthodox church made him a saint. As a bonus, somebody else, about 800 years later, named a vodka drink after him.

Alexander Nevsky

Serve in chilled snifter or wine goblet.

1 oz. vodka

1 oz. apricot liqueur

$^1/_2$ oz. lemon juice

4 oz. orange juice

Orange slice

Combine all ingredients except orange slice in a shaker with cracked ice. Shake vigorously and pour into the serving glass. Garnish with the orange slice.

Doubtless, when the Saint Petersburg hit the scene, its namesake city was still called Leningrad. Now the Soviet Union has dissolved, Leningrad is Saint Petersburg again, and we can all celebrate with this simple combination of vodka and bitters. It tastes best with a premium vodka.

Bar Tips

When you are instructed to drop a fruit wedge into a drink, release more of the flavor by first scoring—scraping—the peel with the tines of a fork.

Saint Petersburg

Serve straight up in a chilled old-fashioned glass.

2 oz. vodka

$^1/_4$ tsp. orange bitters

1 orange wedge

Combine vodka and bitters in mixing glass one-third full of ice. Stir well. Strain into the serving glass. Drop the orange wedge into the drink.

The Vodka...

A vast panoply of drinks not originally made with vodka have time-tested and taste-certified vodka versions.

The Tom Collins can be made with vodka instead of gin. Thus incarnated, it is always called a Vodka Collins, *never* a Vodka Tom Collins.

Vodka Collins

Serve on the rocks in a Collins glass.

1 oz. vodka	Club soda to fill
2 oz. sour mix	Maraschino cherry

Combine all ingredients except for the cherry in the serving glass filled with ice. Stir. Garnish with the maraschino cherry.

Vodka Cooler (Simple)

Serve on the rocks in a Collins glass.

1 oz. vodka	7-Up to fill
$1/2$ oz. sweet vermouth	

Combine the vodka and sweet vermouth in a shaker with ice. Shake vigorously. Strain into serving glass filled with ice. Add 7-Up to fill.

The Grasshopper has seen its heyday come and go. Nevertheless, it survives as a fun retro drink. The traditional Grasshopper is strictly a liqueur drink, but here are two Grasshoppers that add vodka.

Vodka Grasshopper

Serve in a chilled cocktail glass.

$1/2$ oz. vodka	$3/4$ oz. white crème de menthe
$3/4$ oz. green crème de menthe	

Combine the ingredients with cracked ice in a shaker. Shake vigorously, then strain into the serving glass.

Flying Grasshopper

Serve in a chilled old-fashioned or lowball glass.

1½ oz. vodka

½ oz. green crème de menthe

½ oz. white crème de menthe

Combine all the ingredients with cracked ice in a shaker. Shake vigorously, then pour into the serving glass.

In the last chapter, we saw that you can easily substitute gin for the traditional whisky in a sour. Nothing wrong with vodka, either.

Bar Tips
If you don't want to use store-bought sour mix, see Chapter 4 for a fresh recipe.

Vodka Sour

Serve straight-up in a chilled sour glass.

1½-2 oz. vodka

¾ oz. lemon juice

1 tsp. sugar syrup

Lemon slice

Maraschino cherry

Combine all ingredients except the lemon slice and cherry in a shaker with cracked ice. Shake vigorously. Strain into the serving glass and garnish with the lemon slice and maraschino cherry.

The traditional stinger combines brandy with white crème de menthe. Vodka does the job, too.

The words "Gin and Tonic" roll off the tongue so naturally that you may have to stop and think—think *hard*—in order to ask for a *Vodka* Tonic. Make sure the tonic water is fresh and hasn't lost its fizz.

Vodka Stinger

Serve in a chilled cocktail glass.

1¹/₂ oz. vodka

1 oz. white crème de menthe

Combine all ingredients in a shaker with cracked ice. Shake vigorously and strain into the serving glass.

Vodka Tonic

Serve on the rocks in a highball glass.

1¹/₂ oz. vodka   Lime wedge

Tonic water to fill

Pour the vodka into a serving glass one-third full of ice. Add tonic to fill, and garnish with the lime wedge.

Be inventive. The range of possible vodka combinations is limited only by your imagination. Vodka is a neutral spirit you can mix with almost anything. If you need a little help, see Appendix B for more ways to quench your thirst.

The Least You Need to Know

➤ Vodka, which today outsells any other spirit in the United States, achieved popularity only after World War II.

➤ Although nominally colorless, tasteless, and without aroma, vodkas do differ subtly in character. It pays to sample, especially the premium brands.

➤ Most drinkers enjoy vodka libations very, very cold. Consider storing your vodka in the freezer.

➤ Because it adds so little flavor and aroma of its own, vodka is a universal mixer.

The Silver Bullet

The classic "three-martini lunch" has diminished in popularity since the IRS reduced the allowable deduction on business entertaining—and employers realized that *three* martinis at lunch do have a certain impact on the workday. But the martini nevertheless remains at once the most sophisticated, variable, refined, controversial, and popular of cocktails. Self-proclaimed purists have a lot to say about how a martini should be made, and that includes forbidding vodka as an ingredient. "You can make a very nice drink with vodka and vermouth," they say, "but it's not a martini."

Well, this chapter will aim to please the purists, but it will also cover the vodka as well as the gin martini—and a good many variations on these. We trust we will give no lasting offense, but purists may wish to shield their eyes.

The Martini's Controversial Past

As modern mixed drinks go, the martini is pretty old. It probably originated as the *Martinez*, which was invented in San Francisco during the wild Gold Rush years by a celebrated local bartender named Jerry Thomas. Purists—ye who advocate a *dry* martini—take note: Thomas's recipe was anything but dry. It consisted of four parts vermouth to one part Old Tom (*sweet* gin)—practically a mirror opposite of today's drink—and, horror of horrors, it also sported a dash of bitters and two dashes of maraschino liqueur in addition to the vermouth.

> ### Players Script
>
> The Players, steeped as it is in history, offers this historical re-creation of the ancestor of the modern martini, the Martinez. Good luck tracking down a bottle of Old Tom:
>
> In a shaker with cracked ice, shake…
>
> 1 dash bitters
> 2 dashes maraschino liqueur
> 1 pony Old Tom
> 1 wine glass sweet vermouth
>
> Then strain into a chilled cocktail glass and garnish with $1/4$ slice of lemon.

By the 1920s, the Martinez had become the martini, but even a "standard" martini, 1920s-style, went pretty heavy on the vermouth: four parts gin to one part vermouth, and if the opinion of literary scholar Bernard DeVoto is given credence, the standard had not changed much by 1949. In that year, DeVoto published a classic essay on the martini in *Harper's*, decreeing the perfect ratio as 3.7 parts gin to 1 part vermouth.

Buzzed Words

A **dry martini** is one with relatively little vermouth versus gin. Some drinkers prefer 12 parts gin to 1 part vermouth, while others insist on a 20-to-1 ratio. Extremists do away with the vermouth altogether and have a gin and olive on the rocks.

Even in the 1940s—and, one suspects, earlier as well—there were champions of the truly dry martini. Gin to vermouth ratios of 12 to 1 and 20 to 1 were proposed. Sir Winston Churchill, who had strong opinions about everything, believed that a dry martini should be prepared by merely casting a glance toward an unopened bottle of vermouth while pouring the gin into the mixing glass.

And, speaking of mixing, there is the controversy over whether the drink should be stirred or shaken. Agent 007, of course, has always insisted on having his martini "shaken, not stirred." Many bartenders do believe that aerating alcohol by shaking it improves taste, even as others claim that shaking (or even overly vigorous stirring) "bruises the gin." Vigorous shaking can cloud the martini, a strictly cosmetic effect that most drinkers nevertheless find objectionable. The cloudiness, caused by the thousands of tiny air bubbles that form in the drink, does settle—but, by that time, the martini will have started to go warm, and you'll still be thirsty.

You'll also hear differing opinions on just how to chill the drink. Some drinkers prefer their martini on the rocks, while others insist that the real thing *must* be served straight-up—stirring (or shaking) the ingredients with ice, then straining them into the serving glass. Some claim that the ice that melts while shaking actually "marries" the gin to the vermouth, and is therefore crucial to the preparation. Others protest the dilution that occurs by merely *stirring* the drink with ice, and insist that the only way to chill a martini is by storing the gin in the freezer, so that ice becomes wholly unnecessary.

And then there's the issue of added ingredients and garnishes. Wars have been fought with less cause.

Most drinkers welcome a lemon twist or an olive, though some insist that the olive compromises the purity of the drink. A few accept the lemon peel, but insist that it remain untwisted, lest the expressed lemon essence defile the virtue of the libation. A minority insists that absolutely no garnish should contaminate their martini.

Imagine the discomfiture of such a thoroughly chaste drinker confronted by such accents as a few drops of scotch, curaçao, Pernod, bitters, or liqueur! Only the heartless can take pleasure from such a scene.

> **Quick One**
> An Air Force pilot always packed gin and vermouth, olives, a mixing spoon, and a chrome-plated cup. One day, his co-pilot asked, "What good will all that do if we crash in the jungle?" The pilot answered, "We go down in the middle of nowhere, I start making a martini, and somebody will show up and say, '*That's no way to make a martini!*'"

> **Quick One**
> "Let me slip out of these wet clothes and into a dry martini."
>
> —Robert Benchley, Algonquin wit

Martini Secrets

Reader, you've been patient. This is a how-to book, after all, and all we've done thus far is tell you how you might—or might not—make a martini. Here at last are the 10 Secrets of Making a Great Martini:

1. For a gin martini, use a premium-label gin. Which one you use is up to you. As you may recall from Chapter 6, they range in degree of flavorfulness. If you like a martini redolent of aromatic botanicals, veer toward the Bombay end of the gin

spectrum. If you prefer a cleaner taste, lean toward Beefeater. Something in between? Taste Tanqueray. Try them all in your favorite club, then bring home your favorite.

2. For a vodka martini, use a premium-label vodka. The variations in flavorfulness and character among these are less pronounced than among premium-label gins, but you may want to sample several to find a favorite.

3. Use a dry vermouth that you would enjoy drinking by itself, on the rocks. Two brands, Noilly-Prat and Martini and Rossi, dominate the market. Both are excellent. Sample and decide.

Bar Tips

Glasses stored for a long time in a closed cabinet sometimes acquire a musty, dusty taste. Rinse out even clean glasses if they have been stored for any length of time.

Bar Tips

To chill a glass, fill it with ice, add water, and let it sit while you mix the drink. When ready to pour, dump the water and ice, shake the glass to remove the excess, and pour the drink!

4. Use super-clean glassware for mixing as well as for serving. Make certain there is no detergent or soap aftertaste.

5. Whether you serve your martini straight-up or on the rocks, use ice that is entirely free from freezer burn or freezer-borne smells and tastes. Commercial bagged ice is always best.

6. Never use olives stuffed with pimento. They will discolor the drink and give it an unwanted flavor.

7. But… never say never. Some martini lovers like pimento in their olive and don't mind the drink's pinkish hue and peppery flavor one bit.

8. If you are the host, *listen* to the drinker. Based on your taste and experience, you may suggest this or that ratio and this or that gin, but don't force anything on anyone. Accommodate the drinker.

9. Don't let *anyone* tell you there's only one "right" way to make a martini.

10. But it's not worth fighting over. Give peace a chance.

The Classic Dry Martini

We believe that the "dry" martini is the closest thing there is to a "standard" martini. Here's how it's done.

Dry Martini

Serve in a chilled cocktail glass.

2 oz. gin   Olive or lemon twist

$^1/_2$ tsp. dry vermouth

Combine the gin and vermouth in a mixing glass at least half full of ice. Stir well, then strain into the cocktail glass. Garnish with the olive or the lemon twist. If your olives are very small, spear three on a toothpick.

If you want to taste more of the vermouth, make the martini less dry by adding more vermouth. Many drinkers favor a 5-to-1 ratio.

A dry vodka martini should be drier than the dry gin martini. Here's a starting point most drinkers will enjoy.

Dry Vodka Martini

Serve in a chilled cocktail glass.

3 oz. vodka   Olive or lemon twist

Dash of dry vermouth

Combine the vodka and vermouth in a mixing glass at least half full of ice. Stir well, then *quickly* strain into the cocktail glass. Garnish with the olive or the lemon twist. If your olives are very small, spear three on a toothpick.

But wait—there's the *perfect* martini, then there's the *Perfect* Martini. The presumptuous name comes from the exquisite yin and yang of the sweet versus the dry vermouth.

Bar Tips
Both the gin and vodka martinis— but especially the vodka martini— benefit from quick stirring with a lot of ice rather than prolonged stirring with a few ice cubes. The object is to minimize meltage, which dilutes the drink. One of the few things martini drinkers agree on is that a watery drink stinks.

Perfect Martini

Serve in a chilled cocktail glass.

1½ oz. gin   ½ tsp. sweet vermouth
½ tsp. dry vermouth   Olive

Combine all ingredients except the olive in a mixing glass with ice. Stir well and strain into the serving glass. Garnish with the olive.

The Really Dry Martini

There are at least three ways to make a *really* dry martini:

1. Using the same amount of gin or vodka as for the basic dry martini, add just two or three *drops* of vermouth. No, you don't need an eye dropper. Just put your thumb over the mouth of the bottle and sprinkle.

2. Pour an ounce or so of dry vermouth into a chilled cocktail glass. Swirl the vermouth to coat the glass. Pour out the excess vermouth. Stir the gin or vodka in a mixing glass with ice. Strain into the coated cocktail glass.

3. Forget the vermouth altogether. Serve straight gin or vodka on the rocks or straight-up (having stirred the spirit with ice). Call it a *really* dry martini (but it's really just cold gin).

Gibson

The Gibson is the most common variation on the martini theme. At its most basic, it's just a martini with a few (three or more, depending on size and preference) pickled pearl onions instead of the olive or lemon twist. The conscientious Gibson maker, however, varies the underlying martini recipe slightly, yielding a somewhat larger drink that is *always* on the very dry side.

Bar Tips
Take a moment to blot the pickled pearl onions with a paper towel. This will remove excess vinegar, which might otherwise give an unwanted flavor to the drink.

Gibson

Serve in a chilled cocktail glass.

2$^1/_2$ oz. gin   Pickled pearl onions

Dash or two of dry vermouth

Combine the gin and vermouth in a mixing glass at least half full of ice. Stir well, then *quickly* strain into the cocktail glass. Garnish with the pearl onions.

The Vodka Gibson is almost identical to the gin Gibson. Just add a bit more vodka.

Vodka Gibson

Serve in a chilled cocktail glass.

3 oz. vodka   Pickled pearl onions

Dash or two of dry vermouth

Combine the vodka and vermouth in a mixing glass at least half full of ice. Stir well, then *quickly* strain into the cocktail glass. Garnish with the pearl onions.

Vodka Varieties

Now that we've laid out the basic gin and vodka martinis, together with the most basic variation in the form of the Gibson, let's go on to variations on the vodka martini. Indeed, in some future edition of *The Complete Idiot's Guide to Mixing Drinks*, vodka may have supplanted gin as the martini ingredient of choice (perish the thought!). An increasing number of drinkers prefer the cleaner, simpler taste (or non-taste) of vodka to the more assertive and complex savor of gin.

The chief thing to remember about a vodka martini—whatever form it takes—is that the vermouth or other additives and the garnishes occupy center stage. It is *their* flavor that shines through the neutral spirit that is vodka.

The Cajun Martini takes some advance preparation and the acquisition of a few jalapeño peppers.

Cajun Martini

Serve in a chilled cocktail glass.

3 oz. vodka

Dash dry vermouth

Thin slice of garlic

Several slices of pickled jalapeño peppers

Pickled pearl onions

At least one hour before serving, prepare the vodka by steeping the garlic, jalapeño, and onions in it. The steeping vodka should be stored in a closed container in the freezer. Combine the steeped vodka and vermouth in a mixing glass at least half full of ice. Stir well, then *quickly* strain into the cocktail glass. Garnish with a jalapeño slice or some pearl onions.

"Dark Eyes"—"Ochi Chernya"—is a favorite old Russian song, and the name seemed appropriate to the proprietors of Manhattan's celebrated Russian Tea Room to describe a *vodka* martini that uses a *black* olive instead of green. But that's not all.

From Russia to Spain, which lends its characteristic wine—dry sherry—it's on to the Spanish Vodka Martini.

Ochi Chernya

Serve in a chilled cocktail glass.

2 oz. vodka

$^1/_4$ oz. dry vermouth

$^1/_4$ oz. sweet vermouth

Large black olive

Combine the vodka and vermouths in a mixing glass at least half full of ice. Stir well, then *quickly* strain into the cocktail glass. Garnish with the black olive.

Spanish Vodka Martini

Serve in a chilled cocktail glass.

$2^1/_2$ oz. vodka

$^1/_2$ oz. dry sherry

Lemon twist

Combine the vodka and vermouth in a mixing glass at least half full of ice. Stir well, then *quickly* strain into the cocktail glass. Garnish with the lemon twist.

Players Script

The great actor, drinker, and Players member John Barrymore was appearing in San Francisco when the 1906 earthquake wrecked the city. As he emerged from his hotel, the military seized him and put him to work clearing wreckage from the streets. When fellow member and actor John Drew heard of this, he sent Barrymore a telegram: "Glad to hear you are all right but note with regret that it took a convulsion of nature to get you up in the morning and the United States Army to make you work."

Exotic Variations

By now we've either reeducated (fat chance!) or thoroughly alienated the martini purists out there, so let's plunge ahead boldly into the depths of decadence with a catalogue of martini exotica.

What the—a *chocolate* martini?! You bet—and it's quite popular among the ladies. Simple yet sublime… chocolate and cocktails are a girl's best friend.

Chocolate Martini

Serve in a martini glass.

2 oz. vodka

$1/2$ oz. creme de cacao

Combine both ingredients in a shaker filled with ice. Pour into the serving glass.

In Chapter 6, we observed that Dutch—or genever—gin is not generally a good mixer. The sole exception is the Dutch martini. If you like the extremely full-bodied taste of genever, you'll enjoy this drink.

Dutch Martini

Serve in a chilled cocktail glass.

2 oz. genever gin   Lemon peel

¹/₂ tsp. dry vermouth

Combine the gin and vermouth in a mixing glass at least half full of ice. Stir well, then *quickly* strain into the cocktail glass. Garnish with the lemon peel.

If dry gin can be unseated as a principal martini constituent, so can vermouth. We've seen something like this in the Vodka Spanish Martini. Here's the Fino Martini.

Fino Martini

Serve in a chilled cocktail glass.

2 oz. gin   Lemon twist or olive

¹/₄ oz. fino sherry

Combine the vodka and vermouth in a mixing glass at least half full of ice. Stir well, then *quickly* strain into the cocktail glass. Garnish with the lemon twist or olive.

As a love of sushi has spread across the United States, so has an affection for *sake*, the Japanese beverage made from fermented rice. Most of us enjoy it hot, but it is also quite delicious on the rocks, and if you substitute it for the vermouth in a traditional martini, you have—what else?—a Saketini.

Saketini

Serve in a chilled cocktail glass.

2 oz. gin   Olive or lemon twist

¹/₄ oz. sake

Combine the gin and sake in a shaker with ice. Shake well, then strain into the serving glass. Garnish with the olive or lemon twist.

Perhaps you've never thought of the martini in a tropical context. The addition of pineapple juice makes this one downright Hawaiian.

Hawaiian Martini

Serve in a chilled cocktail glass.

1¹/₂ oz. gin

1 tsp. dry vermouth

1 tsp. sweet vermouth

1 tsp. pineapple juice

Combine all the ingredients in a shaker with ice. Shake well, and strain into the serving glass.

We've visited Sicily and Florence, now let's get to Italy's capital, Roma. It's the Campari that nationalizes this martini variation.

Martini Romana

Serve in a chilled cocktail glass.

1¹/₂ oz. gin

¹/₂ tsp. dry vermouth

Few dashes of Campari

Combine all ingredients in a mixing glass with ice. Stir well and strain into the serving glass.

For a revolutionary martini, leave Italy for the Carribean.

Rum Martini

Serve in a chilled cocktail glass.

2 oz. white rum

Several drops of dry vermouth

Olive

Lime twist

Combine the ingredients except the olive and lime twist in a mixing glass with ice. Stir well and strain into the serving glass. Garnish with the olive and lime twist.

If the Saketini bows to Japan, the Tequini doffs a sombrero to the country south of the border. It's a martini made with tequila instead of gin.

Tequini

Serve in a chilled cocktail glass.

$2^1/_2$ oz. tequila   Olive or lemon twist
$^1/_2$ oz. dry vermouth

Combine all ingredients except the olive or lemon twist in a mixing glass with ice. Stir well and strain into the serving glass. Garnish with the olive or lemon twist.

The simplest route to a sweet martini is to use sweet vermouth, mixed in equal proportion to the gin.

Gin and It

Serve in a chilled cocktail glass.

1 oz. gin
1 oz. sweet vermouth

Combine all ingredients in a mixing glass with ice. Stir well and strain into the serving glass.

If Gin and It strikes you as too simple, add a little something else.

Sweet Martini

Serve in a chilled cocktail glass.

2 oz. gin   Dash orange bitters
$^1/_2$ oz. sweet vermouth   Orange peel

Combine all ingredients except the orange peel in a mixing glass with ice. Stir well and strain into the serving glass. Twist the orange peel over the drink and garnish.

The Least You Need to Know

➤ The martini is an American institution: venerable, popular, and subject to endless controversy.

➤ Most martini "purists" insist that drier is better, but they won't find historical precedent for this in the martini's direct ancestor, the decidedly sweet Martinez.

➤ James Bond may like his martini "shaken, not stirred," but most drinkers will object to the clouding this brings to their gin.

➤ Vodka is catching up to gin as the primary ingredient of choice in a martini.

Part 3
Whiskey World

In the world of whiskey, time is measured in slow years of oak-barrel aging, and art is defined by the patient skill of distillers and master blenders. It is a world with a language all its own—bottled in bond, straight, blended, single malt, Coffey still, pot still, wort, and so on—yet with old and familiar boundaries: in Kentucky, Tennessee, Canada, Scotland, Ireland. It is a world filled with strong and varied opinions, tastes, biases, and favorites.

This section walks you through the world of whiskey, bourbon, Tennessee Whiskey, blended whiskey, Canadian whisky, scotch, and Irish whiskey, and provides historical background as well as tips on connoisseurship. And, of course, the drinks. There are a lot of them!

Chapter 9

Bourbon and Tennessee Whiskey: Produce of the Bluegrass and Volunteer States

In This Chapter

➤ Bourbon's ancestors

➤ Bourbon vs. Tennessee whiskey

➤ How to enjoy whiskey neat

➤ Bourbon and whiskey recipes

"The United States is the world's largest producer and consumer of whiskey," the *Encyclopaedia Britannica*'s article on "whiskey" concludes matter-of-factly. But the numbers are anything but matter of fact: Americans have more than *500 brands* of the great American whiskey, bourbon, to choose from. How many other products can you think of that are offered in 500 brands?

Nor is there any product more American than bourbon. It is rooted in colonial times and was among the very first of American industries. It was also among the first products the Feds hit on as a source of tax revenue. And *that* practically caused a war.

This chapter will tell you what all the fuss has been about for all these years.

Let's Talk Whiskey

If you walk into Otto's Bar in Louisville's grand old Seelbach Hotel and ask for a "good Kentucky bourbon," you'll meet with what is best described as a courteous reproof: "*All* bourbon is Kentucky bourbon." You certainly can't go wrong thinking of bourbon as *Kentucky* whiskey (and, in Louisville, it's the *only* way you can think of it), but, looked at another way, you might think of sour mash and other whiskies made in Tennessee as additional varieties of bourbon. In any event, 80 percent of what is called bourbon is, in fact, made in Kentucky.

Why Kentucky?

During the early 18th century, before there was any such thing as the United States, Scotch, Irish, and Dutch colonists were distilling whiskey throughout Maryland, Virginia, and Pennsylvania. Farmers not only made money selling rye and barley to distillers, but often cut out the middleman and set up a still themselves; the farmer's cart could carry no more than four bushels of grain to market, but it could transport two kegs of whiskey, which represented over a dozen bushels of grain. With terrible roads linking farmer and market, this was strong incentive to go into the whiskey business.

By the time the nation achieved independence from Britain, there were more than 5,000 stills steaming away in western Pennsylvania alone—a fact that excited Treasury Secretary Alexander Hamilton, who persuaded Congress to levy an excise tax on whiskey in 1791.

The farmer-distillers responded angrily with the so-called Whiskey Rebellion, and President Washington responded by dispatching troops to enforce the law. In short order, the Whiskey Rebellion was extinguished, the authority of the federal government was affirmed, and the United States has collected liquor taxes ever since.

Not that all the farmers meekly complied. Some lit out for the territories, settling in Kentucky. Not only were the revenuers there fewer and farther between, but the land was rich and abundant—perfect for growing corn—and the water was extraordinarily pure. Much of the state rests on a limestone mantel, a porous rock that makes for great natural filtration of ground water.

It is said that the first man to give up farming in Kentucky for a career as a distiller was Evan Williams, whose fine brand of sippin' whiskey is still marketed. (Williams's original product, however, was apparently none too tasty, since the Louisville town council officially reprimanded him in 1783 not just for bringing whiskey to a meeting, but for bringing *crummy* whiskey.)

But a short time after this, in 1789, Elijah Craig, a Baptist minister and distiller, discovered the enormous boon of aging whiskey in a charred oak barrel. (Hitherto, distillers had aged their product in plain wooden vessels.) The charred oak imparted a smoky, smooth, mellow flavor to the liquor. Realizing he had something very good, Reverend Craig sought a name for his whiskey. The name of his home county had a regal ring to it: Bourbon.

A County in Kentucky

Not all bourbon is produced in Bourbon County, but Kentuckians continue to vigorously defend what they deem their exclusive privilege: to label *bourbon only* that whiskey originating within the state borders. By federal, not state, law, bourbon can be made anywhere in the United States, but it must contain at least 51 percent corn—the grains that make up the balance of the mash are usually rye and barley—and it must be aged in new charred oak barrels.

Like scotch, bourbon comes in "straight" and "blended" varieties. All the whiskey in straight bourbon must have been distilled by a single distiller during a single time period, whereas blended bourbon may contain whiskeys distilled by various distillers at various times—with the proviso that the age given on the bottle label must be that of the *youngest* whiskey in the blend. Speaking of age, bourbons are aged anywhere from two to twelve years; generally, the older the better (and more costly). As with scotch, straight bourbon is usually preferable—and more expensive—than blended brands.

Deep in Tennessee

Tennessee produces many bourbon-like whiskies, but it is best known for its fine sour mashes, the most widely marketed of which are Jack Daniel's, George Dickel, and Evan Williams (whose name was appropriated from neighboring Kentucky). The most distinctive Tennessee whiskies, like these, are readily distinguishable from Kentucky bourbon. They are very mellow, savor less of the aging barrel, and tend to bring the undertones of corn closer to the surface.

Let's Talk Proof

The term *proof*, a designation of alcoholic content, comes from the way early American distillers estimated the strength of what they distilled. "Proving" the alcoholic content of whiskey was accomplished by mixing a sample of the liquor with some gunpowder, lighting the mixture, and observing the resulting flame. Weak whiskey burned with a flickering yellow flame. Whiskey that was *too* strong went up in bright blue flame that soon burned itself out. Whiskey that was just right—that is, "100 proof"—burned with a steady blue flame. You may buy bourbon and other whiskey in proofs ranging from 80 to 100 proof and even somewhat more.

Neat, Rocks, Branch, Soda

Really good whiskey is a pleasure to enjoy neat (straight, no ice, no water), on the rocks, with club soda, or with what Southerners like to call *branch* or *branch water*, which, these days, is just tap water.

Bar Tips

The cowpoke thrusts aside the swinging saloon doors, moseys up to the bar, orders a shot of whiskey, and downs it in a gulp. You can do this, too. But why waste *really good* whiskey? Fine whiskey, like fine wine, is meant to be savored and is best enjoyed slowly.

What do you need to know about enjoying whiskey unadorned? A little:

1. Invest in a premium-label bourbon or Tennessee whiskey. With some 500 brands, you have a lot of sampling to do.

2. Generally speaking, higher-proof whiskies are best for sipping.

3. Use scrupulously clean and thoroughly rinsed glassware.

4. Use ice that is free from freezer burn and freezer odors and tastes. Commercial bagged ice is best.

5. If your tap water tastes good, use it. Otherwise, consider bottled spring water. If you are *really* serious about sampling a variety of whiskies, use distilled water, which is the most neutral mixer available.

6. If you want effervescence, you can mix your whiskey with club soda, soda water, seltzer, or unflavored sparkling water, such as Perrier. If you want the most neutral carbonated mixer, use soda water.

Buzzed Words

To **muddle** is to mash and stir. Mint leaves and other solids are muddled in order to make a suspension or a paste with fluid. A special pestle-like wooden **muddler** can be used to muddle, but any spoon will do.

Juleps: The Schools of Thought

As the subject of the martini sparks debate in the cold North, so, in the sunny South, the Mint Julep is a source of many genteelly heated and arcane discussions. Three juleps that claim to be "standard" follow.

A Mint Julep should be cold and refreshing. If it's a *really* hot day, your guests will cherish their Frozen Juleps.

Mint Julep Version 1

Serve in an old-fashioned glass.

$^1/_2$ tsp. fine-grained sugar   Splash club soda

$2^1/_2$ oz. bourbon   Mint sprig

Put the half teaspoon of sugar in the bottom of the mixing glass. Fill the glass one-third full with ice cubes. Add bourbon. Add the splash of club soda. Garnish with the mint sprig.

Mint Julep #2

Serve in a Collins glass.

2 oz. bourbon   ¹/₂ oz. sugar syrup

6 mint leaves   Mint sprig

Place the mint leaves in the bottom of the serving glass and add the sugar syrup. Mash the leaves in the syrup. Add half the bourbon, then fill the glass with crushed ice. Add the balance of the bourbon and stir vigorously. Garnish with the mint sprig.

Mint Julep #3

Serve in an old-fashioned or Collins glass.

1 cube sugar   Mint sprigs

3 oz. bourbon

Dissolve the sugar cube in the bottom of the serving glass with a few drops of plain water. Add a few mint sprigs. Fill the glass with ice (cubes or crushed) then add the bourbon. Stir well. Cut up some more mint sprigs and add these to the drink. Stir, then allow to stand several minutes before serving.

Frozen Julep

Serve in a large (double) old-fashioned glass.

2 oz. bourbon   6 small mint leaves

1 oz. lemon juice   Mint sprig

1 oz. sugar syrup

In a mixing glass, muddle the mint leaves together with the bourbon, lemon juice, and sugar syrup. Put the muddled ingredients in a blender with crushed ice. Blend until ice becomes mushy. Pour into the serving glass and garnish with a mint sprig.

The Classic Bourbon and Tennessee Cocktails

You can use bourbon or Tennessee whiskey to make any of the recipes in this chapter. Throughout, we've called for "bourbon"; add the equivalent amount of Tennessee whiskey if you prefer. For the more strongly flavored drinks, there is no reason to splurge on premium-label whiskey. Ordinary "bar bourbon" will do just fine.

The idea of *bourbon* and citrus may take a little getting used to, but, aided by a bit of sweet liqueur, the result is a satisfying, full-bodied drink.

Bluegrass Cocktail

Serve in a chilled cocktail glass.

1$\frac{1}{2}$ oz. bourbon

1 oz. pineapple juice

1 oz. lemon juice

1 tsp. maraschino liqueur

Combine all ingredients in a shaker with ice. Shake vigorously, then strain into the serving glass.

Strictly speaking, a *cobbler* is an iced drink made with wine or liqueur plus sugar and fruit juice; however, no one is likely to complain if you throw in some bourbon. Beware. Like the Mint Julep, this is a potent blend. Sugar and carbonated water speed the absorption of alcohol into the bloodstream. The drink goes down so easily that you and your guests will be tempted to gulp. Sip! Please!

Bourbon Cobbler

Serve in a chilled highball glass.

1$\frac{1}{2}$ oz. bourbon

1 oz. Southern Comfort

1 tsp. peach-flavored brandy

2 tsp. lemon juice

1 tsp. sugar syrup

Club soda to fill

Peach slice

Combine all ingredients except the club soda in a shaker with cracked ice. Shake vigorously, then pour into the serving glass. Add several ice cubes, then the club soda to fill. Garnish with the peach slice.

Buzzed Words
Traditionally, a **cobbler** is an iced drink made of wine or liqueur plus sugar and fruit juice.

Made with the traditional gin, it's called a Tom Collins. With bourbon, some call it a John Collins—a nod, doubtless, to the spirit of John Barleycorn, traditional personification of alcohol. You can have yours relatively subdued or jet-assisted, with higher-proof bourbon and a Peychaud's send-off.

Bourbon Collins (Unadorned)

Serve in a chilled Collins glass.

1½ oz. bourbon

½ oz. lime juice

1 tsp. sugar syrup

Club soda to fill

Lime peel

Combine all ingredients except lime peel and club soda in a shaker with cracked ice. Shake vigorously, then pour into the serving glass. Add club soda to fill and garnish with the lime peel.

Bourbon Collins (Augmented)

Serve in a chilled highball glass.

2 oz. 100-proof bourbon

½ oz. lemon juice

1 tsp. sugar syrup

Few dashes of Peychaud's bitters

Club soda to fill

Lemon slice

Combine all ingredients except the lemon slice and club soda in a shaker with cracked ice. Shake vigorously, then pour into the serving glass and garnish with the lemon slice.

The Manhattan is traditionally made with blended—especially Canadian—whiskey, which has much less body than bourbon. We'll look at plenty of Manhattans in the next chapter, but, first, why *not* a Bourbon Manhattan?

Bourbon Manhattan

Serve in a chilled cocktail glass.

2 oz. bourbon

½ oz. sweet vermouth

Dash Angostura or other bitters

Maraschino cherry

Combine all ingredients except the cherry in a mixing glass with ice. Stir well, then strain into the serving glass. Garnish with the cherry.

111

Players Script

Any close friend of John Barrymore's would have known there was fog within as he came out of The Players. With measured tread, he crossed to the waiting cab and took his place, sitting stiffly erect. The driver turned for instructions.

"Take me to The Players," ordered Barrymore. "Excuse me, sir," the driver hesitated. "I didn't quite get that." Barrymore frowned. Raising his voice, he repeated, "I said take me to The Players!"

The puzzled driver was at a loss, but the doorman rushed up to whisper in his ear. Bewildered, the driver proceeded east to the corner of Gramercy Park, north to the corner of the park, west to the corner of the park, south to the corner of the park, then east to the spot he had just left. He jumped down and opened the door. Barrymore descended in majestic silence. He strode toward the entrance from which he had so recently made his exit.

Halfway there, he stopped dramatically. "Young man," he declaimed, "I have been a not-unnoticed figure on the stage for 38 years. And this is positively the first occasion in my entire career when anyone has so much as hinted that my enunciation is defective." And, still majestic, he disappeared within The Players portals.

Bourbon is the spirit of choice for the old-fashioned, which is still a much-requested libation. The drink can also be made with rye, blended whiskey, or Canadian whisky.

Bourbon Old-Fashioned

Serve on the rocks in an old-fashioned glass.

1½ oz. bourbon   Dash sugar syrup
Splash of water   Liberal dash Angostura bitters
Combine all ingredients over ice in the serving glass. Stir well.

These florally named drinks look, smell, *and* taste great.

Bourbon Rose (Dark)

Serve in a chilled highball glass.

1½ oz. bourbon

1 oz. triple sec

4 oz. orange juice

Grenadine

Combine all ingredients except grenadine in a shaker with cracked ice. Shake vigorously, then pour into the serving glass. *Carefully* pour a float of grenadine on top. Do not stir.

Bourbon Rose (Pale)

Serve in a chilled old-fashioned glass.

1½ oz. bourbon

½ oz. dry vermouth

½ oz. crème de cassis

¼ oz. lemon juice

Combine all ingredients in a shaker with cracked ice. Shake vigorously, then pour into the serving glass.

The Sidecar started out life as a brandy drink, but bourbon will do it for you, too.

Bourbon Sidecar

Serve in a chilled cocktail glass.

1½ oz. bourbon

¾ oz. curaçao or triple sec

½ oz. lemon juice

Combine all ingredients in a shaker with cracked ice. Shake vigorously, then strain into the serving glass.

The Whiskey Sour remains one of the most popular sweet mixed drinks. Because it *is* sweet, most folks don't think of using bourbon for this drink; blended whiskey, lighter and thinner than bourbon, is the traditional choice. The Bourbon Sour has more body and depth than the blended whiskey version. It also makes for a more tart sour—hence the lemon instead of lime.

Bourbon Sour

Serve in a chilled Sour glass.

2 oz. bourbon   Orange slice

Juice of $1/2$ lemon   Maraschino cherry

$1/2$ tsp. sugar syrup

Combine all ingredients except the fruit in a shaker with ice. Shake vigorously, then strain into the serving glass. Garnish with the fruit.

New Traditions

Bourbon has a not entirely undeserved reputation as a man's drink—or, more precisely, an "old boy's drink." It summons up visions of conservative gentlemen reading their papers in darkly paneled club rooms thick with cigar smoke. The following are some recipes designed to update the bourbon profile.

While most committed bourbon drinkers shy away from scotch, they usually enjoy gin well enough and have been known to down the occasional martini. Behold—the Dry Mahoney!

Dry Mahoney

Serve in a chilled cocktail glass.

$2^1/2$ oz. bourbon   Lemon twist

$1/2$ oz. dry vermouth

Combine all ingredients except the lemon twist in a mixing glass filled with ice. Stir vigorously, then strain into the serving glass. Garnish with the lemon twist. It is recommended that the drink be served with a few ice cubes on the side, in a second glass.

The addition of Pernod—always an elegant experience—curaçao, and grenadine earn this concoction the title of Millionaire Cocktail.

Millionaire Cocktail

Serve in chilled cocktail glasses.

3 oz. bourbon

1 oz. Pernod

Few dashes curaçao

Few dashes grenadine

1 egg white *

Combine all ingredients in a mixing glass with cracked ice. Stir well, and strain into the serving glasses. *Recipe makes two drinks.*

* Raw egg may be a source of salmonella bacteria. You may wish to avoid drinks calling for raw egg yolk or white.

What is the origin of the name of the following drink? We have so far failed to discern the religious significance of combining ginger ale with club soda. Still, it's a pretty good drink.

Presbyterian

Serve on the rocks in a highball glass.

3 oz. bourbon

Equal portions of ginger ale and

Club soda to fill

Pour bourbon into serving glass half filled with ice cubes. Add equal portions of ginger ale and club soda to fill.

Sooner or later, you'll encounter the legendary Sazerac from the city of New Orleans. The classic version involves some effort, but the effort is worthwhile. Let's work our way up to the classic by beginning with the Simple Sazerac.

The original Sazerac was made with *absinthe*, a powerfully aromatic, bitter liqueur with a high alcoholic content. Its name and principal flavoring come from *Artemisia absinthium*—wormwood—but the beverage also includes licorice, hyssop, fennel, angelica root, aniseed, and star aniseed.

Bar Tips

Most drinks that call for egg white require half an egg white. But it's almost impossible to get *half* an egg white; therefore, all recipes in this book calling for egg white make *two* drinks.

Simple Sazerac

Serve in a chilled old-fashioned glass.

$\frac{1}{4}$ tsp. Pernod or other absinthe substitute

$\frac{1}{2}$ tsp. sugar

1 tbsp. water

Dash Peychaud's bitters

2 oz. bourbon (may also use rye or blended whiskey)

Lemon peel

Coat the serving glass by swirling the Pernod in it. Add the sugar, water, and Peychaud's. Muddle these until the sugar is completely dissolved. Add bourbon with a few ice cubes. Stir vigorously. Garnish with the lemon peel.

Buzzed Words

Absinthe is an aromatic, bitter, very strong liqueur flavored chiefly with wormwood and other botanicals. Absinthe was outlawed in many countries early in the 20th century because of its apparent toxicity.

Absinthe was widely consumed in Paris and elsewhere, even though it seemed to have a nasty knack for inducing convulsions, hallucinations, general mental deterioration, and psychosis. It was subsequently determined that these symptoms were caused not by the liquor itself, but by *thujone*, a toxic substance present in wormwood. A number of substitutes were created, including Pernod, anisette, pastis, ouzo, and raki.

Now, except for the absinthe, here is the original Sazerac. You'll need two old-fashioned glasses. Herbsaint is an absinthe stand-in that may be hard to find outside of New Orleans; you may substitute Pernod.

Original Sazerac

Serve in a chilled old-fashioned glass.

1 sugar cube

2 dashes Peychaud's bitters

Dash Angostura bitters

2 oz. 100-proof bourbon (may substitute rye or blended whiskey)

Dash Herbsaint (may substitute Pernod)

Lemon peel

Use crushed ice to chill *two* old-fashioned glasses. Pour out the ice from one glass. In the bottom of that glass put the sugar cube with a few drops of water. Add the bitters, and muddle the sugar and bitters until the sugar is dissolved. Add bourbon and ice cubes. Stir well. Empty the second glass of ice and add a liberal dash of Herbsaint, swirling to coat the glass. Discard the excess bitters and pour in the mixture from the first glass. Twist the lemon peel over the glass, but *do not garnish with the lemon peel*; discard.

The name of this classic cocktail was meant to suggest that it is just what the doctor ordered.

Ward Eight

Serve in a chilled cocktail glass.

2 oz. bourbon

1 oz. lemon juice

1 oz. orange juice

Sugar syrup to taste

Dash grenadine

Combine all ingredients in a shaker with ice. Shake vigorously and strain into the serving glass.

The Least You Need to Know

➤ Bourbon may not be the most popular spirit in America, but it is the most original. Its precursors have been distilled on American shores since the early 18th century.

➤ Strictly speaking, only whiskey made in Kentucky can properly be called bourbon, although you can consider Tennessee whiskey a bourbon variation.

➤ The flavor and character of bourbon and Tennessee whiskey comes mainly from the aging process. Freshly distilled, whiskey is essentially a neutral spirit.

➤ Bourbon and Tennessee whiskey work well as mixers as long as you remember that they are strongly flavored and full bodied. Some people will prefer the lighter, less characterful flavor of blended whiskey in their mixed drinks.

Chapter 10

'Round the Blend: Canadian and American Blended Whiskeys

Americans tend to enjoy a lighter beverage than Europeans; for example, in the United States, ale and stout have never been as popular as beer. So it is with whiskey. To be sure, many Americans like their bourbon and scotch, but blended whiskey is a North American phenomenon, a beverage that is less filling and lighter in body than bourbon, scotch, or rye. Some of the most popular U.S. and Canadian whiskies are blended. They make great mixers, as you'll see.

The Master Blender at Work

Blended whiskies may combine various straight whiskies (whiskies distilled from the mash of a single grain) only, or may involve combinations of straight, mixed-grain whiskies, grain neutral spirits, and so-called *light whiskies*. The latter are whiskies distilled at high proof—over 160—and stored in used charred oak barrels. The result is more flavorful than neutral spirits, but not as strong as straight whiskey. In a blend, light whiskey imparts character without compromising the light, dry quality desired in a blend.

The creation of a fine blended whiskey is as much art as science; a *master blender* directs the creation of a blended whiskey. The blender may combine as many as 50 whiskies drawn from a "library" of hundreds of products.

Not Whiskey, but Whisky: Enjoying the Canadian Difference

So far as the quality of lightness goes, the Canadian distillers of blended whisky (that's how Canadians spell it) have taken the beverage to its extreme. Light, delicately flavored, and extremely smooth, Canadian whiskies are ideal mixers.

The flavor qualities of blended whiskies, while often subtle, are greatly varied. You would do well to sample a range of these products. Don't forget to use your nose, not just your taste buds. The aroma of a fine blended whiskey is complex and rewarding, and, precisely because of the liquor's light body, much of the pleasure of the product comes from its "nose"—its scent.

Neat, Rocks, Soda, Ginger

You'll want to devote a good deal of pleasurable effort to discovering your favorite blends, particularly if you intend to enjoy the whiskey neat, on the rocks, or with plain soda. Soapy glasses, chlorine-laden tap water, or freezer-burned ice will spoil the taste of delicately flavored American and Canadian blends.

Ginger ale has always been a popular mixer with blended whiskey. Just pour a jigger of whiskey into a highball glass filled with ice and add ginger ale to fill. If you want something a little fancier and quite a bit stronger, try the Horse's Neck.

Manhattan Varieties

The woodwind tones of a good blended or Canadian whiskey are perfectly suited to the Manhattan. Made carefully, the Manhattan is a delicate and subtle drink, despite its essential sweetness. While many people have theirs on the rocks, it is best enjoyed well-chilled, straight-up. The basic, unadorned recipe follows.

Manhattan

Serve in a chilled cocktail glass.

2 oz. blended whiskey

$1/2$ oz. sweet vermouth

Dash Angostura bitters

Maraschino cherry

Combine all ingredients except the cherry with ice in a mixing glass. Stir well, then strain into the serving glass and garnish with the cherry.

As with the dry vermouth in a martini, the amount of sweet vermouth in a Manhattan should be adjusted to suit your taste. Some drinkers specify *Canadian* whisky in their Manhattan. Make it the same way and call it a Canadian Manhattan.

For some hard-bitten Manhattan drinkers, sweet vermouth is just too sweet. For these folks, a Dry Manhattan is called for. If necessary, the Angostura bitters may be excluded, though we prefer to keep this ingredient, even in the *Dry* Manhattan.

Dry Manhattan

Serve in a chilled cocktail glass.

2 oz. blended whiskey

$1/2$ oz. dry vermouth

Dash Angostura bitters (optional)

Lemon twist

Combine all ingredients except the lemon twist with ice in a mixing glass. Stir well, then strain into the serving glass and garnish with the lemon twist.

Some drinkers prefer to garnish the Dry Manhattan with a green olive.

You can substitute Dubonnet for sweet vermouth to make a Manhattan sweeter than a Dry Manhattan, but not as sweet as the standard Manhattan.

The Old-Fashioned Manhattan balances the whiskey against the sweet vermouth for a much sweeter drink. If you like old-fashioneds, this one is for you.

Old-Fashioned Manhattan

Serve in a chilled cocktail glass.

1¹/₂ blended whiskey   Maraschino cherry

1¹/₂ oz. sweet vermouth

Combine ingredients except the cherry in a shaker with cracked ice. Shake vigorously, then pour into the serving glass and garnish with the cherry.

Taking its cue from the Perfect Martini, the Perfect Manhattan balances dry and sweet vermouth. But don't make the proportions *quite* equal.

Perfect Manhattan

Serve in a chilled cocktail glass.

2 oz. blended whiskey   Dash Angostura bitters

¹/₂ oz. sweet vermouth   Maraschino cherry

¹/₄ oz. dry vermouth

Combine all ingredients except the cherry in a mixing glass with ice. Stir well, then strain into the serving glass and garnish with the cherry.

Those familiar with New York City and Long Island know Manhasset as one of the older towns along the island's North Shore. It's moneyed and sedate, and it has a Manhattan variation of its very own.

Manhasset

Serve in a chilled cocktail glass.

1¹/₂ oz. blended whiskey   ¹/₂ oz. lemon juice

¹/₄ oz. dry vermouth   Lemon twist

¹/₄ oz. sweet vermouth

Combine all ingredients except the lemon in a shaker with ice. Shake vigorously, then strain into the serving glass and garnish with the lemon twist.

Fizzes

Blended whiskey is the perfect choice among the "dark spirits" for fizz drinks because its light qualities complement effervescence and don't fight sweet mixers.

Another drink that's especially welcome on a summer evening is a combination of whiskey and curaçao. Consider using Canadian whiskey for a feather-light drink.

Whiskey Curaçao Fizz

Serve in a chilled Collins glass.

2 oz. blended whiskey	1 tsp. sugar
1/2 oz. curaçao	Club soda to fill
1 oz. lemon juice	Orange slice

Combine all ingredients except the orange slice and club soda in a shaker with cracked ice. Shake well, then pour into the serving glass. You may add additional ice cubes, if you wish. Add club soda to fill. Garnish with the orange slice.

Players Script

Crusty, cranky Childe Hassam (1859–1935) was one of America's greatest Impressionist painters—and a hard-drinking member of The Players. He came out of the club one night—drink, as usual, having brought on his dark humor—and angrily repulsed all offers of help.

Some time later a policeman observed a gentleman holding on to Gramercy Park's high iron fence rails and shuffling east a half step at a time. The policeman stopped to observe this phenomenon.

Peering in between the tall iron bars, Hassam worked his way slowly east, shifting his grip at each crablike movement sideways. This laborious progress took him to the corner, where he stopped uncertainly. Then he worked around the right angle and resumed his weary pilgrimage, still looking through the bars into the park.

The friendly cop came up. "Is it anything I can be doin' to help yez, sir?"

"No," snapped Hassam. "Nothing at all. I don't need help." Then, with savage bitterness: "That is—if I can ever get out of this damned *jail* I seem to be in."

The dignified yet cozy library at The Players.

(Photo courtesy of the Walter Hampden Memorial Library, at The Players)

The Whiskey Fizz is the classic whiskey fizz drink. The bitters counterpoint the sugar syrup nicely.

Whiskey Fizz

Serve in a chilled highball glass.

1¹/₂ oz. blended whiskey

Few dashes Angostura bitters

¹/₂ tsp. sugar syrup

Club soda to fill

Combine all ingredients except the club soda in the serving glass one third full of ice. Stir well, then add club soda to fill.

Grapefruit Combos

While the combination of bourbon or scotch with grapefruit juice may raise some eyebrows, the cleaner, lighter taste of blended whiskey makes it all seem perfectly natural.

Most coolers contain a relatively small amount of alcohol. The Grapefruit Cooler packs a full two ounces.

Grapefruit Cooler

Serve in a chilled Collins glass.

2 oz. blended whiskey

4 oz. grapefruit juice

$^1/_2$ oz. red currant syrup

$^1/_4$ oz. lemon juice

$^1/_2$ orange slice

$^1/_2$ lemon slice

Combine all ingredients except the fruit in a shaker with cracked ice. Pour into the serving glass, adding ice cubes, if you wish. Garnish with the orange and lemon.

The Indian River of south Florida runs through the heart of citrus country, which is where the half ounce of grapefruit juice in the Indian River Cocktail comes from.

Indian River Cocktail

Serve in a chilled old-fashioned glass.

$1^1/_2$ oz. blended whiskey

$^1/_4$ oz. raspberry liqueur

$^1/_4$ oz. sweet vermouth

$^1/_2$ oz. grapefruit juice

Combine all ingredients in a shaker with cracked ice. Shake vigorously and pour into the serving glass.

Old-Fashioneds and a Rickey

As some people see it, only an old-fashioned made with bourbon is a *real* old-fashioned. They like the full body of the Kentucky whiskey and the play of the sugar syrup and bitters against a spirit with loads of character and strong flavor. Others prefer to lighten up with blended or Canadian whiskey.

Blended Whiskey Old-Fashioned

Serve on the rocks in an old-fashioned glass.

$1^1/_2$ oz. blended whiskey

Dash water

Dash sugar syrup

Liberal dash Angostura bitters

Combine all ingredients in a serving glass half full of ice.

For a Canadian Old-Fashioned, use Canadian whisky, of course, and make a few other adjustments.

Canadian Old-Fashioned

Serve in a chilled old-fashioned glass.

1¹/₂ oz. Canadian whisky

¹/₂ tsp. curaçao

Dash lemon juice

Dash Angostura bitters

Lemon twist

Orange twist

Combine all ingredients except twists in a shaker with cracked ice. Shake vigorously, then pour into the serving glass. Garnish with the twists.

A rickey is a drink made with sugar and lime juice. The classic spirit is gin, and while most drinkers would find bourbon or scotch too rich for their rickey, blended whiskey or Canadian works just fine.

Whiskey Rickey

Serve on the rocks in a Collins glass.

1¹/₂ oz. blended whiskey

Juice of ¹/₂ lime

1 tsp. sugar syrup

Club soda to fill

Lime twist

Combine all ingredients except the lime twist and club soda in the serving glass at least half filled with ice. Stir well. Add club soda to fill and garnish with the lime twist.

Pucker Up

The Whiskey Sour may be the most popular blended whiskey cocktail. The basic sour can be made with commercial powdered sour mix or with freshly prepared sour mix. Check out Chapter 4 for a sour-mix recipe.

Whiskey Sour

Serve in a chilled sour glass.

2 oz. blended whiskey

1 oz. sour mix

Maraschino cherry

Orange slice

Combine all ingredients except fruit in a shaker with cracked ice. Shake vigorously. Pour into the serving glass and garnish with fruit.

If you don't want to use commercial sour mix or make sour mix yourself, just use lemon juice and sugar syrup. You will sacrifice the creamy foam.

Alternative Whiskey Sour

Serve in a chilled sour glass.

2 oz. blended whiskey

1 oz. lemon juice

1 tbs. sugar syrup

Maraschino cherry

Orange slice

Combine all ingredients except fruit in a shaker with cracked ice. Shake vigorously. Pour into the serving glass and garnish with fruit.

The secret of a distinctive Horse's Neck is the preparation of the lemon peel. This is no simple twist. Peel a whole lemon in one continuous curlicue strip. Put the peel in the glass. Then add the liquids and ice.

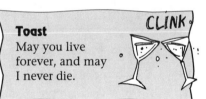

Toast
May you live forever, and may I never die.

Horse's Neck

Serve in a Collins glass.

1 lemon

3 oz. blended whiskey

Ginger ale to fill

Peel the lemon in one continuous strip and place it in the serving glass. Fill the glass one third with ice cubes. Add whiskey. Squeeze a few drops of lemon juice over the whiskey, then add ginger ale to fill.

On the Sweet Side

The mild flavor of blended whiskey makes it a natural for the sweeter mixers.

If you like the New York Sour, try the New Yorker.

New Yorker

Serve in a chilled cocktail glass.

1¹/₂ oz. blended whiskey

¹/₂ oz. lime juice

1 tsp. sugar syrup

Dash grenadine

Lemon twist

Orange twist

Combine all ingredients except fruit in a shaker with ice. Shake vigorously, then pour into the serving glass and garnish with the twists.

Buzzed Words
A **daisy** is a whiskey- or gin-based drink that includes some sweet syrup and a float of (usually golden) liqueur.

Daisy drinks are characterized by a float of liqueur. Golden liqueur is traditional—hence the name—but you can float any light liqueur on a daisy, including curaçao, maraschino liqueur, Grand Marnier, green Chartreuse, Benedictine, Galliano, or others.

Whiskey Daisy

Serve in a chilled highball glass.

2 oz. blended whiskey

1 tsp. red currant syrup (may also use raspberry syrup or grenadine)

¹/₂ oz. lemon juice

Club soda to fill (optional)

1 tsp. yellow Chartreuse (or other light liqueur)

Lemon slice

Combine all ingredients except liqueur, club soda, and lemon slice in a shaker with cracked ice. Shake vigorously and pour into the serving glass. Carefully add the liqueur for a float. Do not stir. Garnish with the lemon slice.

From Chicago, the classic Black Hawk, named after the hotel that was, in turn, named for the combative early 19th-century leader of the Sauk and Fox Indian tribes.

Black Hawk

Serve in a chilled cocktail glass.

1 oz. blended whiskey	$^1/_2$ oz. lemon juice
1 oz sloe gin	Maraschino cherry

Combine all ingredients except the cherry in a shaker with ice. Shake vigorously and strain into the serving glass. Garnish with the maraschino cherry.

Long a favorite among mainstream blended whiskies, Seagram's 7-Crown soon developed a natural affinity for its soft drink counterpart, 7-Up. Can you use a different blended whiskey in a 7&7? Sure, but then it wouldn't really be a *Seven* & 7, would it?

7&7

Serve on the rocks in a highball glass.

$1^1/_2$ oz. Seagram's 7-Crown

4 oz. 7-Up

Pour the whiskey into the serving glass filled with ice. Add 7-Up.

With Wines and Liqueurs

If the 7&7 has a reputation as a working person's drink, blended whiskies also contribute to a battery of more genteel creations.

The Ladies' Cocktail was born of an age when it was assumed that women were "ladies" who liked their alcohol with frills and frou-frous. Today, the Ladies' Cocktail makes a marvelous "retro" drink.

Ladies' Cocktail

Serve in a chilled cocktail glass.

$1^1/_2$ oz. blended whiskey	Few dashes Angostura bitters
1 tsp. anisette	Pineapple stick
Few dashes Pernod	

Combine all ingredients except the pineapple stick in a shaker with cracked ice. Shake vigorously and strain into the serving glass. Garnish with the pineapple stick.

The Lawhill is practically the definition of a cocktail: a combination of diverse ingredients on top of an alcohol base.

The Lawhill

Serve in a chilled cocktail glass.

1¹/₂ oz. blended whiskey

1/₂ oz. dry vermouth

1/₄ oz. Pernod

1/₄ tsp. maraschino liqueur

1/₂ oz. orange juice

Dash Angostura bitters

Pineapple stick

Combine all ingredients except pineapple stick in a shaker with ice. Shake vigorously and strain into the serving glass. Garnish with pineapple stick.

Malmsey is the sweetest of the fortified wines named for their place of origin, the Portuguese island of Madeira in the Atlantic. Madeira is fortified with brandy during fermentation and achieves an alcoholic content of 18 to 20 percent.

Madeira Cocktail

Serve in a chilled old-fashioned glass.

1¹/₂ oz. blended whiskey

1¹/₂ oz. Malmsey Madeira

1 tsp. grenadine

Dash lemon juice

Orange slice

Combine all ingredients except the orange slice in a shaker with cracked ice. Shake vigorously and pour into the serving glass. Garnish with the orange slice.

O, Canada!

All of the recipes in this chapter can be made with Canadian whisky instead of American blended whiskey, if you prefer. But here are a few drinks especially for Canadian whisky.

Dog Sled

Serve in a chilled old-fashioned glass.

2 oz. Canadian whisky

2 oz. orange juice

1 tbsp. lemon juice

1 tsp. grenadine

Combine all ingredients with cracked ice in a shaker. Shake vigorously, then pour into the serving glass.

Frontenac was an early colonial governor of Canada; it's possible this orangey cocktail was named for him.

Frontenac Cocktail

Serve in a chilled cocktail glass.

1^1/$_2$ oz. Canadian whisky

^{1}/$_2$ oz. Grand Marnier

Few dashes kirsch

Dash orange bitters

Combine all ingredients with cracked ice in a shaker. Shake vigorously, then pour into the serving glass.

Saskatoon is a city in south-central Saskatchewan, founded in 1883 as the proposed capital of a temperance colony. The best-laid plans....

Saskatoon Stinger

Serve on the rocks in an old-fashioned glass.

2 oz. Canadian whisky

1 oz. peppermint schnapps (may substitute white crème de menthe)

Lemon twist

Pour the whisky and schnapps into the serving glass half filled with ice cubes. Stir well, and garnish with the lemon twist.

The Least You Need to Know

➤ Blended whiskey and Canadian whisky are considerably lighter in flavor and body than bourbon, scotch, or rye; therefore, many people find them more "mixable."

➤ Fine blended whiskey is the work of a master blender, who chooses and proportions a variety of whiskies to create the blend.

➤ Clean glassware, pure water, and pristine ice cubes are essential to making a good drink with a subtly flavored blended whiskey.

➤ In most recipes, U.S. and Canadian blends can be used interchangeably; just be aware that Canadian whisky is generally lighter and more subtly flavored than its U.S. counterparts.

Chapter 11

Comin' Through the Rye: Enjoying The Drinker's Drink

> **In This Chapter**
>
> ➤ Why rye is a "drinker's drink"
>
> ➤ Where rye comes from
>
> ➤ A good reason to avoid *cheap* rye
>
> ➤ Rye recipes

Rye is one of those spirits people call a "drinker's drink," which means that a lot of folks just don't like the stuff. It does come on strong, but if you like scotch, rye is worth giving a chance. This chapter has some suggestions for enjoying this black sheep among whiskies.

The Black Sheep

Rye is a cereal grain that has been cultivated at least since 6500 B.C. Despite its lengthy lineage, it's always been something of a second-class grain, grown mainly where the climate and soil are unfavorable for other, more favored cereals, or cultivated as a winter crop in places too cold to grow winter wheat. You can make a loaf of bread with rye, but, even here, it doesn't measure up to wheat because it lacks the requisite elasticity. The rye bread most of us eat is almost always a blend of rye and wheat; traditionally, black bread, made entirely from rye, has been associated with poverty (though the moderately increasing popularity of pumpernickel in the United States has upgraded the stature of rye grain somewhat).

Quick One

Commuter to train conductor: "This morning I accidentally left a small bottle of rye on the train. Was it turned into the Lost-and-Found?"

"No," the conductor replied, "but the guy who found it was."

Bar Tips

Rye has fallen so far out of the loop that drinkers who ask for "rye and ginger," are probably expecting to be served a blended whiskey with ginger ale. Respond to the request thus—"Do you want rye or blended whiskey?"

So there it is: the rather sad story of this hearty, but hard-pressed cereal grain. And it gets sadder.

While pumpernickel bread has increased in popularity in the United States over recent years, the popularity of rye whiskey has steadily declined. Most liquor stores carry but few brands, and many drinkers give it scarcely a thought.

Rye, Unadorned

The fact is, rye offers a full-bodied, up-and-at-'em alternative to scotch and Irish whiskey, the two whiskey types it most resembles in flavor. Invest in a good rye. Cheap brands give new meaning to the term *rotgut* and are characterized by a musty taste—like sipping something that's been sitting in a damp basement for far too long. Drinking rye should not be a punishment. In many liquor stores, you'll find but a single premium brand, Old Overholt, the most widely marketed rye. Fortunately, it's quite good.

Serious drinkers take their rye neat, period: in a shot glass, at room temperature. Like other whiskies, it can also be served on the rocks, straight-up (having been chilled on ice), with club soda, or with ginger ale. The usual rules and recommendations apply:

➤ Use scrupulously clean glassware

➤ Use pure water

➤ Use unsullied ice cubes

Rock and Rye: What It Is and What To Do with It

Some day, if it hasn't occurred already, you will have a conversation something like this:

You: Have you ever tried rye?

Them: I've heard of *rock* and rye. Is that what you mean?

You: No.

Rock and rye is not rye whiskey on the rocks. It is a liqueur, marketed under various brand names, made with rye whiskey, whole fruits—you'll see them in the bottle—and rock candy. Since every time you say *rye*, the phrase "rock and rye" will jump up like a leg whose knee has been tapped by a rubber mallet, you'd better know what to do with rock and rye.

Basically, there are two things you can do. You can make a *cooler* or you can make a *heater*.

Rock and Rye Cooler

Serve in a highball glass.

1¹/₂ oz. vodka   Lemon-lime soda to fill

1 oz. rock and rye   Lime slice

2 tsp. lime juice

Combine all ingredients except soda in a shaker with ice. Shake vigorously, then strain into the serving glass half filled with ice cubes. Add lemon-lime soda to fill and garnish with a lime slice.

Rock and Rye Toddy

Serve in a heat-proof mug.

2 oz. rock and rye   Lemon slice

3 oz. boiling water   Cinnamon stick

2 dashes Angostura bitters   Grated nutmeg

Combine rock and rye with bitters in the mug. Drop in the lemon slice, then pour on boiling water. Garnish with the cinnamon stick and grated nutmeg.

Certain old-timers swear by the Rock and Rye Toddy as very comforting to cold sufferers. We make absolutely no claim to any health benefits, but just pass on this fragment of folk wisdom.

Fizz and Flip

A *fizz* is just about any drink made with sugar and soda, and a *flip* is a drink with liquor, sugar, spice, and egg. Both types of drinks have pleasantly old-fashioned qualities, which makes them perfect for rye, itself an old-fashioned spirit.

Buzzed Words
A **toddy** is a hot drink consisting of liquor (often rum), water, sugar, and spices.

Buzzed Words
Flip drinks contain liquor, sugar, spice, and egg. They were most popular in the 18th and 19th centuries.

135

Rye Fizz

Serve on the rocks in a highball glass.

1¹/₂ oz. rye

Dash Angostura bitters

Dash sugar syrup

Club soda to fill

Combine all ingredients except the soda in a mixing glass. Stir well and pour into the serving glass filled with ice. Add club soda to fill.

 Bar Tip

The best way to chill a brandy snifter is with crushed ice. Pour it into the snifter, allow the snifter to chill, then pour out the ice when you are ready to pour in the drink. Putting a delicate snifter in a refrigerator or freezer may crack it.

Rye Flip

Serve in a chilled brandy snifter.

1¹/₂ oz. rye

1 egg

1 tsp. sugar syrup

Ground nutmeg

Combine all ingredients except nutmeg in a shaker with ice. Shake vigorously, then strain into the serving glass. Sprinkle with nutmeg.

Fortifiers

The assertive quality of rye gives you the distinct feeling that you are, indeed, having a *drink*. For that reason, rye works well in the kind of drinks people used to call pick-me-ups.

The Hesitation, like the Kungsholm cocktail (which you'll learn about later in the chapter) combines rye with a characteristic Swedish liqueur called *punsch*. Why hesitate?

Hesitation

Serve in a chilled cocktail glass.

1¹/₂ oz. rye

1¹/₂ oz. Swedish *punsch*

Few liberal dashes lemon juice

Combine all ingredients in a shaker with cracked ice. Shake vigorously, then pour into the serving glass.

The Hunter's Cocktail is an old-timey classic. Not only is it meant to recruit flagging energies after a ride to hounds, its bright red maraschino cherry is intended not to clash with the color of one's riding coat.

Hunter's Cocktail

Serve on the rocks in an old-fashioned glass.

1¹/₂ oz. rye

¹/₂ oz. cherry brandy

Maraschino cherry

Combine rye and brandy over ice in the serving glass. Stir, then garnish with the cherry.

Players Script

Henry Dixey was a late 19th-century comedian and an early Player. One day, a waiter mistakenly brought him a glass of milk intended for somebody else.

"What is this?" Dixey demanded.

"Milk, sir," the waiter replied.

"Is it *fresh* milk?" Dixey frowned.

"Oh, yes sir," the waiter assured him.

"Then take it away," Dixey said grandly, returning to his newspaper.

Movie buffs may remember the 1956 film *Lisbon*, which featured Grace Kelly and Ray Milland, and brought into the world the popular melody "Lisbon Antigua," which has graced elevator music systems ever since. It also lent brief popularity to the Lisbon Cocktail, which is something very much worth reviving.

Lisbon Cocktail

Serve in chilled old-fashioned glasses.

3 oz. rye

4 oz. port

1 oz. lemon juice

2 tsp. sugar syrup

1 egg white *

Combine all ingredients in a shaker with cracked ice. Shake vigorously, then pour into the serving glasses. *Recipe makes two drinks.*

* *Raw egg may be a source of salmonella bacteria. You may wish to avoid drinks calling for raw egg yolk or white.*

Citrus Varieties

The origin of rye whiskey, in a cereal grain that thrives at high altitudes and in cold, inhospitable climates, is about as far from the citrus realm as one can get. Nevertheless, the two worlds meet joyously in a few good drinks.

Bal Harbour is a Florida coastal community so upscale that it had to spell its name the British way. Its namesake cocktail smacks of easy living among old money.

Bal Harbour Cocktail

Serve in a chilled cocktail glass.

$1^1/_2$ oz. rye

$1/_2$ oz. dry vermouth

1 oz. grapefruit juice

Maraschino cherry

Combine all ingredients except the cherry in a shaker with cracked ice. Shake vigorously, then strain into the serving glass. Garnish with the maraschino cherry.

Founded in 1868 as a New York City drinking club, the Benevolent and Protective Order of Elks is the most venerable of the "Big Three" American lodge-type orders named after wildlife. (The others are the Moose and the Eagles.) With 1.5 million members, mostly in smaller towns across the country, the Elks certainly *deserve* their own cocktail. (You don't have to know the secret handshake to partake.)

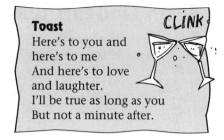

Toast
Here's to you and here's to me
And here's to love and laughter.
I'll be true as long as you
But not a minute after.

Note that the Elk's Own is an *exception* to the rule governing most drinks that include egg white. You'll need one egg white—not half—per drink.

Elk's Own

Serve in a chilled old-fashioned glass.

1^1/$_2$ oz. rye	1 egg white
^{3}/$_4$ oz. port	1 tsp. powdered sugar
Juice of ^{1}/$_2$ lemon	Pineapple stick

Combine all ingredients except the pineapple stick in a shaker with cracked ice. Shake vigorously, then pour into the serving glass and garnish with the pineapple stick.

We've already seen an Indian River Cocktail made with blended whiskey (in Chapter 10). The version based on rye uses orange juice rather than grapefruit juice and adds dry rather than sweet vermouth.

Indian River Rye Cocktail

Serve in a chilled old-fashioned glass.

1 oz. rye	2 oz. orange juice
1 oz. dry vermouth	Few dashes raspberry syrup

Combine all ingredients in a shaker with cracked ice. Shake vigorously, then pour into the serving glass.

With Liqueurs and Bitters

Rye really comes into its own when combined with liqueurs and bitters. These drinks are decidedly not for people who want a "lite" experience. They'll take you the whole nine yards.

True to form, the cocktail named for the City on the Bay is decidedly on the sweet side.

Frisco Cocktail

Serve in a chilled cocktail glass.

1¹/₂ oz. rye

1¹/₂ oz. Benedictine

¹/₂ oz. lemon juice

Orange twist

Combine all ingredients except the orange twist in a shaker with ice. Shake vigorously, then strain into the serving glass and garnish with the twist.

Lord Baltimore's Cup is probably the best known rye cocktail, and it remains popular. Made with care, it is nothing less than spectacular.

Lord Baltimore's Cup

Serve in a chilled large wine glass or wine goblet.

¹/₂ tsp. sugar syrup

Few dashes Angostura bitters

1 oz. rye

Champagne to fill

1 tsp. Pernod for float

Combine the sugar and bitters in the serving glass. Add rye, along with several ice cubes, then fill with champagne. Carefully add Pernod as a float. Do not stir.

Bitters bring out the best in really good rye. The name of the Pink Rye comes from the tinge added by the Angostura.

Pink Rye

Serve on the rocks in an old-fashioned glass.

$1^1/_2$ oz. rye

Liberal dashes Angostura syrup

Combine the ingredients in the serving glass filled with ice. Stir well.

Rye Manhattans

The versatile Manhattan can be made with bourbon, blended whiskey, scotch, and rye. The basic recipe follows.

Rye Manhattan

Serve in a chilled cocktail glass.

$1^1/_2$ oz. rye

$^1/_4$ oz. sweet vermouth

Maraschino cherry

Combine the rye and vermouth in a mixing glass filled with ice. Stir well, then strain into the serving glass and garnish with the cherry.

A variation on the Rye Manhattan is the Dry Rye Manhattan. Rye combines amazingly well with dry vermouth.

Dry Rye Manhattan

Serve in a chilled cocktail glass.

$1^1/_2$ oz. rye

$^1/_4$ oz. dry vermouth

Maraschino cherry

Combine the rye and vermouth in a mixing glass filled with ice. Stir well, then strain into the serving glass and garnish with the cherry.

"Perfect" Manhattans, like Perfect Martinis, combine sweet and dry vermouths.

Perfect Rye Manhattan

Serve in a chilled cocktail glass.

2 oz. rye

1/2 tsp. sweet vermouth

1/2 tsp. dry vermouth

Few dashes Agnostura bitters

Maraschino cherry

Combine all ingredients except cherry in a shaker with ice. Shake vigorously, then strain into the serving glass and garnish with the cherry.

The Least You Need to Know

➤ Rye is the most neglected of the whiskies, but it is well worth reviving as a change of pace from bourbon or scotch.

➤ Rye is often confused with rock and rye, which is a rye-based liqueur laden with fruit and rock candy.

➤ While the cheaper brands of bourbon and scotch aren't all that bad, cheap rye is terrible. Invest in a premium brand.

➤ While dedicated rye drinkers usually prefer their rye neat, the whiskey mixes very well with bitters, liqueurs, and, surprisingly, citrus.

Chapter 12

Scotch Snobs and Irish Spirits: Blends and Single Malts

In This Chapter

- ➤ How scotch is made
- ➤ Malt vs. grain scotch, and single-malt vs. blended scotch
- ➤ Scotch vs. Irish whiskey
- ➤ Scotch recipes

Of all distilled spirits, scotch comes closest to wine in terms of commanding a legion of connoisseurs both dedicated and disputatious. Like making wine, creating scotch is theoretically quite simple. There is fermentation, distilling, aging, then bottling. In the case of blended scotch, there is the added complication of blending 15 to 50 whiskies. Yet, still, as the saying goes, this isn't rocket science. Nevertheless, scotch varies greatly in taste from label to label, and just why this is the case is a subject of deep mystery.

As to Irish whiskey, its following is much smaller than the host of scotch fanciers; yet, thanks to the great popularity of a number of liqueurs based on Irish whiskey (paramountly Irish Mist and Bailey's Original Irish Cream), the whiskey itself is enjoying increasing demand in the United States. It's certainly worth trying.

Scotland the Brave

No one has yet been able to make truly satisfying scotch whisky (remember, that's how the Scots prefer to spell it) outside of Scotland. Is there magic there? Or is it just the right barley and water and peat for the barley roasting? Most authorities attribute at least some of the variation among whiskeys of the great scotch-producing regions—Highlands, Lowlands, Campbeltown, and the Isle of Islay—to differences in the amount of exposure to peat firing each malt receives.

> **Buzzed Words**
> **Malt** is grain (usually barley) that has been allowed to sprout.

Speaking of malt, there are two broad categories of scotch, defined by their use of malted versus unmalted grain.

The process of malting barley goes like this:

1. The grain is soaked for two or three days in water, then allowed to sprout.

2. As a result of sprouting, the barley releases an enzyme called *diastase*, which renders the starch in the barley soluble and therefore readily converted into sugar.

3. After eight to twelve days, the sprouting process is stopped by drying the malted barley in a *kiln* (oven) fired with peat fuel. This ultimately imparts a smoky savor to the finished whisky.

4. Once it has been dried, the malt is ground in a mill and mixed with hot water.

5. After eight hours, a soluble starch (called the *wort*) is drawn off and transferred to fermentation vats, where the wort is fermented by yeast for 48 hours.

6. The result is a weak alcohol called *wash*, which is now distilled into whisky.

> **Buzzed Words**
> **Wort** is a soluble starch in the form of an infusion of malt. It is used in the fermentation processes of making whiskey and beer.

Malt scotches are made entirely from malted barley and are laboriously distilled, like cognac, one batch at a time, in relatively small *pot stills*. *Grain scotches* combine malted barley with unmalted barley and corn and are distilled in greater volume in more modern *"continuous"* stills.

> **Buzzed Words**
> The **continuous still** (also called a **Coffey still**, after the inventor, Aeneas Coffey) allows for continuous high-volume production, as opposed to the **pot still**, which must be emptied and "recharged" one batch at a time.

The raw whisky that comes from the still is aged in oak casks, which may be new or used (having either aged sherry or even American bourbon). By Scottish law, the whisky must age for at least three years, but six to eight years is deemed optimum for grain whisky and 14 to 15 years for malt whisky.

The casual scotch drinker may or may not be familiar with the distinction between malt and grain whiskies, but all except the absolute neophyte have heard something about *single-malt* versus blended scotches.

By far, most scotch consumed in the United States (and in Scotland, for that matter) is blended from products produced by several different distilleries. As with blended whiskey (see Chapter 10) blending is the painstaking work of a highly skilled master blender, who ensures uniformity of brand and a high level of quality control. After blending, the scotch is typically aged in wooden vats for another six to nine months to "marry" the blend. There is nothing arbitrary about blending. A premium blended scotch is a delicately orchestrated combination of malt and grain whiskies from the characteristic regions of Scotland, each combined in exacting proportion.

> **Buzzed Words**
> **Malt scotches** are made entirely from malted barley and are distilled in relatively small pot stills. **Grain scotches** combine malted barley with unmalted barley and corn and are distilled in "continuous" stills.

Despite the effort that goes into creating blended scotch, it is much less expensive than single-malt scotch, which, despite growing American popularity, accounts for a scant two percent of scotch sales. As the name implies, single-malt scotch is made exclusively from malted barley, which means that it is aged at least 14 years. The whisky in a bottle of single-malt scotch has been distilled and aged during a single period and by a single distillery. The best-known names among the malted scotches ring out with Celtic grandeur: The Glenlivet, Knockando, Glenfiddich, Laphroaig, Glenmorangie, and Macallan. They cost as much as *very* fine wine, and you will want to enjoy them neat, on the rocks, or with unflavored mixers.

> **Bar Tips**
> For mixed drinks, use blended scotch. There is no sane reason to expend the precious nectar of single-malt scotch in combination with strongly flavored mixers.

Ireland the Source

As we first observed in Chapter 1, Ireland is where whiskey was born; it was given its modern name in the 12th century by soldiers of England's Henry II returning from an Irish campaign. Today's Irish whiskey starts out much the way scotch does, with barley (some malted, some not) and water. The drying process, however, is carried out in smokeless kilns rather than over a peat fire. The result: Irish whiskey lacks the smoky flavor of scotch (and is therefore perceived as less sharp, mellower, and lighter than most scotches). The barley is mixed with other grains (especially rye, wheat, and corn), fermented, distilled, and aged from four to fifteen years. Good Irish whiskey has a predominantly barley malt flavor and is very mellow.

Unmixed Pleasure: Neat, Rocks, Water, Soda

For the lover of fine scotch, few gustatorial pleasures exceed that of sampling the many blended and single-malt varieties available. Any of the premium-priced blended labels make for enjoyment, especially served on the rocks or with a plain mixer. The single-malt scotches are best enjoyed neat—and absolutely *any* of these is sure to delight. Irish whiskey is likewise rewarding neat or on the rocks. Just remember the rules of enjoying fine whiskey in its unadorned state:

➤ Use super-clean glassware that is free from soap and detergent residue.

➤ Make certain any water that you add has no unwanted flavors or odors.

➤ Use the best ice possible. If you must take it from your freezer, run some water over it to get rid of freezer burn and any stray odors or flavors.

Wine-tasting parties have been around for a long time. Scotch is sufficiently varied and complex in flavor that it, too, can become the focus of a tasting party. Practiced connoisseurs cut the scotch 50/50 with distilled water—and don't feel obliged to swallow all they sample. The object of a scotch-tasting party is to experience refined enjoyment, not to get hammered. Much of the "tasting" is done with the nose. The "bouquet" of the scotch speaks volumes. Another word of advice: A scotch-tasting party is often a BYOB (bring your own bottle) affair. To supply a dozen or more bottles of premium scotch will strain any pocketbook. Work out a list of scotches to try, and arrange for each guest to bring a bottle.

Classic Scotch Concoctions

Scotch is as mixable as you let it be and certainly as mixable as bourbon. Because it has loads of character and stands so perfectly on its own, its repertoire is somewhat more limited than blended whiskey's. Nevertheless, there are plenty of great scotch drinks. See Appendix B for some scotch versions of the usual classics, and below for a few unique scotch specialties.

> **HA HA HA Quick One**
> Two men meet in a sleazy dockside bar.
> "Lemme tell ya. It's gotten to the point where I get drunk mostly on water."
> "That's crazy," the other man said. "Impossible!"
> "It's a fact. Especially when you're cooped up with nothin' but men on the ship."

The Rob Roy is essentially a Manhattan made with scotch instead of bourbon or blended whiskey. The drink commands a small but intensely loyal following. The namesake, Robert Macgregor (1671–1734), was a ruthless Highland outlaw who called himself Rob Roy and who achieved the kind of exaggerated fame conferred earlier on Robin Hood (and, later, on Jesse James), when Sir Walter Scott published his sensational novel *Rob Roy* in 1818.

Rob Roy

Serve in a chilled cocktail glass.

2 oz. scotch

1/2 oz. sweet vermouth

Maraschino cherry

Combine the scotch and sweet vermouth in a mixing glass with ice. Stir well, then strain into the serving glass and garnish with the cherry. For a Dry Rob Roy, substitute dry vermouth and garnish with a lemon twist. You'll find variations in Appendix A.

This simple combination of scotch and scotch liqueur is among the most popular of scotch-based mixed drinks.

Rusty Nail

Serve on the rocks in an old-fashioned glass.

1 1/2 oz. scotch

1 oz. Drambuie

Combine ingredients in the serving glass half filled with ice cubes. Stir. (If you prefer, the Drambuie can be floated without stirring.)

Highland Fling is the name attached to two scotch drinks, which have nothing in common, aside from the fact that both are based on a jigger of scotch.

Highland Fling with Milk

Serve in a chilled old-fashioned glass.

1 1/2 oz. scotch   1 tsp. sugar syrup

3 oz. milk   Ground nutmeg

Combine all ingredients except nutmeg in a shaker with cracked ice. Shake vigorously, then pour into the serving glass and sprinkle with the ground nutmeg.

Highland Fling with Sweet Vermouth

Serve in a chilled cocktail glass.

1¹/₂ oz. scotch

¹/₂ oz. sweet vermouth

Few dashes orange bitters

Olive

Combine all ingredients except the olive in a shaker with cracked ice. Shake vigorously, then strain into the serving glass and garnish with the olive.

Scotch with Liqueurs

CLINK · Toast

Women have many faults, but men have only two: everything they say and everything they do!

Scotch marries well with liqueurs, especially Drambuie, Scotland's immensely popular scotch-based liqueur.

A *bairn* is what the Scots call a child, and the word has become an expression of particular affection. Here's a wee drink worth cherishing—pronounce it *bear-r-r-r-r-nnn*, trilling the 'R' thoroughly.

Bairn

Serve in a chilled cocktail glass.

1¹/₂ oz. scotch

³/₄ oz. Cointreau

Few dashes orange bitters

Combine all ingredients in a shaker with ice. Shake vigorously, then pour into the serving glass.

Named in honor of a famous Scottish military regiment, the Blackwatch is both highly unusual and highly refreshing.

Dundee is a large industrial city that is also noted for its marmalade. None of that here, however, in the Dundee Dream, a bracing combination of scotch and gin.

Blackwatch

Serve on the rocks in a highball glass.

1½ oz. scotch   Lemon slice

½ oz. curaçao   Mint sprig

½ oz. brandy

Combine all ingredients except the lemon slice and mint sprig in the serving glass half filled with ice cubes. Stir gently, then garnish with the lemon slice and mint sprig.

Dundee Dram

Serve in an old-fashioned glass.

1 oz. scotch   1 tsp. lemon juice

1 oz. gin   Lemon twist

½ oz. Drambuie   Maraschino cherry

Combine all ingredients except fruit in a shaker with cracked ice. Shake vigorously, then pour into the serving glass and garnish with the twist and cherry.

On the Sweet Side

Scotch is naturally the sweetest of whiskies and takes well to the more sugary mixers. The Scotch Orange Fix, for example, pairs scotch with sugar syrup and curaçao.

Players Script

For two years the great American writer Samuel Langhorne Clemens, better known as Mark Twain, lived at The Players and ate most of his meals there. He had the same breakfast every morning: coffee, rolls, and three soft-boiled eggs, served to him broken in a water tumbler, because the regular egg glasses would not hold three at a time.

One morning his regular waiter, John, was late getting to work, and, without even stopping for his own breakfast, hurried to prepare Twain's usual order. In his haste, he broke two eggs into a regular egg glass and kept the third for himself. Twain put down his morning paper as John served him, but before the waiter left the room, he heard Twain pounding his call bell furiously. John returned to the table.

"Just how many eggs are in this cup?" Twain wanted to know.

"Three, sir," John said, looking embarrassed.

"Hmm." Twain looked straight at the waiter. "Is Walter about?"—referring to the Club's celebrated major domo. Walter was summoned.

"I want to congratulate you on your waiter," Twain said. "He really is a wonder. I've been staying in this house for several months, and I've tried over and over to get three eggs into one of these egg glasses. This young man comes along and does with ease what I have failed to do after countless efforts. I say he's a wonder."

Samuel Clemens, a.k.a. Mark Twain, author and Player. (Photo courtesy of Culver Pictures.)

Sangaree is the Anglicized version of the word *sangria*, which, in Spanish, pertains (unappetizingly enough) to the act of bleeding and has, therefore, lent itself to naming the rich red combination of sweetened red wine and fruit we enjoy in Mexican, Spanish, and Cuban restaurants. Unlike the Hispanic *sangria* drinks, however, the Scotch Sangaree has no red wine and is merely garnished with a lemon twist. It is a spiritous drink graced by nutmeg.

Scotch Sangaree

Serve in a large (double) old-fashioned glass.

1 tsp. heather honey

1½ oz. scotch

Lemon twist

Club soda to fill

Grated nutmeg

Mix the honey and a few splashes of the club soda in the serving glass. Stir until the honey is dissolved. Add the scotch and lemon twist, along with a few ice cubes. Stir. Add club soda to fill, and sprinkle with the nutmeg.

Smashes are drinks with loads of crushed ice.

Scotch Smash

Serve in a large (double) old-fashioned glass.

6 mint leaves

Heather honey (may substitute sugar syrup)

3 oz. scotch

Orange bitters

Muddle (mash and stir) the honey (or sugar syrup) with the mint leaves in the serving glass, then fill the glass with finely crushed ice. Add scotch and stir well. Dash on a topping of orange bitters and garnish with the mint sprig.

Vermouth Combinations

Both sweet and dry vermouths are used in a number of scotch-based mixed drinks. In addition to those we've already seen, here's a collection of some of the best.

Blood and Sand

Serve in a chilled old-fashioned glass.

$^3/_4$ oz. scotch

$^3/_4$ oz. cherry brandy

$^3/_4$ oz. sweet vermouth

$^3/_4$ oz. orange juice

Combine all ingredients in a shaker with cracked ice. Shake vigorously, then pour into the serving glass.

Blood and Sand is named for the smash-hit Rudolph Valentino film about the doomed romance of a Spanish bullfighter. Robert Burns, the perpetual poet laureate of Scotland, is another hero who lends his name to a scotch-and-vermouth combination.

Bobby Burns

Serve in a chilled cocktail glass.

$1^1/_2$ oz. scotch

$^1/_2$ oz. dry vermouth

$^1/_2$ oz. sweet vermouth

Dash Benedictine

Combine all ingredients in a shaker with ice. Shake vigorously, then strain into the serving glass.

Blood and Sand was a popular film that had nothing to do with Scotland, while *Brigadoon* was a 1947 Broadway hit musical by Lerner and Loewe that had *everything* to do with the Highlands. How *are* things in Glocamora, anyway?

Brigadoon

Serve in a chilled old-fashioned glass.

1 oz. scotch

1 oz. grapefruit juice

1 oz. dry vermouth

Combine all ingredients in a shaker with cracked ice. Shake vigorously, then pour into the serving glass.

Loch Ness

Serve in a chilled old-fashioned glass.

1^1/$_2$ oz. scotch ^{1}/$_4$ oz. sweet vermouth

1 oz. Pernod

Combine all ingredients in a shaker with cracked ice. Shake vigorously, then pour into the serving glass.

The Irish Collection

You could easily substitute Irish whiskey for scotch in the drinks for which we've just given the recipes. However, a good many drinks are especially suited to the mellow, lighter, drier taste of Irish whiskey.

Liqueur and Aperitif Drinks

The thinner, lighter quality of Irish whiskey combines well with a variety of liqueurs and aperitifs. Best known among the Irish whiskey-aperitif combinations is the Blackthorn.

Blackthorn

Serve in a chilled old-fashioned glass.

1^1/$_2$ oz. Irish whiskey   Liberal dashes Pernod

1^1/$_2$ oz. dry vermouth   Liberal dashes Angostura bitters

Combine all ingredients in a shaker with cracked ice. Shake vigorously and pour into the serving glass.

County Sligo is mostly rugged pastureland, mountainous and punctuated by peat bogs. It includes the wild island of Innisfree, celebrated in a poem by no less a figure than William Butler Yeats.

Innisfree Fizz

Serve in a large wine glass or goblet.

2 oz. Irish whiskey

1 oz. lemon juice

1 oz. curaçao

$^1/_2$ tsp. sugar syrup

Club soda to fill

Combine all ingredients except the club soda in a shaker with ice. Shake vigorously, then strain into the serving glass and add club soda to fill.

The Irish Rainbow combines liqueurs and Pernod, which provide a spectrum of tastes and color.

Irish Rainbow

Serve in a chilled old-fashioned glass.

$1^1/_2$ oz. Irish whiskey

Liberal dashes Pernod

Liberal dashes curaçao

Liberal dashes maraschino liqueur

Liberal dashes Angostura bitters

Orange twist

Combine all ingredients except the twist in a shaker with cracked ice. Shake vigorously, then pour into the serving glass. Garnish with the orange twist.

Mists

Irish Mist is a highly popular and readily available liqueur based on Irish whiskey. Combined with more of its mother ingredient, it makes for some tempting whiskey-and-liqueur libations.

Ballylickey Belt

Serve in an old-fashioned glass.

$^1/_2$ tsp. heather honey

$1^1/_2$ oz. Irish whiskey

Club soda to fill

Lemon twist

Dissolve the honey with a few splashes of the club soda in the bottom of the serving glass. Add the whiskey and a few ice cubes, then club soda to fill. Garnish with the twist.

Irish Fix

Serve in a chilled old-fashioned glass.

2 oz. Irish whiskey

$1/2$ oz. Irish Mist

$1/2$ oz. lemon juice

$1/2$ oz. pineapple syrup (may substitute pineapple juice sweetened with a little sugar)

Orange slice

Lemon slice

Combine all ingredients except fruit in a shaker with cracked ice. Shake vigorously, then pour into the serving glass. Garnish with the fruit slices.

Sweet Drinks

Here is a nosegay of sweet drinks.

Bow Street Special

Serve in a chilled cocktail glass.

$1^1/2$ oz. Irish whiskey

$3/4$ oz. triple sec

1 oz. lemon juice

Combine the ingredients in a shaker with cracked ice. Shake vigorously, then pour into the serving glass.

Grafton Street Sour

Serve in a chilled cocktail glass.

$1^1/2$ oz. Irish whiskey

$1/2$ oz. triple sec

1 oz. lime juice

$1/4$ oz. raspberry liqueur

Combine all ingredients except the raspberry liqueur in a shaker with ice. Shake vigorously, then strain into the serving glass. Carefully top with the liqueur.

Paddy Cocktail

Serve in a chilled cocktail glass.

1½ oz. Irish whiskey
¾ oz. sweet vermouth

Liberal dashes Angostura bitters

Combine the ingredients in a shaker with cracked ice. Shake vigorously, then pour into the serving glass.

Players Script

While he was living at The Players, Mark Twain took William Bispham, a prim New York City merchant, to the New Amsterdam Hotel to dine one night. It was an unusual occasion for Bispham. He had his home and his church, and never dined at the club or elsewhere unless a board meeting ran past six o'clock. He was a proper, rather conventional man, so it was not surprising that the conversation began to lag halfway through dinner. Then Bispham noted that his companion had stopped talking entirely—quite uncharacteristic of Twain. Looking up, Bispham saw that he was staring at a lovely young woman dining alone at another table—remarkable in itself for those days.

"Mark!" Bispham exclaimed, shocked. "Don't you see that you're embarrassing her?"

"She's wonderful, William, isn't she wonderful?" Twain murmured, not taking his eyes away.

"Yes, but you mustn't, you mustn't," Bispham said, rising in his agitation and trying to draw Twain's attention from the object of his desire.

But Twain rose, too, and said with an intensity that could only have shocked poor Bispham even more, "Why, I'd rather lie down beside that young woman naked than beside General Grant in full uniform!"

The Least You Need to Know

➤ Scotch comes in blended varieties and in an unblended variety known as single-malt scotch.

➤ Ideal for sipping neat, expensive single-malt scotch is wasted on most mixed drinks.

➤ Blended scotch is the work of a master blender, and not only are the constituent whiskies aged before blending, the blended product is also aged for several months to "marry" the combined whiskies.

➤ Irish whiskey is similar to scotch and may be substituted for it in many recipes calling for scotch. However, it lacks the smoky flavor of scotch.

Part 4
Almost Tropical

Whereas the nature of the ideal martini is the subject of endless debate, and whiskey is a topic of which some people never tire, the two light spirits of the tropics, rum and tequila, are understood by few and fully appreciated by even fewer. Here is your introduction to the wonderfully complex, rich, and flavorful realm of rum, in which each country of origin defines its own style and taste—from New England (yes, New England) down to the islands of the Caribbean, and into Central and even South America.

As for tequila, it has long lived in the shadows, tainted by an unfounded reputation as slightly sleazy—perhaps even downright gross, what with that little worm in the bottle. Well, no worm has ever gotten into a bottle of tequila, and the spirit is actually produced in a legally defined region of Mexico in accordance with stringent standards. Good tequila is carefully crafted, and sometimes even aged.

It pays to know something about rum and tequila: not only have both gained greatly in popularity in the United States, they are the key ingredient in a host of much-requested, delicious, provocative, and refreshing drinks.

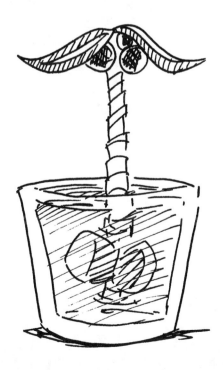

Chapter 13

Carribean Sugarcane: A Rum Résumé

> ## In This Chapter
>
> ➤ Rum—a spirit of great variety
>
> ➤ The distinctive characters of rums from different countries
>
> ➤ Rums to drink straight and rums to mix
>
> ➤ Rum recipes

If you think of rum only as a clear, sweet liquor to mix with a Coke or throw into a daiquiri, you've got a vast tropical and semitropical world to explore. The fact is, even drinkers who are sophisticated in the nuances of bourbon and Tennessee whiskey and blended versus single-malt scotches often know very little about rum. It is produced in a dazzling variety of flavors in countries spanning the Carribean and the Atlantic coast of Central and South America. This chapter opens the door to the varied realm of rum.

A Little Travelogue

The existence of rum was first reported in records from Barbados about 1650. By the early 18th century, rum was made part of the official ration of Royal Navy sailors, and British Navy Pusser's Rum was the Royal Navy's official rum purveyor for almost three centuries, until the rum ration was discontinued in 1970. In 1862, Bacardi and Company produced the first clear, light-bodied rum, operating a small still at Santiago de Cuba. Today, Bacardi rum—in its light-bodied as well as darker incarnations—is the most widely distributed rum in the world, penetrating markets in at least 175 countries.

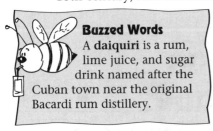

Buzzed Words
A **daiquiri** is a rum, lime juice, and sugar drink named after the Cuban town near the original Bacardi rum distillery.

Bacardi makes a very fine product, but it is not the only rum whose acquaintance you should make. Unfortunately, even well-stocked liquor stores in major U.S. cities rarely carry more than a few brands. You'll probably find Mount Gay, which is a fine example of the smooth, mellow gold rums produced in Barbados; you may find Bermudez, from the Dominican Republic; Rhum Barbancourt, from Haiti; and perhaps one or two of the products of Martinique. Jamaican rums, including Myers's, Appleton, Captain Morgan, and British Navy Pusser's, are also stocked in the large stores—with Myers's and Captain Morgan receiving quite wide distribution. Guyana's remote Demerara River produces a 151-proof product distilled and marketed by Hudson's Bay and Lemon Hart & Sons. Large liquor stores often stock it.

CLINK Toast
May you have health, love, money, and time to spend it!

If this sounds like quite a few rums are available, wait till you run down a list of countries noted for their rums: Antigua, Barbados, Bermuda, Cuba, Colombia, Costa Rica, Dominican Republic, Guyana, Haiti, Jamaica, French West Indies, Panama, Puerto Rico (home base for Bacardi since the advent of Castro in Cuba), St. Lucia, St. Vincent, British Virgin Islands, U.S. Virgin Islands, Trinidad, and Venezuela. Many of these countries produce several brands of rum, most of which are consumed domestically and never exported.

So Near and Yet So Far

As with most spirits, the basic process of making rum is simple. Most rums are made from molasses, which is the residue that remains after sugar has been crystallized from sugar-cane juice.

It is significant that the sugar necessary for fermentation is present in the molasses, which means that, more than any other distilled spirit, rum retains the flavor of the raw material from which it is made. This accounts in large part for the great variation in flavor and character among rums produced in different regions.

Another determinant of taste and character is the type of yeast employed to trigger the fermentation process. Each producer of rum closely guards its unique strain of yeast. Finally, distillation methods, aging duration and conditions, and blending also contribute to distinctive flavor. As with the blending of whiskey, the blending of rum is the work of a master blender, who tests, chooses, and combines the products of various distilleries and various ages to achieve a rum of distinctive character and consistent quality.

As I said, the process *looks* simple, but the variables involved are *so* varied—geography, climate, natural processes, human invention, and human judgment—that the making of a fine rum is, as much as the creation of a great whiskey, an art.

Colonial Benders

While Royal Navy grog—a combination of rum and water—might be considered the first rum highball, legend holds that it was the Buccaneer Henry Morgan who invented the first rum *cocktail*. Mixing the grog with lime juice and sugar, he created the ancestor of the daiquiri. But it was in colonial America that rum first became popular as the primary ingredient of a genuine mixed drink. George Washington, Ben Franklin, Thomas Jefferson—everyone—flipped for something called Flip. It could be made cold or hot, but hot Flip was by far the favorite: rum was mixed with beer (at a time when beer was a common substitute for water of uncertain purity), beaten eggs, cream, and spices, then *mulled* (heated and spiced) with a red-hot poker. "Flip-iron" pokers were made especially for this purpose.

> **Buzzed Words**
> To **mull** a drink is to heat and spice it. Traditionally, the heating was done by inserting a hot poker into the drink; today, mulled drinks are usually heated on a stove.

Rum Solo

In general, the characteristic rums of Jamaica and the Demerara River region of Guyana are dark, heavy, and sweet. Barbados rums are golden or dark amber and neither as heavy nor as sweet as those of Jamaica or Demerara. Today, the characteristic rums of Puerto Rico and the Virgin Islands follow the pattern set by Bacardi in the mid-19th century in that they are dry and light. Long-aged rums—some of the best of which are produced in Colombia (Ron Medellin) and Venezuela (Cacique Ron Anejo)—take on a rich golden-amber color from the American Oak barrels in which they are stored for as much as 10 years.

It is a pleasure to sample rum on the rocks or, like fine cognac, neat, in a snifter. The dark and gold rums are best for drinking this way. Most people enjoy the light rums in mixed drinks. However, while light rum works with most mixed rum drinks, a number of recipes call for dark or gold rum, some call for rum from a specific country, and others even call for a particular brand. Be aware that rum flavors vary widely, so you will get the most pleasing results if you follow the recipe recommendations for rum type.

Bacardis

Not surprisingly, the most widely known name in rum has lent itself to one of the most frequently requested rum drinks. The Bacardi can be made with Bacardi light or gold rum.

Bacardi

Serve in a chilled cocktail glass.

1 ¹/₂ oz. light or gold Bacardi rum   ¹/₂ tsp. grenadine

¹/₂ oz. lime juice

Combine all ingredients in a shaker with cracked ice. Shake vigorously, then pour into the serving glass.

Light rum marries well with gin. Here's the Bacardi Special.

Bacardi Special

Serve in a chilled cocktail glass.

1¹/₂ oz. light Bacardi rum   ¹/₂ oz. lime juice

³/₄ oz. gin   ¹/₂ tsp. grenadine

Combine all ingredients in a shaker with cracked ice. Shake vigorously, then pour into the serving glass.

Players Script

During the Depression, James Kirkwood, famed on the stage during the '10s and '20s, had fallen on hard times. Kirkwood was nursing a beer at The Players one night when, as he later recalled, he was "embraced from behind and kissed on the back of the neck, and heard an unforgettable voice say, 'You beautiful bastard.' It was John Barrymore."

After their fifth scotch, Barrymore asked his friend how things had been going.

"I'm broke," Kirkwood replied. "One play—$60."

"Jim, I'm splitting up the bankroll," Barrymore said. "I'm going to write you a check for $2,500."

"Not tonight, Jack. Don't spoil it."

"Why not?" Barrymore insisted. "The girls will get it anyway."

¡Cuba Libre!

In a more innocent age ("more innocent age" being that period of time in which you happened to grow up) rum and Coke was a common introduction to alcoholic beverages. The virtue and vice of rum and Coke is that it goes down, well, like Coke, and inexperienced drinkers may quickly consume far more than they should.

If you wish to reduce calories in the rum and Coke, use diet cola. And if you want to add a touch of sophistication to the drink, transform it into a Cuba Libre.

Cuba Libre

Serve on the rocks in a highball glass.

1$\frac{1}{2}$ oz. light or gold rum   Lime wedge
Coca-Cola or other cola soft drink to fill

Combine all ingredients except the lime in the serving glass filled with ice. Garnish with the lime wedge.

No, you haven't misread the recipe: A Cuba Libre is a Rum and Coke—garnished with a wedge of lime.

If you really want to transform this familiar drink into something special, use dark rum and some cherry brandy plus cola for the Cherry Cola.

Cherry Cola

Serve on the rocks in a lowball glass.

2 oz. dark rum   2 oz. Coca-Cola or other cola soft drink to fill
$\frac{1}{2}$ oz. cherry brandy   Lemon twist

Combine the ingredients in the serving glass filled with ice. Garnish with the twist.

Coladas

The piña colada may be the most popular rum cocktail, and it has spawned a number of variations. These may be made with light or gold rum. The first recipe is specially adapted to light rum; the second, to gold.

Piña Colada with Light Rum

Serve in a chilled Collins glass.

1¹/₂ oz. light rum

1 oz. cream of coconut

2 oz. canned pineapple chunks

2 oz. pineapple juice

Splash cream

Maraschino cherry

Orange slice

Pineapple stick

Combine all ingredients except fruit in a blender with 3 oz. of crushed ice. Blend until smooth, then pour into the serving glass and garnish with fruit.

Piña Colada with Gold Rum

Serve in a chilled Collins glass.

2 oz. gold rum

2 oz. cream of coconut

4 oz. pineapple juice

Pineapple stick

Maraschino cherry

Combine all ingredients except fruit in a shaker with crushed ice. Shake vigorously, then pour into the serving glass. Garnish with fruit.

CLINK Toast

To love and laughter and happily ever after!

Bar Tips

Exotic rum drinks are best served in fun vessels—the kitschier the better. Comb flea markets and second-hand stores for Hurricane glasses, totem cups, and the like. Freely substitute these for the glassware recommended in this chapter.

Daiquiris

Named for the little Cuban town near Santiago de Cuba, where the first Bacardi began operation, the daiquiri has a deceptively genteel reputation. Often considered a "ladies' drink," an unsweetened daiquiri made with 151-proof rum was a favorite of no less a macho figure than Ernest Hemingway.

The classic daiquiri uses light rum. Shake long and hard in order to get a thoroughly chilled drink. You'll find recipes for frozen daiquiries in Appendix B.

Daiquiri

Serve in a chilled cocktail glass.

2 oz. light rum $\frac{1}{2}$ tsp. sugar syrup

Juice of $\frac{1}{2}$ lime Orange slice

Combine all ingredients except the orange slice in a shaker with ice. Shake vigorously, then strain into the serving glass.

If you prefer dark rum, try the Daiquiri Dark.

Daiquiri Dark

Serve in a chilled Collins glass.

2 oz. Jamaica rum $\frac{1}{2}$ tsp. sugar syrup

$\frac{1}{2}$ oz. lime juice

Combine all ingredients in a shaker with ice. Shake vigorously, then strain into the serving glass.

A delightful and popular variation on the classic Daiquiri is made with banana.

Banana Daiquiri

Serve in a chilled cocktail glass.

$1\frac{1}{2}$ oz. light rum 1 tsp. sugar syrup

$\frac{1}{2}$ oz. lime juice $\frac{1}{2}$ ripe banana, sliced

Combine all ingredients in a blender with cracked ice. Blend until smooth, then pour into the serving glass.

Strawberry Daiquiri

Serve in a chilled cocktail glass.

1¹/₂ oz. light rum   1 tsp. sugar syrup

¹/₂ oz. lime juice   6 large strawberries (fresh or frozen)

Combine all ingredients in a blender with cracked ice. Blend until smooth, then pour into the serving glass.

Peach-flavored drinks are gaining in popularity.

Peach Daiquiri

Serve in a chilled cocktail or wine glass.

2 oz. light rum   1 tsp. sugar syrup

¹/₂ oz. lime juice   ¹/₂ oz. peach juice

Combine all ingredients in a blender with cracked ice. Blend until smooth, then pour into the serving glass.

Citrus Creations

Not surprisingly, the spirit of the tropics has a natural affinity for the fruit of the tropics. Black Stripe is a rich, thick combination of dark rum, molasses (whence the rum came), and lemon juice.

Buzzed Words

Grog was originally nothing more than rum diluted with water and rationed to sailors of the 18th-century Royal Navy. Its namesake was Admiral Edward Vernon (1684-1757), who first ordered the ration: Vernon's nickname was Old Grogram, after his habit of wearing a grogram (coarse wool) cloak.

The original Navy Grog was nothing more than rum cut with water. The following version, for civilian consumption, is rather more elaborate.

A zombie is one of the walking dead, a soulless body reanimated by voodoo. One of the most famous rum drinks combines three kinds of rum with curaçao and Pernod as well as a host of citrus juices to create a libation whose effect can indeed rob one of consciousness, if not the soul. The Zombie takes a bit of effort to build.

Black Stripe

Serve in a chilled cocktail glass.

2 oz. dark Jamaica rum

$^1/_2$ oz. golden molasses

$^1/_2$ oz. lime juice

Combine all ingredients in a blender with cracked ice. Blend until smooth, then pour into the serving glass.

Navy Grog

Serve in a chilled large (double) old-fashioned glass.

1 oz. light rum

1 oz. dark Jamaica rum

1 oz. 86-proof Demerara rum

$^1/_2$ oz. orange juice

$^1/_2$ oz. guava juice

$^1/_2$ oz. lime juice

$^1/_2$ oz. pineapple juice

$^1/_2$ oz. orgeat syrup

Lime slice

Mint sprig

Combine all ingredients except the lime slice and mint sprig in a shaker with cracked ice. Shake vigorously, then pour into the serving glass and garnish with the lime slice and mint sprig.

Zombie

Serve in a chilled Collins glass.

2 oz. light rum

1 oz. dark Jamaican rum

$^1/_2$ oz. 151-proof Demerara rum

1 oz. curaçao

1 tsp. Pernod

1 oz. lemon juice

1 oz. orange juice

1 oz. pineapple juice

$^1/_2$ oz. papaya juice

$^1/_4$ oz. grenadine

$^1/_2$ oz. orgeat syrup

Mint sprig

Pineapple stick

Combine all ingredients except the pineapple stick and mint sprig in a blender with 3 oz. of cracked ice. Blend until smooth, then pour into the serving glass and garnish with the mint sprig and pineapple stick.

Island Hopping

The allure of rum is that it's the tropics in a bottle and can transform any social gathering into an exotic vacation. Here's a collection of drinks that summon up faraway places.

Elvis Presley devotees will want to sample the Blue Hawaiian, which you may like to think was named after the King's 1961 film. Go ahead. Think what you want.

Blue Hawaiian

Serve in a chilled Collins glass.

2 oz. light rum

1 oz blue curaçao

1 oz. sour mix

1 oz. orange juice

1 oz. pineapple juice

Combine all ingredients in a blender with 3 oz. cracked ice. Blend until smooth, then pour into the serving glass.

Players Script

In 1911, the newspaper editor Isaac Marcosson gave a dinner party at The Players for U.S. Postmaster General Frank Hitchcock. Marcosson arranged for a miniature airplane, with a mailbag suspended from it, to be floated over the table. Later, a guest very much in his cups boldly predicted that airmail delivery *might* be expected by the middle of the 20th century. His prediction was greeted with expressions of sympathy for his condition.

Long a favorite tourist drink in New Orleans, this is the straight-up cocktail version of the Hurricane.

Hurricane

Serve in a chilled cocktail glass.

1 oz. light rum

1 oz. gold rum

$1/2$ oz. passion fruit syrup

$1/2$ oz. lime juice

Combine all ingredients in a shaker with ice. Shake vigorously, then strain into the serving glass.

The featured drink of kitschy "Oriental" restaurants all across North America, the Mai Tai is a classic that belongs in every bartender's repertoire. Break out the miniature paper umbrellas. The first recipe is the "original" Mai Tai, as prepared in the Trader Vic's restaurant chain.

Mai Tai

Serve in a chilled old-fashioned glass.

1 oz. Jamaica rum	$1/4$ oz. orgeat syrup
1 oz. Martinique rum	Lime twist
$1/2$ oz curaçao	Mint sprig
$1/4$ oz. rock-candy syrup	Pineapple stick

Combine all ingredients except the twist, sprig, and stick in a shaker with cracked ice. Shake vigorously, then pour into the serving glass and garnish with the lime, mint, and pineapple.

Rum with Liqueurs and Brandy

We begin with the following salaciously named drink. Enough said.

Between the Sheets

Serve in a chilled cocktail glass.

$3/4$ oz. light rum	$3/4$ oz. Cointreau
$3/4$ oz. brandy	$1/2$ oz. lemon juice

Combine all ingredients with ice in a shaker. Shake vigorously, then strain into the serving glass.

Nothing savors more of the islands than an outrigger.

Outrigger

Serve in a chilled cocktail glass.

1 oz. gold rum

1 oz. brandy

1 oz. triple sec

$1/2$ oz. lime juice

Combine all ingredients in a shaker with ice. Shake vigorously, then strain into the serving glass.

A fabled drink, Tiger's Milk is something you really should know how to make.

Tiger's Milk

Serve in a chilled wine goblet.

$1^1/_2$ oz. Bacardi Anejo gold rum

$1^1/_2$ oz. cognac

4 oz. half-and-half

Sugar syrup to taste

Grated nutmeg

Combine all ingredients except nutmeg in a shaker with cracked ice. Shake vigorously, then pour into the serving glass. Dust with grated nutmeg.

CLINK

Toast

All that we have rank, sang, and dance, no one will ever take away from us.

Planter's Punch Variations

Planter's Punch is claimed as the property of the folks who make Myers's Rum. This is the recipe you'll find on a bottle of their dark rum.

The *Plantation* Punch throws Southern Comfort and brown sugar into the mix.

Planter's Punch

Serve in a chilled Collins glass.

2 oz. Myers's dark rum

3 oz. orange juice

Juice of $1/2$ lemon or lime

1 tsp. sugar

Dash grenadine

Orange slice

Maraschino cherry

Combine all ingredients except fruit in a shaker with cracked ice. Shake vigorously, then pour into the serving glass. Garnish with the orange slice and maraschino cherry.

Plantation Punch

Serve in a chilled Collins glass.

$1^1/2$ oz. dark Jamaica rum

$3/4$ oz. Southern Comfort

1 tsp. brown sugar

1 oz. lemon juice

Club soda to fill

Orange slice

Lemon slice

1 tsp. port

Combine all ingredients except club soda, fruit, and port in a shaker with cracked ice. Shake vigorously, then pour into the serving glass. Add club soda to fill and garnish with the fruit. Top off with the port.

Coffee Drinks

Jamaican coffee is also called a Calypso and makes a splendid after-dinner drink.

Jamaican Coffee (a.k.a Calypso)

Serve in a coffee mug.

$3/4$ oz. Tia Maria

$3/4$ oz. Jamaican rum

Hot coffee

Whipped cream

Pour Tia Maria and rum into the mug and add coffee. Top with whipped cream.

Café Foster

1 oz. light or dark rum   Hot coffee
¹/₂ oz. crème de banana   Whipped cream

Pour rum and crème de banana into mug. Add coffee to fill, then top with whipped cream.

In addition to the many original mixed drinks featuring rum, the tropical spirit can stand in for a variety of liquors in familiar drinks. See Appendix B for all the rum variations of classics like the martini, the Collins, and the screwdriver.

The Least You Need to Know

➤ Few people know or appreciate the wide variety of rums produced; unfortunately, only a relatively small fraction of these spirits are available in most American liquor stores.

➤ Rum starts out as molasses, which contains the sugar that is the basis of the spirit's fermentation. For this reason, you will taste more of the raw ingredient in rum than in any other spirit.

➤ The taste and character of rum varies greatly from one country of origin to the next.

➤ Light or gold rum is usually best for mixing; except in a few special recipes, the dark rums are best enjoyed on the rocks or in a snifter, like brandy.

Chapter 14

From the Halls of Montezuma: Tequila!

In This Chapter

➤ How to drink tequila, Pancho-Villa style

➤ The origin of tequila

➤ How tequila is made

➤ Tequila in white and gold

➤ Tequila recipes

Tequila—at least on the U.S. side of the border—has long been shrouded in disreputable myth. The truly callow still regard it as a hallucinogen—rendered particularly vile by the inclusion of a worm in the bottle—but, even among more sophisticated drinkers, tequila often has a reputation as a crude, harsh beverage redolent of raw yeast and industrial solvent.

The mistaken idea that tequila is a hallucinogen comes from confusing it with another spirit, *mescal*, which, like tequila, is made from the *agave* plant, albeit a different species. But all mescal shares with *mescaline*—a true hallucinogen—are the first two syllables. The origin of mescal is agave, whereas mescaline comes from *peyote*.

What's more, reports of raw, harsh, and otherwise disagreeable qualities are unfounded with regard to genuine tequila, which must meet strict standards set by the Mexican government. The standards came about partly because tourists were often sold cheap, inferior products, which gave tequila that bad rep. As to the worm, you may find it in a bottle of mescal, but never in tequila.

If you're surprised by what you've read so far, I've got quite a bit more to tell you about this pungent, faintly sweet, deliciously yeasty spirit, which continues to grow in popularity north of the border.

The Mexican Itch

As mixologist John J. Poister describes in *The New American Bartender's Guide*, the "Mexican Itch" is the "original" way to imbibe tequila. You walk into any Mexican *cantina*, belly up to the bar, and say, "Tequila estilo Pancho Villa, por favor." Tequila, Pancho-Villa style.

It seems that Villa (1878–1923), a folk hero who combined the roles of bandit and revolutionary guerrilla, enjoyed his tequila in shots served with a lime wedge and coarse salt. The Mexican Itch is now known as a tequila shooter.

Tequila's Royal Heritage

The Toltec people ruled central Mexico from the 10th to the 12th century. They amassed an empire, which was subsequently invaded and conquered by the Aztecs in the middle of the 12th century.

Toast

Here's looking up your old address!

Some Toltec person—legend says he was of royal blood—discovered what he called a miracle plant, the pineapple. Like agave, the base of the pineapple plant fills with sweet sap, which this Toltec called *agua miel*—"honey water." The Toltecs fermented the honey water to produce what Mexicans today call *pulque,* a refreshing and only mildly alcoholic beverage.

Anyway, the rest of the story goes that the Toltec discoverer of honey water sent his daughter, the beautiful Princess Xochitl, to the principal ruler of the Toltecs. The ruler liked the honey water, and he loved Xochitl, whom he made his queen. Presumably everyone lived happily ever after.

Until, of course, the Aztecs invaded. Four hundred years later, the Aztecs made the mistake of welcoming a band of highly dubious Spanish visitors led by one Hernan Cortés. Aztec-Spanish relations quickly deteriorated, and eventually the great Indian empire was pillaged, ravished, and conquered.

Although they destroyed Aztec civilization, the conquistadors did do something constructive. They introduced distillation into the conquered realm and tried it out on fermented honey water. Tequila was born.

Geography South of the Border

Or *something* was born. Maybe it was mescal. By Mexican law, to be called *tequila*, the spirit must have been distilled from mash derived exclusively from the blue agave, a plant that takes a full 10 years to mature and is cultivated in a strictly defined region surrounding the town of Tequila in the state of Jalisco. Mescal production is not subject to strict government regulation or geographical restrictions.

To make tequila, the hearts of the agave are harvested and taken to steam ovens for roasting. They are then shredded, their juice expressed; sugar is added to promote fermentation; and then, after four days, the fermented fluid is double-distilled to produce a clear spirit that, after filtration, may be bottled directly or aged in oak casks from less than a year to as long as seven years.

Tequila Varieties

Sample the various tequila brands imported into this country and choose your favorite. You should be aware of the two basic varieties, whatever the brand: the white tequila and the gold. White is unaged, bottled immediately after distillation. The gold, which sometimes shades into the brown range, called *tequila añejo*, is aged in oak casks. It acquires its color just as whiskey does, from the chemical interaction with the oak.

> **Buzzed Words**
> **Tequila añejo** is tequila that has been aged in oak casks, acquiring a gold coloring. Unaged tequila is clear and called **white** tequila.

The difference between white tequila and *tequila añejo* is immediately apparent to the drinker. The aged product is much smoother and mellower, and the longer it has aged, the smoother and mellower it will be. It also costs more. White tequila is not a sipping drink. Either mix it or take it as a shooter, with salt and a lime wedge. *Tequila añejo*, however, may be mixed or savored slowly, like good whiskey or a fine cognac.

Tequila Estilo Pancho Villa con Sangrita, Por Favor!

Okay, we've made such a fuss about Pancho Villa's version of a shooter, let's make with the details:

1. The tequila part is easy. Just pour a shot—a jigger—of white tequila in a shot glass.
2. Take a lime wedge between the thumb and forefinger of your left hand. (Unless you're left-handed. You're doing the shot with your good hand.)
3. Put a liberal pinch of coarse kitchen salt (not fine table salt) directly behind the held wedge, in the little hollow on the back of your hand between the base of your thumb and the base of your forefinger. (It helps to lick your hand first, so the salt stays put.)

4. Pick up the shot of tequila in your right hand.

5. Lick the salt, immediately down the tequila in a gulp, then suck the lime.

At this point, feel free to bang the bar several times as you struggle to resume respiration.

Alternatively, you may chase the shooter with *sangrita*, a traditional Mexican concoction without alcohol. Sangrita is available premixed in stores that specialize in Mexican foods, or you can mix your own:

Sangrita

Yields $3^1/_2$ cups.

2 cups tomato juice	2 tsp. very finely minced onion
1 cup orange juice	2 tsp. Worcestershire sauce (or to taste)
2 oz. lime juice	3 pinches white pepper
2 tsp. Tabasco sauce (or to taste)	Pinch celery salt (to taste)

Combine all ingredients in a blender. Blend thoroughly, then strain into a container for chilling in the refrigerator.

You'll see a recipe for a tequila-based Bloody Mary later in the chapter; be also advised that sangrita makes an extremely fiery Bloody Mary or Tequila Maria mix. Just add $1^1/_2$ oz. of vodka (for a Bloody Mary) or tequila (for a Tequila Maria) to 4 oz. of Sangrita.

Margaritas

The margarita, the most popular tequila cocktail, is a natural evolution from the tequila shooter. It is essentially tequila combined with lime. The combining takes place not in your mouth and gullet, but more genteelly, in a glass. A half-ounce of triple sec sweetens the deal.

Bar Tips
Traditionally, bartenders rim margarita glasses with coarse salt. (See Chapter 5 for information on how to rim a glass.) Many drinkers find a 50/50 mixture of salt and sugar more palatable. Try it.

The following margarita recipes are all served in glasses rimmed with coarse salt. See Chapter 5 for information on how to rim a glass.

Some prefer their margarita on the rocks, but it goes down great as a frozen drink and is often requested as such. You'll need a *large* cocktail glass or a *large* wine goblet to serve one.

Margarita

Serve in a chilled cocktail glass, optionally rimmed with coarse salt.

1¹/₂ oz. tequila (white or gold)

¹/₂ oz. triple sec

Juice of ¹/₂ large lime (or whole small lime)

Coarse salt

Lime slice

Combine all ingredients except the lime slice in a shaker with ice. Shake vigorously, then strain into the serving glass. Garnish with the lime slice.

Frozen Margarita

Serve in a large chilled cocktail glass or large chilled wine goblet rimmed with salt.

1¹/₂ oz. white tequila

¹/₂ oz. triple sec

1 oz. lemon or lime juice

Coarse salt

Lime slice

Put approximately 2 cups of cracked ice in a blender. Add all ingredients except salt and lime slice. Blend until slushy. The mixture should be firm rather than watery. Pour into the serving glass. Garnish with the lime slice.

An exciting variation on the Frozen Margarita is the Frozen *Fruit* Margarita. *You* pick the fruit—such as raspberries with raspberry liqueur, or bananas with banana liqueur.

Frozen Fruit Margarita

Serve in a large, chilled cocktail glass or wine goblet rimmed with salt.

1¹/₂ oz. white tequila

¹/₂ oz. triple sec

¹/₂ oz. sour mix

Fresh fruit to taste

1 oz. fruit liqueur to harmonize with fresh fruit chosen

Dash Rose's lime juice

Coarse salt

Lime slice

Put approximately 2 cups of cracked ice in a blender. Add all ingredients except salt and lime slice. Blend until slushy. The mixture should be firm rather than watery. Pour into the serving glass. Garnish with lime slice.

You may also depart from the familiar straight-up margarita. This blue one should shake things up.

Blue Margarita

Serve in a large, chilled cocktail glass or wine goblet rimmed with salt.

2 oz. white tequila

$^3/_4$ oz. blue curaçao

2 oz. sour mix

$^1/_2$ oz. lime juice

Coarse salt

Lime slice

Combine all ingredients except salt and lime slice in a shaker with ice. Shake vigorously, then strain into the serving glass. Garnish with the lime slice.

Top-Shelf Margarita

Serve in a chilled cocktail glass rimmed with salt.

$1^1/_2$ oz. gold tequila

$^1/_2$ oz. Grand Marnier

1 oz. sour mix

1 oz. lime juice

Coarse salt

Lime slice

Combine all ingredients except the salt and lime slice in a shaker with ice. Shake vigorously, then strain into the serving glass. Garnish with the lime slice.

Other Tequila Classics

The margarita may be the only tequila cocktail many people know, but it is hardly the end of this spirit's repertoire. Three tequila classics follow.

Sneaky Pete

A lot of tequila's off-color rep derives from its confusion with mescal, which, in days gone by, was often indifferently made and palmed off on unsuspecting tourists, who discovered that the libation had all the charm of a Mickey Finn. "It just snuck up on me," many a groggy gringo must have said. Anyway, cheap mescal was christened Sneaky Pete—and that name is all it shares with this modern drink.

Sneaky Pete

Serve in a chilled cocktail glass.

2 oz. white tequila

$1/2$ oz. white crème de menthe

$1/2$ oz. pineapple juice

$1/2$ oz. lime or lemon juice

Lime slice

Combine all ingredients except the lime slice in a shaker with cracked ice. Shake vigorously, then pour into the serving glass. Garnish with lime slice.

Players Script

Prohibition hardly brought an end to the serving of alcoholic beverages at The Players. New York's finest were especially cooperative during this difficult period. The celebrated architect Aymar Embury, a longtime Players member, organized a Christmas party at his home one Prohibition year and discovered in panic that a case of scotch was not on hand. Embury contacted Charlie Connolly, The Players' chief bartender, and asked if he had any scotch. Charlie said he did, but that delivery would be a problem. Then Charlie realized that a New York City beat cop was just that minute being entertained in the club kitchen. Charlie approached him.

"Certainly," the officer replied. "Mr. Embury must have his scotch. I'll take it right up in the police car."

Tequila Sunrises

A popular drink that's pretty to look at, the Tequila Sunrise is not so much layered as it is shaded, one level dissolving into another. Make it carefully, and you'll quickly see where the name came from.

Tequila Sunrise

Serve in a chilled Collins glass.

1¹/₂ oz. white or gold tequila

Juice of ¹/₂ lime

3 oz. orange juice

³/₄ oz. grenadine

Lime slice

Combine all ingredients except grenadine and lime slice in a shaker with cracked ice. Shake vigorously, then pour into the serving glass. *Carefully* add the grenadine. *Do not stir!* Garnish with lime slice.

The tequila also sets, as shown in the Tequila Sunset.

Tequila Sunset

Serve in a chilled Collins glass.

1¹/₂ oz. white tequila

3 dashes lime juice

Orange juice to fill

¹/₂ oz. blackberry brandy

Combine the tequila and lime juice in the serving glass filled with ice. Add orange juice to fill. Stir. *Carefully* pour the blackberry brandy into the drink down a twisted-handle bar spoon (see Chapter 5). Allow the brandy to rise from the bottom. *Do not stir!*

Citrus Mixers

You can combine tequila with any drinkable citrus juice and have a refreshing, great-tasting beverage. An ounce and a half of tequila to four ounces of orange, grapefruit, or pineapple juice makes a fine on-the-rocks libation. A few more inventive concoctions follow.

Matador

Serve in a chilled cocktail glass.

1¹/₂ oz. white or gold tequila

3 oz. pineapple juice

1 oz. lime juice

¹/₂ tsp. sugar syrup

Combine all ingredients in a shaker with ice. Shake vigorously, then strain into the serving glass.

If you prefer, the Matador may be sweetened with the likes of honey, grenadine, coconut syrup, triple sec, or other sweeteners instead of the simple sugar syrup.

Changuirongo

Serve on the rocks in a Collins glass.

1$\frac{1}{2}$ oz. white or gold tequila   Lime or lemon wedge

Citrus-flavored soda

Combine tequila and soda over ice in the serving glass. Garnish with the fruit wedge.

Tequila with Liqueur

Tequila blends beautifully with a number of liqueurs. If neither the Bloody Bull nor the Matador appeals to you, how about the Brave Bull?

Brave Bull

Serve in a chilled old-fashioned glass.

1$\frac{1}{2}$ oz. white tequila   Lemon twist

$\frac{3}{4}$ oz. Kahlúa

Combine all ingredients except the twist in a shaker with cracked ice. Shake vigorously, then pour into the glass. Garnish with the twist.

Mexico has a pervasive Catholic heritage, which influenced the naming of this drink: Monja Loca—Crazy Nun.

Crazy Nun

Serve in an old-fashioned glass filled with finely crushed ice.

1$\frac{1}{2}$ oz. white or gold tequila

1$\frac{1}{2}$ oz. anisette

Combine all ingredients in the serving glass filled with finely crushed ice. Stir well.

The Crazy Nun may be made drier by adding less anisette.

Tequila with Rum—Yes, Rum

Mexico is quite a distance from the islands of the Carribean, but tequila has made the acquaintance of rum, and these two light spirits marry beautifully.

Berta's Special is also called a Taxco Fizz and was invented at Bertita's Bar in Taxco, a town in south-central Mexico. The town had been a silver mining center since pre-Columbian times. It is still renowned for its silver—and for little saloons like Bertita's. The Berta's Special requires an entire egg white for one drink.

The Coco Loco—crazy coconut—is a blast to make and great fun to drink. You'll need some straws! And, please, read the directions before you tackle the coconut. (Don't try handling the saw after you've had one of these!)

Berta's Special

Serve in a chilled tall Collins glass.

2 oz. tequila	1 egg white
Juice of 1 lime	Club soda to fill
1 tsp. sugar syrup (may substitute honey)	Lime juice
Liberal dashes orange bitters	

Combine all ingredients except the club soda in a shaker with cracked ice. Shake vigorously, then pour into the serving glass. Add club soda to fill. Garnish with the lime slice.

Coco Loco

Serve in a coconut (see directions).

1 coconut	1 oz. pineapple juice
1 oz. white tequila	Sugar syrup to taste
1 oz. gin	$1/2$ fresh lime
1 oz. light rum	

Prepare the coconut by carefully sawing off the top. Do not spill out the coconut milk. Add cracked ice to the coconut, then pour in the liquid ingredients. Squeeze in the lime juice, then drop in the lime shell. Stir. Sip through straws.

As popular as it has become in the United States, tequila is still *relatively* new to American drinkers, and there is a great deal of room for new tequila inventions. In the meantime, bold bartenders and drinkers have found places for tequila in a host of trusted stand-bys. For example, the sour turns out to be a natural with tequila. Don't use sour mix, but lime or lemon juice instead. The Tequila Manhattan requires a premium-label *tequila añejo*. Go easy on the sweet vermouth. See Appendix B for a full list of classic tequila variations.

> **Bar Tips**
> You'll find a recipe for a tequila martini—the Tequini—in Chapter 8.

The Least You Need to Know

➤ Contrary to its reputation in some quarters, tequila is a highly refined spirit, which is made in conformity with strict standards set by the Mexican government.

➤ Tequila was born when the Spanish conquistadors began distilling the fermented juice of the agave.

➤ Folklore aside, tequila contains no hallucinogens.

➤ Choose gold tequila—*tequila añejo*—for sipping and for selected mixed drinks; white tequila is for shooters and most mixed drinks.

Part 5
Just Desserts

Most drinkers enjoy different spirits at different times of day and evening. After dinner is the hour for brandy or cognac and perhaps a cordial. And it is the festive time, too, for hot or flaming drinks or, perhaps, the layered miniatures known as pousse-cafés.

Here is a chapter on what to look for in good brandy or fine cognac, and how to use them in a delicious array of mixed drinks. Next, we turn to the liqueurs, exploring their origins in medieval medicine and describing the palette of flavors available to those who would drink them.

Then there comes a time in every bartender's life when he or she wants to do something truly spectacular. Enter the flambé—*the flaming drink*—*and the* pousse-café, *miniature architectural masterpieces built of delectable liqueur layers. The last two chapters in this section teach you how to flame drinks safely and splendidly, and how to create magically layered drinks sure to command grateful awe from anyone you want to impress.*

Chapter 15

Snifter's Bouquet: The Brandy/Cognac Mystique

In This Chapter

➤ V.S.O.P. and other coded messages

➤ How brandy is made

➤ The brandy-producing regions

➤ Brandy vs. cognac

➤ "Flavored" or "fruit" brandies

➤ Brandy and cognac recipes

Brandy used to be a lot more important than it is now. It was called "water of life" in French—*eau de vie*. Brandy was employed as a tonic and as a medicine. In fact, the St. Bernard dogs of the hospice founded by Saint Bernard of Montjoux in the Pennine Alps carried miniature brandy kegs. In 300 years of service as rescuers and pathfinders, these animals carried *eau de vie* to some 2,500 snowbound or lost travelers.

Even more importantly, through the many centuries when Europe's water supplies were rife with disease, brandy was mixed with the water to render it potable. Brandy was, in fact, Europe's first distilled spirit and was almost universally consumed.

Today, brandy—and especially its regal incarnation as cognac—is regarded with feelings ranging from respect to awe, and, like fine champagne, it has earned a place of honor as a ceremonial libation, typically reserved for special occasions. That's fine, but brandy also makes a delicious and very useful mixer in a host of drinks that you can enjoy any time.

That's VSOP, Not RSVP

Part of the brandy/cognac mystique is locked within the letters *V.O.* or *V.S.O.P.* printed on the label. You need be puzzled no longer. V.O. just stands for *very old*, but is, in fact, applied to brandies of a rather young age (as brandy goes), at least four and a half years. V.S.O.P. stands for *very superior old pale* and indicates a truly old brandy, usually 10 years old or more.

Bar Tips

Unlike wine, brandy stops aging once it is removed from the wooden cask and bottled, so the bottling date is of no significance. There is a practical limit to how long brandy may age. After about 60 years, aging becomes deterioration.

Costly premium cognacs sport a few additional appellations, the best-known of which is "Napoleon." At one time, a Napoleon brandy really had been put in the cask during the reign of the French emperor. Nowadays, it just indicates a very, very old brandy. There is no standard, but some Napoleons exceed 50 or 60 years!

What does aging do to brandy? The effect is twofold. To begin with, there is simply something magical about consuming a drink that was prepared years ago. You're dipping, quite literally, into history. More directly, however, aging renders the flavor of brandy or cognac more complex, more subtle, more interesting, and makes the drink smoother and mellower.

The Story of Eau de Vie

Like basic wine, basic brandy is the product of fermented grape juice. Unlike wine, the fermented liquid is distilled, thereby significantly raising its alcohol content, before aging in wooden casks.

Those are the basics. But brandy comes in many variations, in terms of region, distillation method, aging duration and method, and even the fruit used—for brandies are not limited to the grape.

Brandies from France and Elsewhere

The most celebrated brandy-producing nation in the world is France, but brandies are also distilled in Switzerland, Germany, Hungary, Spain, Italy, Greece, Peru, Mexico, and South Africa. Three out of every four bottles of brandy sold in the United States come from California.

Cognac—The Regal

In France, the Cognac region produces the most universally esteemed brandy in the world, cognac. Now, the Cognac region is large, and the label of a bottle of cognac will give a further indication of the spirit's place of origin: Grande Champagne, Petite Champagne, Borderies, Fin Bois, Bois Ordinaires, and Bois Communs. Of these districts, the Grande and Petite Champagnes are considered to produce the finest cognacs.

> **Buzzed Words**
> Champagne, as applied to cognac, has nothing to do with the sparkling wine. The word is French for flat, open country, and its English equivalent is *plain*.

Everything about cognac takes time and care. Not only are the grapes carefully cultivated and selected, but distillation is carried out in *alembics*, which are ancient devices that turn out distillate one batch at a time (in contrast to modern continuous stills, which are suited to mass production). Less expensive brandies are distilled in continuous stills rather than in the much more demanding alembics.

Cognac is aged in storehouses above ground, in casks made of particularly porous wood. Much of the distillate simply evaporates over the years. Cognac distillers accept this loss as a cost of doing business and refer to it as *la part des anges*—the angels' share.

After 10 years or more, the cognac is bottled, and, as with other distilled spirits, once the liquid is removed from contact with the wood, the aging ceases.

Armagnac—The Nutty

Armagnac, in the southwestern quadrant of France, is renowned for its namesake brandy. Armagnac is made by a process almost identical to that used to create cognac, but the raw materials and the subsequent blending process produce a brandy that has a distinctively nutty flavor, with earthy undertones and, many insist, high notes redolent of violets, plum, and peach.

Calvados—The Big Apple

Due north of Armagnac, in northwestern France, the coastal region of Normandy produces a distinctive brandy from apples. Americans have made *applejack* (apple brandy) since colonial times, but the Norman Calvados is a much subtler, mellower product, the result of 10 to 15 years of aging. If you see a label indicating "Calvados du Pays d'Auge," you will know that you are drinking Calvados from the region recognized as the source of the finest.

While it is traditional to enjoy most brandies after a meal, the Norman French typically drink Calvados in the midst of a large meal. It clears the palate while simultaneously whetting the appetite for more.

The Brandies from Elsewhere

While most drinkers deem French cognac and (to a lesser extent) Armagnac the brandies of choice, connoisseurs also admire the light California brandies (especially good in mixed drinks) and the interesting products of other nations. Italian *grappa* is a very strong, aggressive, and bracing brandy (as is another product of France, Burgundian *marc*). Spanish brandies recall sherry (the greatest sherries are produced in Spain), and the most highly prized is *amontilado*, made famous (or infamous) by Edgar Allan Poe's story of a man who buries his enemy alive in a cellar containing a "Cask of Amontilado." Like Armagnac, amontilado has a delicious, nutlike quality. Farther afield, you'll find *Metaxa*, a Greek brandy sweetened with sugar; *Asbach-Uralt* from Germany; *Pisco* from Peru; *Presidente* from Mexico; and *K.W.V.* from South Africa. All are worth sampling.

Flavored Brandies

Calvados is an example of a *flavored brandy*—that is, a brandy based on a fruit other than the grape. The French—as well as distillers in other countries—offer a wide range of flavored or "fruit" brandies, including pear brandy (which typically comes bottled with an entire Bartlett pear inside), raspberry brandy (known as *framboise*), strawberry brandy (*fraise*), plum brandy (*mirabelle*), and cherry brandy (*kirsch*). Burgundy's *marc* is made from the *pomace* (skin and pulp) of grapes, rather than the grape juice. The result is a most aggressive and flavorful brandy.

> ### Players Script
>
> The Roaring '20s brought Prohibition to The Players, as it did to the entire nation. Sort of. The cops who patrolled the Gramercy Park district adjacent to The Players had an easy-going attitude toward its enforcement. Artist Jules Guerin left The Players with a couple bottles of gin stuffed into his overcoat. Seeing his pendulous pockets, a beat cop confronted Guerin.
>
> "What's that you've got there?"
>
> "Booze," Guerin confessed.
>
> "I thought so. Be on your way now."

Numerous drinks that include brandy call for flavored or fruit brandies. For those that require ordinary brandy, however, you are best off choosing a reasonably priced V.O., perhaps from a California distiller. Reserve the V.S.O.P. cognacs and the Armagnacs for snifter savoring and for the select group of subtle mixed drinks that truly benefit from the premium spirit.

Versatile as a mixer, brandy makes a provocative and refreshing stand-in for "the usual" in a variety of standard drinks. See Appendix B for recipes for the Brandy Julep, Brandy Collins, Brandy Sour, and other brandy versions of the classics.

The Alexanders

The Alexander family consists of a brother and sister. The Brandy Alexander is one of the most popular brandy-based mixed drinks—and perhaps the most popular dessert drink as well.

Brandy Alexander

Serve in a chilled cocktail glass.

$1^1/_2$ oz. brandy

1 oz. crème de cacao

1 oz. heavy cream

Combine all ingredients in a shaker with ice. Shake vigorously, then strain into the serving glass.

Some drinkers prefer a straight 1-1-1 ratio—one ounce of brandy to one ounce of liqueur to one ounce of cream.

Now, while the Alexander family is small—a brother and sister—there is some doubt as to the precise identity of the sister. Here's one opinion:

Alexander's Sister de Menthe

Serve in a chilled cocktail glass.

$1^1/_2$ oz. brandy

1 oz. white crème de menthe

1 oz. heavy cream

Combine all ingredients in a shaker with ice. Shake vigorously, then strain into the serving glass.

And here's another:

Alexander's Sister Kahlúa

Serve in a chilled cocktail glass.

1¹/₂ oz. brandy   1 oz. heavy cream

1 oz. Kahlúa

Combine all ingredients in a shaker with ice. Shake vigorously, then strain into the serving glass.

Again, for either of these, you may use a 1-1-1 ratio, if you prefer.

Other Brandy Classics

Brandy is an eminently mixable spirit, and you as well as your guests would do well to venture occasionally beyond the familiar territory of the Alexanders.

A simple brandy and soda is one of the most popular brandy drinks.

Brandy and Soda

Serve on the rocks in a lowball glass.

1¹/₂ oz. brandy

4 or 5 oz. club soda

Combine the ingredients over ice in the serving glass.

Flips made with all kinds of spirits were all the rage—about 200 years ago. Today, only the Brandy Flip survives as a reasonably popular drink.

Brandy Flip

Serve in a chilled wine glass.

2 oz. brandy   ¹/₂ oz. cream (optional)

1 egg   Ground nutmeg

1 tsp. sugar syrup

Combine all ingredients except nutmeg in a blender with cracked ice. Blend until smooth, then pour into the serving glass. Sprinkle with nutmeg.

A sidecar can be made with whiskey, but it was born as a brandy drink.

Sidecar

Serve in a chilled cocktail glass.

1¹/₂ oz. brandy   ¹/₂ oz. lemon juice

³/₄ oz. curaçao

Combine all ingredients in a shaker with ice. Shake vigorously, then strain into the serving glass.

We've seen a Whiskey Stinger, but, by birthright, it is a brandy drink.

Stinger

Serve in a chilled cocktail glass.

1¹/₂ oz. brandy

1¹/₂ oz. white crème de menthe

Combine all ingredients in a shaker with ice. Shake vigorously, then strain into the serving glass.

The hallowed yet comfortable reading room at The Players.

(Photo courtesy of the Walter Hampden Memorial Library, at The Players)

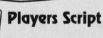

Players Script

In the spirit of Players camaraderie, Samuel Clemens—Mark Twain—could forgive many things, but a lawyer called Phineas Alvah Ludlum had obtrusive manners that infuriated Twain.

Having his breakfast late one morning, Twain saw Ludlum come in. Ludlum greeted Twain in his usual bumptious manner. Twain eventually moved to the reading room and absorbed himself in magazines, observing that it had begun to rain.

Meanwhile, Ludlum finished breakfast and went to the coatroom. He asked the attendant if there was an umbrella. "I'm sorry, sir, but there isn't," the attendant told him.

"I see one in there," Ludlum said impatiently.

"That belongs to Mr. Clemens. I can't give you that."

Ludlum took it anyway. "Don't worry," he said. "Mark Twain is a great friend of mine. Tell him that Mr. Phineas Alvah Ludlum has taken it, as he had to go to a funeral."

Later, Twain prepared to leave. The cloakroom attendant told him what had happened. Furious, he roared, "I hope Mr. Ludlum's damned funeral is a failure!"

Applejack and Calvados are among the most popular flavored or fruit brandies. And even if you don't have apple brandy, regular brandy and apple juice make a surprisingly good drink. Like regular brandy, apple brandy or applejack can be used as the principal ingredient in a host of traditional drinks.

Apple Blossom with Juice

Serve in a chilled cocktail glass.

1¹/₂ oz. brandy	1 tsp. lemon juice
1 oz. apple juice	Lemon slice

Combine all ingredients except the lemon slice in a shaker with ice. Shake vigorously, then strain into the serving glass. Garnish with the lemon slice.

Apricot Excursions

If you're accustomed to thinking about apricot brandy as something your maiden aunt imbibes, here are a few recipes to help you revise your thinking.

Apricot Brandy Fizz

Serve in a chilled old-fashioned glass.

2 oz. apricot brandy

Liberal dash or two grenadine

Orange slice

Lemon twist

Club soda to fill

Combine brandy and grenadine in the serving glass one third filled with ice. Garnish with orange slice and lemon twist, then add club soda to fill.

Apricot Brandy Sour

Serve in a chilled cocktail glass.

2 oz. apricot brandy

1 oz. lemon juice

1 tsp. sugar syrup

Lemon slice

Combine all ingredients except the lemon slice in a shaker with ice. Shake vigorously, then strain into the serving glass. Garnish with the lemon slice.

Cherry Mixtures

At least two cherry brandy drinks are worth your attention.

Toast
May you never lie, cheat, or drink— but if you must lie, lie in one another's arms, and if you must cheat, cheat death, and if you must drink, drink with all of us.

CLINK

Cherry Blossom

Serve in a chilled cocktail glass.

1¹/₂ oz. brandy

³/₄ oz. cherry brandy (may substitute cherry liqueur)

¹/₂ oz. curaçao

¹/₂ oz. lemon juice

¹/₄ oz. grenadine

1 tsp. sugar syrup

Combine all ingredients in a shaker with cracked ice. Shake vigorously, then strain into the serving glass. If you wish, rim the glass with brandy and powdered sugar.

Cherry Hill

Serve in a chilled cocktail glass.

1 oz. brandy

1 oz. cherry brandy (may substitute cherry liqueur)

¹/₂ oz. dry vermouth

Orange twist

Combine all ingredients except orange twist in a shaker with cracked ice. Shake vigorously, then pour into the serving glass. Garnish with orange twist.

Peachy Potables

Peach brandy forms the perfect foundation for some *very* sweet drinks.

Peach Fizz

Serve in a chilled Collins glass.

1¹/₂ oz. brandy

1¹/₂ oz. peach brandy

¹/₂ oz. lemon juice

1 tsp. crème de banana

1 tsp. sugar syrup

Club soda to fill

Fresh or brandied peach slice

Combine all ingredients except soda and peach slice in a shaker with cracked ice. Shake vigorously, then pour into the serving glass. Add club soda to fill and garnish with the peach slice.

Peachtree Sling

Serve in a chilled Collins glass.

1¹/₂ oz. brandy

1¹/₂ oz. peach brandy

¹/₂ oz. lemon juice

¹/₂ oz. sugar syrup

Club soda to fill

Brandied or fresh peach slice

1 tsp. peach liqueur

Combine all ingredients except soda, peach slice, and peach liqueur in a shaker with cracked ice. Shake vigorously, then pour into the serving glass. Add club soda to fill, then garnish with the peach slice. Spoon on the peach liqueur as a float. Do not stir.

B&B Variations

B&B is a classic combination of Benedictine and brandy—preferably premium-label cognac. It is a delicious after-dinner drink.

B&B

Serve in a snifter.

1 oz. cognac

1 oz. Benedictine

Combine all ingredients in snifter and swirl.

Another B&B favorite is the B&B Collins. Brandy works well here, but, for a special treat, use cognac.

B&B Collins

Serve in a chilled Collins glass.

2 oz. cognac

1–2 oz. lemon juice

1 tsp. sugar syrup

Club soda to fill

¹/₂ oz. Benedictine

Lemon slice

Combine all ingredients except soda, Benedictine, and lemon slice in a shaker with cracked ice. Shake vigorously, then pour into the serving glass. Add club soda to fill. Carefully pour on the Benedictine as a float. Do not stir. Garnish with the lemon slice.

Brandy and Champagne

Brandy and champagne make a sophisticated combination. You might begin with a Champagne Cooler.

Champagne Cooler

Serve in a chilled wine goblet.

1 oz. brandy	Champagne to fill
1 oz. Cointreau	Mint sprig

Combine brandy and Cointreau in the serving glass. Add champagne to fill and stir very gently. Garnish with mint sprig.

The Chicago is a classic brandy and champagne combination.

Chicago

Serve in a chilled wine goblet rimmed with sugar.

Lemon wedge	Dash curaçao
Superfine sugar	Dash Angostura bitters
1¹/₂ oz. brandy	Champagne to fill

Run the lemon wedge around the serving glass rim to moisten. Roll the moistened rim in sugar to coat. Combine brandy, curaçao, and bitters in a mixing glass with ice. Stir well, then strain into the serving glass. Add champagne to fill.

The simplest thing to do with brandy and champagne is just to mix 'em. Use brut champagne and good-quality cognac for a royal treat.

King's Peg

Serve in a chilled wine goblet.

3 oz. cognac

Brut champagne to fill

Pour cognac into the serving glass, then add champagne to fill. Optionally, include two or three ice cubes.

Mayfair Cocktail and Other Brandy Drinks

The famed Mayfair Cocktail is named for one of London's traditionally most fashionable districts. It leads off our small collection of brandy-and-bitters, brandy-and-aperitif drinks.

Mayfair Cocktail

Serve in a chilled cocktail glass.

1 oz. cognac

1 oz. Dubonnet rouge

$^1/_2$ oz. lime juice

1 tsp. sugar syrup

Liberal dashes Angostura bitters

Orange twist

Combine all ingredients except orange twist in a shaker with ice. Shake vigorously, then pour into the serving glass. Garnish with the twist.

The East India summons up the days when the sun never set in the British Empire.

East India

Serve in a chilled cocktail glass.

$1^1/_2$ oz. brandy

$^1/_2$ oz. curaçao

$^1/_2$ oz. pineapple juice

Dash Angostura bitters

Combine ingredients in a shaker with ice. Shake vigorously, then strain into the serving glass.

The Phoebe Snow is a delicate drink that needs to be violently shaken in order to get it thoroughly chilled.

Phoebe Snow

Serve in a chilled cocktail glass.

$1^1/_2$ oz. cognac

$1^1/_2$ oz. Dubonnet rouge

Dash Pernod

Combine all ingredients in a shaker with ice. Shake vigorously, then strain into the serving glass.

The Least You Need to Know

➤ The designation *V.O.* on a bottle of brandy means that the brandy has been aged for at least four and a half years; *V.S.O.P.* is reserved for cognac aged at least ten years.

➤ Brandy ages only in contact with the oak of the aging casks. Once bottled, it no longer ages.

➤ While the most celebrated brandies come from France, the product of other nations is very much worth sampling as well.

➤ A variety of fruits besides grapes can form the basis of brandy; most widely used is the apple, from which American applejack and French Calvados are made.

Chapter 16

Cordially Yours:
The Liqueurs

In This Chapter
➤ Origin and history of liqueurs
➤ How liqueurs are made
➤ Liqueur innovations
➤ A guide to liqueurs
➤ Liqueur recipes

Liqueurs—also called cordials—occupy a realm between the manufacture of spirits and the esoteric lore of alchemy. Ounce for ounce, you won't find stronger, more compelling, or more varied flavors than those distilled into liqueur. No distilled spirit has a more varied, more venerable, or more interesting past than the liqueurs, which partake both of ancient tradition and modern top-secret technology.

It is a great delight to shop around and taste a variety of liqueurs to identify those that will become your favorites. And don't just look in this chapter for liqueur recipes. You'll find them used throughout this book, in conjunction with many other spirits. Here, however, they take center stage.

Good for What Ails You

During the Dark Ages, distillation was a way of extracting and preserving the essences of such powerful medicinals as roots, barks, seeds, leaves, herbs, spices, fruit, and flowers. Indeed, distillation is the basis of modern pharmacology as well as modern chemistry, because it allows the extraction of the active portion of many natural materials, which then may be combined and compounded in new ways.

Buzzed Words
Cordial is a synonym for **liqueur**, but the word originally designated only those liqueurs thought to have tonic or medicinal use.

During the Middle Ages, alcohol, especially alcohol in which herbal and other natural substances had been distilled, was regarded as a medicine. But the inescapable fact was that many alcoholic concoctions tasted good and made you feel good. Thus, even after their medicinal virtues fell into doubt and disrepute, liqueurs remained popular.

A good example is curaçao. In the 1600s, British navy "surgeons" (as they were officially called) noticed that scurvy appeared among crew members when their supplies of fresh citrus fruit ran out. In an era before refrigeration, what better way to preserve fruit than in alcohol? Curaçao distills dried orange peel in alcohol. Unfortunately, it doesn't distill the vitamin C along with the orange flavor, so curaçao proved wholly ineffective against scurvy—but that didn't prevent its becoming a popular drink nonetheless, and it survives as a widely used liqueur.

How Liqueurs Are Made

Liqueurs combine alcohol with various natural substances in one of four ways:

1. **Infusion**   The flavoring agents are steeped in water, then combined with alcohol.
2. **Maceration**   The flavoring agents are steeped in alcohol, thereby extracting the essence of the agent.
3. **Distillation**   The flavoring agents are mixed with alcohol and then distilled together.
4. **Percolation**   Alcoholic spirits are percolated or dripped through flavoring agents in order to extract the essence of the agents.

In addition to the flavoring agents, all liqueurs are sweetened. In the United States, this is actually regulated by law. A liqueur must contain at least 2.5 percent sugar by weight—though most are considerably sweeter than this.

State of the Art

Although liqueur production is rooted in the Dark Ages, it is still a source of innovation. For example, innovations in distillation technology have produced a series of dairy cream-based liqueurs, which require no refrigeration and have a remarkably long shelf life. Not long ago *schnapps* was something your grandparents or great-grandparents remembered fondly from "the Old Country." Today, thanks to innovations in processes for extracting flavors from botanicals, a rainbow of flavored schnapps has emerged, offering remarkably natural fruit flavors.

> **Buzzed Words**
> **Schnapps** may be used to describe any number of strong, dry liquors, but, recently, has been applied to a variety of flavored liqueurs. The word derives from the German original, spelled with one *p* and meaning "mouthful."

Generic vs. Proprietary Liqueur

The range of liqueurs may be sharply divided into two broad categories: *generic* and *proprietary*.

The generic category accounts for somewhat less than half of all liqueurs on the market and encompasses the basic and most popular flavors, including almond, anise, peppermint, and others.

The proprietary liqueurs include Benedictine, Chartreuse, Drambuie, Grand Marnier, and Cointreau. There are many more, each made from closely guarded secret formulas—family recipes handed down over many generations. The Benedictine liqueur-making "family," for example, is the Benedictine order of monks, who still produce this popular cordial faithfully from a recipe formulated in 1510.

> **Buzzed Words**
> **Generic liqueurs** are prepared according to standard formulas by a number of distillers. **Proprietary liqueurs** are "brand-name" products prepared according to closely guarded trade-secret formulas that are the property of specific distillers.

Review of the Essential Liqueurs

Chapter 4 lists the bare-bones essential set of liqueurs that should form a part of your spiritous arsenal. But if you're at all serious about mixing liqueur-based drinks, you'll need more.

The most widely used generic liqueurs include the following:

➤ amaretto (made with almond extract)

➤ anisette (anise)

➤ crème de banana (banana)

➤ crème de cassis (black currants)

➤ crème de cacao (cocoa and vanilla)

➤ crème de menthe, white or green (peppermint)

➤ curaçao (curaçao orange peel)

➤ sambuca (coffee beans)

➤ triple sec (oranges)

➤ crème de café (coffee beans)

➤ sloe gin (sloe berries)

Bar Tips
Some European producers do offer "true" fruit brandies that are sweetened and bottled at a low 48 proof. These are still considered brandies rather than liqueurs.

In addition, some authorities would class the fruit-flavored brandies not with brandy, but with generic liqueurs. Fruit-flavored brandy is conventional brandy, distilled from grapes, but flavored with the essences of other fruit. In contrast, the fruit brandies discussed in the preceding chapter are actually distilled from the fermented juice of fruit other than grapes.

There is another difference between fruity liqueurs and fruit-flavored brandies. Fruit liqueurs are very sweet and relatively low in alcoholic content, at 48 to 60 proof. Fruit-flavored brandies are less sweet and higher in alcoholic content than fruit liqueurs—around 70 proof or higher. Finally, the "true" fruit brandies are not sweet and pack a proof well in the range of hard liquor, anywhere from 86 to 100 proof.

The best-known proprietary liqueurs include:

➤ Benedictine

➤ Chartreuse

➤ CocoRibe

➤ Cointreau

➤ Drambuie

➤ Frangelico

➤ Galliano

➤ Grand Marnier

➤ Irish Mist

➤ Kahlúa

➤ La Grande Passion

➤ Midori

➤ Peter Heering

➤ Southern Comfort

Bar Tips
If you or a guest spills a sticky, colored liqueur on a fancy suit or dress, immediately soak the stain with club soda. Follow with plain water, and rub a bit of Ivory bar soap directly on the stain. Rinse with cold water, then blot dry.

Liqueurs with Brandy

Liqueurs combine very naturally with brandy or cognac to make delicious dessert or after-dinner drinks. The most often requested brandy-liqueur combination, B & B, is covered in Chapter 15. Our first offering is decidedly different from that dignified, even rather staid libation.

Acapulco Joy

Serve in a chilled wine goblet.

1¹/₂ oz. Kahlúa

1 oz. peach brandy

1 scoop vanilla ice cream

¹/₂ banana, sliced

Pinch ground nutmeg

Maraschino cherry

Combine all ingredients except the nutmeg and cherry in a blender. Blend until smooth, then pour into the serving glass. Sprinkle with nutmeg and garnish with the cherry.

The name of the next drink is appealing in itself, especially to fans of Marlene Dietrich.

Blue Angel

Serve in a chilled cocktail glass.

¹/₂ oz. blue curaçao

¹/₂ oz. crème de violette

¹/₂ oz. brandy

¹/₂ oz. lemon juice

¹/₂ oz. cream

Combine all ingredients in a shaker with ice. Shake vigorously, then strain into the serving glass.

The Cap Martin is a delightful combination of crème de cassis, cognac, and pineapple juice.

Cap Martin

Serve in a chilled cocktail glass.

1 oz. crème de cassis

¹/₂ oz. cognac

1 oz. pineapple juice

Orange slice

Combine all ingredients except the orange slice in a shaker with ice. Shake vigorously, then strain into the serving glass. Garnish with the orange slice.

The aptly named Festival is a bright, delicious, and highly refreshing fruity, creamy drink.

Festival

Serve in a chilled cocktail glass.

³/₄ oz. crème de cacao   ³/₄ tsp. cream

1 oz. apricot brandy   1 tsp. grenadine

Combine all ingredients in a shaker with cracked ice. Shake vigorously, then pour into the serving glass.

Rolls-Royce

Serve in a chilled cocktail glass.

1 oz. Cointreau   1 oz. orange juice

1 oz. cognac

Combine all ingredients in a shaker with cracked ice. Shake vigorously, then pour into the serving glass.

Liqueur with Liquor

Combinations of liqueur with hard liquor are deceptively potent. The liqueur makes the liquor go down easy and, before you know it, you're buzzed. Enjoy—but pace yourself by drinking responsibly.

Afraid of sharks? Try tangling with a Barracuda! You can serve this tropical drink in a highball glass, in a novelty tropical drink glass, or—most fun of all—in a freshly carved-out pineapple shell.

Barracuda

Serve in a carved-out pineapple shell.

¹/₂ oz. Galliano   Champagne to fill

1 oz. gold rum   Lime slice

1 oz. pineapple juice   Maraschino cherry

¹/₄ oz. lime juice   Pineapple shell

¹/₄ oz. sugar syrup

Combine all ingredients except champagne, lime slice, and cherry in a shaker with cracked ice. Shake vigorously, then pour into the pineapple shell. Add champagne to fill. Garnish with the lime slice and the cherry.

Kahlúa is a delicious coffee liqueur that takes on a tawny appearance and texture when combined with gold rum and fresh cream in a Café Kahlúa.

Café Kahlúa

Serve in a chilled old-fashioned glass.

3 oz. Kahlúa

1¹/₂ oz. gold Jamaica rum

2 oz. cream

Cinnamon stick

Combine all ingredients except cinnamon stick in a shaker with cracked ice. Shake vigorously, then pour into the serving glass. Garnish with the cinnamon stick.

Grand Hotel! The name of this libation summons up the opulence of an age gone by—not to mention yet another Marlene Dietrich movie. This is a drink to be savored slowly and, preferably, in delightful company.

They call Mazatlán the Pearl of the Pacific. Bring a little of Mazatlán to your own private Peoria with its namesake drink.

Bar Tips
Serve drinks containing dairy products fresh, just as you would serve milk alone.

Grand Hotel

Serve in a chilled cocktail glass.

1¹/₂ oz. Grand Marnier

1¹/₂ oz. gin

¹/₂ oz. dry vermouth

Dash lemon juice

Lemon twist

Combine all ingredients except the twist in a shaker with cracked ice. Shake vigorously, then pour into the serving glass. Garnish with the twist.

Mazatlán

Serve in a chilled cocktail glass.

1 oz. white crème de cacao

1 oz. light rum

¹/₂ oz. coconut cream

1 oz. cream

Combine all ingredients in a shaker with ice. Shake vigorously, then strain into the serving glass.

Melon liqueur—especially Midori—has become increasingly popular. Join the Melon Ball crowd in the Melon Patch.

Melon Ball

Serve on the rocks in a highball glass.

1 oz. vodka   5 oz. orange juice

$^1/_2$ oz. Midori melon liqueur

Combine the vodka and Midori in the serving glass filled with ice. Add orange juice and stir well.

Melon Patch

Serve in a chilled highball glass.

1 oz. Midori melon liqueur   Club soda to fill

$^1/_2$ oz. triple sec   Orange slice

$^1/_2$ oz. vodka

Combine all ingredients except club soda and orange slice in the serving glass one third full of ice. Stir well, then add club soda to fill and garnish with the orange slice.

Players Script

Prohibition was repealed on December 5, 1933. The *New York Herald Tribune* reported that "some index of the business done over at The Players in Gramercy Park on the first day of legal drinking within the club's premises may be found in the circumstance that members wore down three full-length, extra heavy lead copy pencils signing their names to bar checks. While no standing is permitted against the bar itself of this historic club, tables have been laid out in the billiard room and the new freedom has attracted unusually large numbers during the last two days."

*The grill room at
The Players.*

*(Photo courtesy of the Walter Hampden Memorial Library, at
The Players)*

Liqueurs with Other Liqueurs

Not surprisingly, one of the best mixers to combine with liqueur is another liqueur. Here are some combinations to try.

Blue Lady

Serve in a chilled cocktail glass.

1¹/₂ oz. blue curaçao   ¹/₂ oz. light cream

¹/₂ oz. white crème de cacao

Combine all ingredients in a shaker with cracked ice. Shake vigorously, then pour into the serving glass.

Is it "Kiss Me Quick" or "Kiss Me, Quick"? Grammarians need not apply.

Kiss Me Quick

Serve in a chilled brandy snifter.

2 oz. Pernod

$^1/_2$ oz. curaçao

Liberal dashes Angostura bitters

Club soda to fill

Combine all ingredients except club soda in a shaker with cracked ice. Shake vigorously, then pour into the serving glass. Add club soda to fill.

Mocha Mint

Serve in a chilled cocktail glass.

$^3/_4$ oz. Kahlúa

$^3/_4$ oz. white crème de menthe

$^3/_4$ oz. crème de cacao

Combine all ingredients in a shaker with ice. Shake vigorously, then strain into the serving glass.

The Pernod Cocktail is another classic—as are most drinks built on Pernod.

Pernod Cocktail

Serve in an old-fashioned glass.

$^1/_2$ oz. water

Liberal dashes sugar syrup

Liberal dashes Angostura bitters

2 oz. Pernod

Into the serving glass half filled with crushed ice add water, sugar syrup, and bitters. Stir well, then add the Pernod. Stir again.

Simple and frequently requested, the Sombrero.

Sombrero

Serve on the rocks in an old-fashioned glass.

1¹/₂ oz. Kahlúa

1 oz. cream

Pour Kahlúa into the serving glass half filled with ice. Use a spoon to float the cream onto the Kahlúa. *Do not stir!*

The Velvet Hammer, one of the most celebrated liqueur-plus-liqueur drinks, is also among the simplest.

Velvet Hammer

Serve in a chilled cocktail glass.

1 oz. Cointreau   1 oz. heavy cream

1 oz. white crème de cacao

Combine all ingredients in a shaker with ice. Shake vigorously, then strain into the serving glass.

Liqueur with Fruit Juices

Based on fruit to begin with, most liqueurs are delightful when combined with fruit juices. Here are some examples.

Bar Tips
Use only ripe bananas in recipes calling for banana.

Abbot's Delight

Serve in a chilled parfait glass.

1¹/₂ oz. Frangelico   ¹/₂ banana, sliced

3 oz. pineapple juice   Liberal dashes Angostura bitters

Combine all ingredients in a blender with ice. Blend until smooth, then pour into the serving glass.

The Cape Cod Cooler is as sweet as they come.

Cape Cod Cooler

Serve in a chilled Collins glass.

2 oz. sloe gin

1 oz. gin

5 oz. cranberry juice

$^1/_2$ oz. lemon juice

$^1/_2$ oz. orgeat syrup

Lime slice

Combine all ingredients except the lime slice in a shaker with cracked ice. Shake vigorously, then pour into the serving glass. Garnish with the lime slice.

Cordial Favorites

The following is a clutch of classics—some of the liqueur drinks that are most often requested.

The Alabama Slammer may be made as a highball or as a shooter.

Alabama Slammer Highball

Serve in a highball glass.

$^1/_2$ oz. sloe gin

$^1/_2$ oz. Southern Comfort

$^1/_2$ oz. triple sec

$^1/_2$ oz. Galliano

3 oz. orange juice

Maraschino cherry

Orange slice

Combine all ingredients except fruit in a shaker fill with ice. Shake vigorously, then strain into the serving glass. Add more ice, if you wish. Garnish with the cherry and orange slice.

Alabama Slammer Shooter

Serve in shot glasses.

$1^1/_2$ oz. sloe gin

$1^1/_2$ oz. amaretto

$1^1/_2$ oz. Southern Comfort

$1^1/_2$ oz. orange juice

Combine all ingredients in a shaker with ice. Shake vigorously, then strain into shot glasses. Yields four shots.

Sloe Gin Fizz

Serve in a chilled Collins glass.

1 oz. sloe gin

2 oz. sour mix

club soda to fill

Maraschino cherry

Combine the sloe gin and sour mix in a shaker filled with ice. Shake vigorously, then strain into the serving glass. Add club soda to fill, then garnish with the cherry.

Reach into the retro closet, and you'll find the Grasshopper. This green, creamy drink is long past its heyday, but nostalgia is evergreen—and these drinks may well be coming back into vogue.

Grasshopper

Serve in a chilled cocktail glass.

1 oz. green crème de menthe

1 oz. white crème de cacao

1 oz. light cream

Combine all ingredients in a blender with ice. Shake vigorously, then strain into the serving glass.

Let's close with another retro favorite: the Pink Squirrel.

Pink Squirrel

Serve in chilled cocktail glass.

1 oz. crème de noyaux

1 oz. white crème de cacao

1 oz. cream

Combine all ingredients in a shaker with ice. Shake vigorously, then strain into the serving glass.

The Least You Need to Know

➤ Liqueur started out as medicine in the Middle Ages.

➤ Liqueurs are compounded by infusion, maceration, distillation, or percolation.

➤ Try a wide variety of liqueurs. Compile your own personal list of favorites.

➤ Liqueurs fall into two broad categories: generic (marketed under many brand names and made according to standard recipes) and proprietary (prepared according to jealously guarded trade secrets and marketed under a single brand name).

Up in Flames: Hot and Flaming Drinks

The human body is a furnace. Heat is precious to it, and what is precious feels good. That, in essence, is the attraction of hot drinks, whether it's tea, coffee, or hot chocolate. Add alcohol to a hot drink, and that thermal glow spreads, mellows, and is sustained. In the days before central heating, no self-respecting inn would fail, in wintertime, to offer toddies or mulled drinks. The flip, an American colonial favorite consisting of spirits, ale, eggs, sugar, cream, and assorted spices, was heated on demand with a "flip iron"—a poker kept hot on the fireplace grate for the purpose of heating and frothing drinks.

While it may no longer be customary or practical to offer hot alcoholic drinks at all times, such libations are welcome and delightful on chilly or rainy evenings or as après-ski relaxers. Sharing a warm drink seems to invite good conversation and general conviviality. A number of hot drinks add the element of drama as well. Offer even the most jaded of adults a flaming drink, and you are sure to get plenty of childlike ooohs and ahhhs.

Fortified Coffees of All Nations

Bar Tips
When mixing spirits with coffee, pour the spirit in first. Then add the coffee.

The most obvious hot drink vehicle is America's favorite hot beverage: coffee. The most popular fortified coffees have national themes, derived from the kind of spirit used to fuel them.

The Italian part of the Italian Coffee is amaretto. Your favorite coffee will do, regardless of its nationality.

Amaretto Café (Italian Coffee)

Serve in a coffee mug.

1¹/₂ oz. amaretto   Whipped cream
Hot coffee to fill

Pour the amaretto into the mug and add hot coffee to fill. Top with whipped cream.

Combine Galliano with hot coffee for a Roman libation.

Roman Coffee

Serve in a coffee mug.

1¹/₂ oz. Galliano   Whipped cream

Coffee to fill

Pour Galliano into the mug. Add coffee to fill and top with whipped cream.

Café Mexicano hails from south of the border.

Café Mexicano

Serve in a coffee mug.

1 oz. Kahlúa   Hot coffee

¹/₂ oz. white or gold tequila   Whipped cream (optional)

Pour the Kahlúa and tequila in the mug. Add coffee. Top with whipped cream, if you wish.

The French love their coffee, and while the Café Bonaparte and Café Marnier don't proclaim their nationality in their names, their Gallic identity is unmistakable.

Café Bonaparte

Serve in a coffee mug or hot drink glass.

1¹/₂ oz. brandy   Cappucino to fill

Pour the brandy into the serving glass, then fill with cappuccino.

Café Marnier

Serve in a coffee mug.

1¹/₂ oz. Grand Marnier   Whipped cream (optional)

Espresso to fill

Pour the Grand Marnier into the mug. Add espresso to three-fourths full. Stir and add whipped cream, if you wish.

By far, Irish Coffee is probably the most popular hot spiritous drink. Here's the classic version.

Irish Coffee

Serve in a coffee mug.

1¹/₂ oz. Irish whiskey	Coffee
1 tsp. sugar	Whipped cream

Pour whiskey into the mug. Add sugar. Add coffee to fill and top with whipped cream.

If you prefer a smoother drink, use Bailey's Irish Cream liqueur, which is made with Irish whiskey. Do not add extra sugar.

Creamy Irish Coffee

Serve in a coffee mug.

1¹/₂ oz. Bailey's Irish Cream	Whipped cream
Coffee to fill	

Pour the liqueur into the mug. Add coffee to fill and top with whipped cream.

Flavors Jamaican have become more and more popular of late, whether it's jerked chicken or Jamaican Coffee.

Jamaican Coffee

Serve in a coffee mug.

1 oz. Tia Maria	Whipped cream
³/₄ oz. rum (white, gold, or dark)	Grated nutmeg
Coffee to fill	

Pour Tia Maria and rum into the mug. Add coffee to fill, top with whipped cream, and sprinkle with nutmeg.

In the name of Switzerland, we have the Café Zurich, the most elaborate of the national coffee drinks.

Café Zurich

Serve in a coffee mug.

1^1/$_2$ oz. anisette

1^1/$_2$ oz. cognac

^{1}/$_2$ oz. amaretto

Coffee

1 tsp. honey

Whipped cream

Pour the spirits into the coffee mug. Add hot coffee to three-fourths full. Float a teaspoon of honey on top of the drink, then top the honey with whipped cream.

What is more comforting than a hot cocoa? Well...

Comfort Mocha

Serve in a mug.

1^1/$_2$ oz. Southern Comfort

1 tsp. instant cocoa

1 tsp. instant coffee

Boiling water to fill

Whipped cream

Combine all ingredients except the whipped cream in a mug with boiling water. Top with whipped cream.

Hot Rum Drinks

In its simplest original incarnation, grog was nothing more than rum diluted with water, and in Chapter 13 we introduced a more elaborate recipe. But grog may also be served hot.

Hot Grog

Serve in a mug.

1 tsp. sugar

1^1/$_2$ oz. rum

Juice of ^{1}/$_4$ lemon

Boiling water to three-fourths full

Place sugar in the mug, then add rum and the lemon juice. Finally, add boiling water to three-fourths full. Stir.

Hot Buttered Rum is talked about a lot more than it is actually served.

Hot Buttered Rum

Serve in a mug.

1 tsp. sugar

1 tsp. butter

2 oz. white, gold, or dark rum

Boiling water to three-fourths full

Put the sugar and butter in the mug, then add the rum. Pour in boiling water to three-fourths full. Stir.

Buzzed Words
A **hot toddy** is any alcohol-based sweetened hot drink. It may be shortened simply to **toddy**. There is no such thing as a cold toddy.

Toddy Collection

Originally, a *hot toddy* was a hot drink made from the fermented sap of certain Asian palm trees. Nowadays, a toddy is any alcohol-based sweetened hot drink. Here are some classic toddies.

Your Basic Hot Toddy

Serve in a mug.

1 tsp. sugar

2 oz. blended whiskey

Boiling water to three-fourths full

Put the sugar in the mug, then add the whiskey. Add boiling water to three-fourths full. Stir.

Hot Toddy with Bourbon

Serve in a mug.

1 tsp. sugar

3 whole cloves

Cinnamon stick

Lemon slice

4 oz. boiling water

1 oz. bourbon

Grated nutmeg

Put the sugar, cloves, cinnamon stick, and lemon slice into the mug. Add 1 oz. of the boiling water and stir. After letting the mixture steep for five minutes, pour in the bourbon and the rest of the boiling water. Stir. Dust with nutmeg.

You may vary either of these toddies by using brandy, rum, gin, or vodka instead of blended whiskey or bourbon.

Comfort Drinks

Just about any hot drink you can make is soothing, but the following recipes will summon up visions of true nirvana.

Bar Tips
Wine and most liqueurs cannot endure boiling. The flavor as well as much of the alcoholic content will go up in steam.

To mull a drink is to spice and heat it. We begin with two ways of mulling claret. The first recipe is for an individual drink; the second, for a batch.

Mulled Claret

Serve in a mug.

5 oz. red Bordeaux

1 oz. port

³/₄ oz. brandy

Pinch ground cinnamon

Pinch grated nutmeg

A few whole cloves

Lemon twist

Combine all ingredients in a saucepan and heat, but do not boil. Pour into the mug.

Mulled Claret Batch

Yield: 13 drinks

2 oz. honey

1 750 ml. bottle red Bordeaux

1 pt. ruby port

1 cup brandy

6 whole cloves

Few cinnamon sticks, broken

¹/₂ tsp. grated nutmeg

Lemon twist

In the flaming pan of a chafing dish over direct heat, dissolve the honey with 1 cup water. Add the Bordeaux, port, brandy, spices, and lemon. Heat over a low flame, stirring occasionally. Do not allow to boil.

A delicious Mulled Cider can be made quite simply.

Simple Mulled Cider

Serve in mugs.

3 oz. sugar

3 pints hard cider

4 oz. rum

1 cinnamon stick per mug

Pinch allspice per mug

Combine ingredients in a pot. Heat and stir, but do not boil. Strain into the mug. The recipe yields three large or five smaller drinks.

If you prefer your Mulled Cider one drink at a time, here is a very elegant recipe.

Mulled Cider (Single Serving)

Serve in a mug.

2 oz. gold rum

Dash Angostura bitters

4 whole cloves

Cinnamon stick

Pinch ground allspice

1 tsp. honey

1 cup apple cider

Lemon twist

Heat all ingredients in a saucepan and stir well. Strain into the mug.

Buzzed Words
Hard cider is fermented cider and, therefore, alcoholic. **Sweet cider** is nonalcoholic apple cider.

The classic hot drink Tom and Jerry predates the cartoons by many years and takes its name from two characters—Corinthian Tom and Jerry Hawkins—in *Life in London*, a popular novel by Pierce Egan. Some authorities believe the Egan characters are less important to the name of the drink than the apparent fact that it was invented by a bartender named Jerry Thomas.

Here are two popular versions:

Tom and Jerry 1

Serve in a mug.

1 egg white *

2 tsp. sugar

Pinch baking soda

2 oz. rum

Hot milk

$^1/_2$ oz. cognac

Grated nutmeg

Combine in a bowl the egg white, sugar, baking soda, and $^1/_2$ oz. of the rum. Beat until stiff. Combine this mixture with an additional $1^1/_2$ oz. rum and 2 tbsp. hot milk. Pour into the mug, then add hot milk to fill. Float cognac on top and dust with nutmeg.

* Raw egg may be a source of salmonella bacteria. You may wish to avoid drinks calling for raw egg yolk or white.

The alternative recipe that follows is simpler.

Tom and Jerry 2

Serve in a mug.

1 egg *

$^1/_2$ oz. sugar syrup

1 oz. dark Jamaica rum

1 oz. cognac

Boiling water to fill

Grated nutmeg

Separate the egg and beat white and yolk separately, then fold white and yolk together. Add sugar syrup, then pour mixture into the serving mug. Add the rum and cognac, followed by boiling water to fill. Dust with nutmeg.

* Raw egg may be a source of salmonella bacteria. You may wish to avoid drinks calling for raw egg yolk or white.

Going to Blazes

Few acts of mixology are more impressive than setting a drink ablaze. The effect is not only theatrical; done correctly, it enhances the flavor of the drink and, most importantly, results in no injury to onself or one's guests.

Bar Tips
The Tom and Jerry has long been enjoyed as a punch. See Chapter 23 for a punch recipe.

Don't Try This at Home!

Most liquor has a relatively low concentration of alcohol. If what you're working with is 80 proof, the liquid is only 40 percent alcohol. This means that it probably won't burn unless it is vaporized; therefore, your first step is to heat a *small* amount of alcohol before igniting it.

Bar Tips

The flaming drink is definitely not child's play. *Flaming alcohol is intensely hot and can cause serious burn injuries!* In addition to safety, it is important to flame drinks properly in order to preserve as well as enhance their flavor.

Bar Tips

A flaming drink is *not* to be consumed while it is flaming. This may sound like superfluous advice. Who'd be dumb enough to drink fire? But in some college bars and elsewhere, the idea is to down a flaming drink at once, so that the alcohol vapor burns off above the glass, while the liquor is safely downed. Raising a flaming drink to your face, then trying to drink it, is always a very bad idea.

This said, it must be observed that *vaporized* alcohol, even at relatively low concentrations, is *very* flammable. So, before we get into the details of how to flame drinks, let's take time for a safety check:

➤ Use the smallest amount of liquor possible to flame drinks. For a single drink, an ounce is sufficient.

➤ Respect alcohol as a flammable liquid, which can cause severe injury or property damage.

➤ Do not flame drinks near draperies, curtains, paper banners, bunting, streamers, or other combustible materials.

➤ When flaming or heating spirits in a saucepan or chafing dish, stand back. Do not put your face directly over the pan. The vapors may flare up!

➤ Never heat or flame spirits in a chafing dish at the serving table. If the hot or flaming liquid should spill, you could end up burning a number of people. Instead, heating and flaming should be done on a stable cart or serving table apart from guests.

➤ Do not keep uncorked spirits near an open flame.

➤ Never add spirits into a flaming dish! There is a good chance that the vapors will ignite and the fire will blow back on you or someone else.

➤ Alcohol burns with a pale flame. If the lights in the room are bright, you and your guests may not see the flame. This is not only dangerous, but insufficiently spectacular. Dim the room lights before flaming.

➤ When flaming drinks, be especially careful of small children in the area.

➤ Generally, alcohol burns off quickly; however, always have a sufficiently large lid on hand to cover the chafing dish in order to put out a fire gone awry.

➤ Although you can expect the alcohol to burn off quickly, never leave a flaming drink—especially in a large chafing dish—unattended.

Ignition...Lift Off!

To flame a drink successfully and safely, begin by taking a single teaspoonful of the liquor you want to flame. Warm this over a lighted match in order to vaporize some of the alcohol. Ignite the liquor in the spoon, then carefully pour the flaming alcohol over the prepared recipe. Do *not* put your face near the drink you are flaming. Stand back.

> **Buzzed Words**
> As a verb, **flambé** means to drench with liquor and ignite. The word may also be used as a noun, synonymous with flaming drink.

Achieving Spectacular Effects

Flaming drinks can appear disappointing if you fail to:

➤ Heat a small amount of the liquor first, in order to vaporize it.

➤ Turn down the lights. An alcohol flame is pale. Make certain you and your guests can see it.

A lot of the spectacle of the flambé is in the performance rather than the flame. Make the flambé a full-dress presentation. Put on a show, and look like you're enjoying what you're doing. (Be certain, too, to observe the safety rules listed above.)

Flaming Rum

Rum is well suited to the flambé because the flaming process creates a delicious collection of concentrated natural flavors.

Burning Blue Mountain

Serve in a egg nog-style mug.

5 oz. dark Jamaican rum

2 tsp. powdered sugar

Orange rind, cut up

Lime rind, cut up

Lemon twist

Pour rum into a chafing dish and warm. Add sugar and fruit rinds. Stir to dissolve sugar, then ignite. Ladle the drink into the serving glass and garnish with the lemon twist.

Christmas Rum Punch

Serve in a punch bowl.

6 oranges	$1/2$ gallon sweet cider
Cloves	Powdered cinnamon
1 bottle dark rum	Grated nutmeg
Sugar to taste	

Prepare the oranges by sticking them with cloves, then baking until the oranges begin to brown. Slice the oranges and place in a punch bowl. Add rum. Add sugar to taste. Carefully ignite and allow to burn for a few minutes before extinguishing with the cider. Garnish with cinnamon and nutmeg.

Flaming Brandy

Brandy is the most frequently used fuel for flamed drinks.

Big Apple

Serve in a warmed 10 oz. mug.

3 oz. apple juice	3 tbs. baked apple
Pinch ground ginger	1 oz. apple brandy

Combine the apple juice and ginger in a saucepan. Heat and let simmer for a few minutes. Put the baked apple in the serving mug. Pour the apple brandy into a ladle. Warm the ladle over a match or a low gas flame. Ignite the brandy in the ladle, then pour over the baked apple. Extinguish the fire with the warm ginger-spiced apple juice. Stir. Serve warm, with a spoon for eating the apple.

Another flaming coffee drink…

Coffee Blazer

Serve in an old-fashioned glass.

1 tbs. Kahlúa	Lemon slice
1 tbs. cognac	Hot coffee to fill
Sugar	Whipped cream

Warm the Kahlúa and cognac over a match or low gas flame. Moisten the rim of the serving glass with the lemon slice, then roll the rim in sugar; drop the lemon slice in the glass. Warm the glass over a low flame to melt the sugar on the rim. Pour in the warmed Kahlúa and cognac and ignite. Extinguish with the coffee. Stir well and top with whipped cream.

The Least You Need to Know

➤ Hot liquor-based drinks were most popular in the days before central heating.

➤ Before the advent of convenient refrigeration, more drinks were served hot than on ice.

➤ Today, coffee and liquor combinations are the most popular hot drinks.

➤ Flambés—flaming drinks—make for high drama and fun, but it is important to flame and serve them safely.

Chapter 18

Architectural Masterpieces: Building the Pousse-Café

For mountaineers, it's Everest. For concert pianists, it's the Rachmaninoff Third Piano Concerto. For a Renaissance painter, it was a great cathedral ceiling. For the bartender, it's the pousse-café.

These little gems—little, because they are characteristically served in pony glasses (1-2 oz.) or pousse-café glasses (3–4 oz.)—evoke unbridled admiration of the bartender and his or her art. They are colorful layers of liquid. Liquid! In layers! It's magic!

Actually, it's specific gravity, and this chapter will show you how to take advantage of the laws of physics to create tasty and visually appealing dessert drinks.

Many-Layered Drinks

Pousse-cafés are drinks made with two, three, four, or more liqueurs and, often, cream. Because the different spirits have differing specific gravities, some will float on top of some others. Poured carefully and in the proper order—from heaviest to lightest—the liqueurs will remain unmixed, layered like a wedding cake, some strangely beautiful geological formation, or a miniature work of architecture, depending on your imagination.

> **Buzzed Words**
> A **pousse-café** is a drink made with two or more liqueurs and, sometimes, cream. The different spirits vary in specific gravity, so float in discrete layers if carefully combined. The layered effect is novel and pretty.

These drinks are miniature spectaculars, and, as such, they require practice, patience, and a bit of good luck. It is almost impossible to create pousse-cafés in a busy bar humming with jarring and jolting activity. While making a pousse-café is not as difficult as building a model clipper ship in a bottle, you will need some measure of peace and quiet.

Do You Have What It Takes?

In addition to peace and quiet, to make a pousse-café you'll need:

➤ A steady hand

➤ A little patience

➤ A good sense of humor

➤ Guests with a little patience and a good sense of humor

➤ Practice

➤ A twisted-handle bar spoon

➤ A set of pony glasses or, better yet, pousse-café glasses

Let's address the last two requirements. (The necessity and nature of the other prerequisites will become self-evident as soon as you start experimenting with these drinks.) In Chapter 4, we described the bar spoon. That long handle with its spiral twist serves an important purpose in pulling off a successful pousse-café. Here's how you use the bar spoon:

1. Measure out the appropriate amount of the first liqueur. (We'll talk about amounts in just a minute or two.)

2. From the measuring glass, pour the first—that is, the heaviest—ingredient into the serving glass.

3. Measure out the next—lighter—liqueur.

Okay. That was easy. But there are two schools of thought about just how to use the bar spoon to add the next—and subsequent—layers. Here are steps 4 and 5 according to School of Thought #1:

4. Hold the spoon upside down; that is, with the bottom of the spoon facing up. Place the handle of the spoon nearest the bowl against the mouth of the measuring glass containing the liquid you want to pour. The handle should cover the entire diameter of the measuring glass. Insert the other end of the spoon handle into the serving glass, against the inside wall of the glass and just above the level of the liquid already inside the glass.

5. *Slowly* pour, so that the liqueur slides down the handle, is slowed by the spiral twist, then slips down along the inside wall of the glass. This avoids agitating the liquids, enabling the lighter liquid to float on the heavier one without blending with it. Do this for each successive layer of liqueur, always proceeding, of course, from light, to lighter, to lightest spirit.

Pousse-café pouring method #1.

Here are steps 4 and 5 according to School of Thought #2:

4. Hold the bar spoon so that the bowl of the spoon will be inserted into the serving glass. The convex back of the bowl should be toward you, so that the liqueur will slip around the back of the bowl. Put the other end of the spoon, the handle, against the measuring glass, so that it spans the entire diameter of the glass. Insert the bowl end into the serving glass, touching the back of the bowl against the inside wall of the glass, just above the level of the liqueur already present in the glass.

233

5. Pour *slowly*, so that the liqueur slides down the handle, is slowed by the spiral twist, then slips down over the back of the spoon bowl, along the inside wall of the glass, and onto the first layer of liqueur. This avoids agitating the liquids, enabling the lighter liquid to float on the heavier one without blending with it. Do this for each successive layer of liqueur, always proceeding, of course, from light, to lighter, to lightest spirit.

Pousse-café pouring method #2.

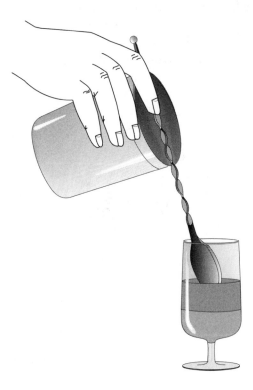

Now to the glasses. A large pony glass (2 oz.) or a small pousse-café glass (3 oz.) is best. To create and maintain the layering effect, it is crucial that the glass be quite a bit taller than it is wide. A tubelike configuration is best.

The foundation of your creation.

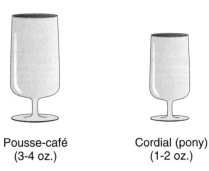

Pousse-café
(3-4 oz.)

Cordial (pony)
(1-2 oz.)

You see, while one layer of liquid is lighter than the layer that preceded it, each layer still has weight. It is the surface tension of each of the lower layers that helps support and maintain separation of layers. To the extent that the surface of the liquid is made larger—by a wider-mouthed glass—the weaker the surface tension and the less stable the layering becomes.

Pousse-café recipes usually call for a teaspoon—that is, $1/4$ ounce—of liqueur for each layer. That's why a 3-ounce serving glass is ideal. A 1-ounce pony will severely limit the number of layers you can build, and if you try to compensate for this by reducing the amount of liqueur in each layer, you'll end up with layers that are either too thin to sustain or simply too thin to have much visual impact. A 4-ounce pousse-café glass is fine for many-layered drinks, but a three- or four-layer creation will get lost in such a glass—unless you increase the amount of liqueur in each layer, which is perfectly acceptable.

> **Bar Tips**
> You can get along without a bar spoon. You'll probably get satisfactory results pouring your layers down a long, glass stirring rod. If you're skilled, you may be able to tilt the serving glass slightly, and pour each succeeding layer slowly down the side of the glass. But why don't you just go out and get a bar spoon? Accessories make the bar.

If you can't obtain 3-ounce glasses, adjust the amount of each liqueur to fill a larger glass adequately or, if your glass is small, restrict the number of layers you build.

Layering Logistics

In all the recipes you'll find here, ingredients are listed in descending order, with the heaviest ingredient listed first, and the lightest last. It is imperative that the ingredients be added in order—the top-listed ingredient first, the next one next, and so on.

What can go wrong with a pousse-café?

➤ You can inadvertently pour the ingredients out of order. The result: total disaster (although nobody will be permanently injured).

➤ An over-eager guest can slap a hand on your back while you are pouring. Result: Ditto.

➤ A rowdy guest can slap a hand down on the bar or table on which you are preparing the drink. Result: Ditto again.

➤ You discover that you are in the flight path of a major airport. Result: Double ditto.

➤ You become overconfident and pour too fast. Result: More ditto.

➤ The bar spoon slips into the drink. Result: Ditto upon ditto.

➤ You complete your work, then move the glass too quickly. Result: Ditto, ditto, ditto.

➤ Your guest seizes the drink you have so lovingly prepared, grabs a swizzle stick, and....

A Host of Angels

Pousse-cafés are by nature small, delicate, airy, and ephemeral of taste and appearance divine—at least more or less. For these reasons, a number of the classic pousse-cafés are called Angel's something-or-other.

Remember to pour the ingredients of the Angel's Delight exactly in the order listed. Grenadine is heaviest, the cream is the lightest.

Angel's Delight

Serve in a 3 oz. pousse-café glass.

$1/4$ oz. grenadine

$1/4$ oz. triple sec

$1/4$ oz. Crème Yvette

$1/4$ oz. cream

Use a bar spoon to pour each layer into the serving glass, exactly in the order listed. One layer should float upon another. *Do not stir!*

Be certain to use cognac, not only for taste, but to ensure the proper specific gravity of the Angel's Kiss.

Angel's Kiss

Serve in a 3 oz. pousse-café glass.

$1/4$ oz. white crème de cacao

$1/4$ oz. Crème Yvette

$1/4$ oz. cognac

$1/4$ oz. cream

Use a bar spoon to pour each layer into the serving glass, exactly in the order listed. One layer should float upon another. *Do not stir!*

Some bartending books clean this one up by calling it Angel's Tip (like the overeager TV censor who overdubbed "Frankly, my dear, I'm going to build a dam," for Clark Gable's celebrated parting shot in *Gone with the Wind*). There are two versions of this drink.

First Angel's Tit

Serve in a 3 oz. pousse-café glass.

$^1/_4$ oz. brown crème de cacao

$^1/_4$ oz. cream

Maraschino cherry

Use a bar spoon to pour each layer into the serving glass, exactly in the order listed. One layer should float upon the other. *Do not stir!* Pierce the cherry through with a toothpick and balance it across the glass as a garnish.

Second Angel's Tit

Serve in a 3 oz. pousse-café glass.

$^1/_4$ oz. brown crème de cacao

$^1/_4$ oz. maraschino liqueur

$^1/_4$ oz. cream

Maraschino cherry

Use a bar spoon to pour each layer into the serving glass, exactly in the order listed. One layer should float upon another. *Do not stir!* Pierce the cherry through with a toothpick and balance it across the glass as a garnish.

The Angel's Wing is one part of the angel's anatomy no one finds objectionable in mixed company.

Angel's Wing

Serve in a 3 oz. pousse-café glass.

$^1/_4$ oz. white crème de cacao

$^1/_4$ oz. cognac

$^1/_4$ oz. cream

Use a bar spoon to pour each layer into the serving glass, exactly in the order listed. One layer should float upon another. *Do not stir!*

Royal Palaces

The gaze of some folks is directed earthward, to corporeal rather than angelic glories. Here are three regal pousse-café creations.

The King Alphonse is a First Angel's Tit without the cherry.

King Alphonse

Serve in a 3 oz. pousse-café glass.

$1/4$ oz. brown crème de cacao

$1/4$ oz. cream

Use a bar spoon to pour each layer into the serving glass, exactly in the order listed. One layer should float upon the other. *Do not stir!*

The King's Cup is a simple drink, for a pousse-café, which calls for two-thirds Galliano and one-third cream.

King's Cup

Serve in a 3 oz. pousse-café glass.

$1/2$ oz. Galliano

$1/4$ oz. cream

Use a bar spoon to pour each layer into the serving glass, exactly in the order listed. One layer should float upon the other. *Do not stir!*

The Princess is another modest libation.

Princess

Serve in a 3 oz. pousse-café glass.

$3/4$ oz. apricot brandy

$1/4$ oz. cream

Use a bar spoon to pour each layer into the serving glass, exactly in the order listed. One layer should float upon the other. *Do not stir!*

Patriot's Pride: Red, White, and Blue Creations

Here is a trio of patriotic pousses. (Patriotic, provided that you are American—or French—with a fondness for your national colors.)

Stars and Stripes Version 1

Serve in a 3 oz. pousse-café glass.

$^1/_4$ oz. grenadine

$^1/_4$ oz. heavy cream

$^1/_4$ oz. Crème Yvette

Use a bar spoon to pour each layer into the serving glass, exactly in the order listed. One layer should float upon the other. *Do not stir!*

Stars and Stripes Version 2

Serve in a 3 oz. pousse-café glass.

$^1/_4$ oz. grenadine

$^1/_4$ oz. maraschino liqueur

$^1/_4$ oz. Parfait Amour

Use a bar spoon to pour each layer into the serving glass, exactly in the order listed. One layer should float upon the other. *Do not stir!*

Stars and Stripes Version 3

Serve in a 3 oz. pousse-café glass.

$^1/_4$ oz. crème de cassis

$^1/_4$ oz. Green Chartreuse

$^1/_4$ oz. maraschino liqueur

Use a bar spoon to pour each layer into the serving glass, exactly in the order listed. One layer should float upon the other. *Do not stir!*

Spectaculars

Here are three of the more spectacular pousse-cafés you can make.

The Classic

Serve in a 3 oz. pousse-café glass.

$^1/_4$ oz. grenadine

$^1/_4$ oz. crème de cacao

$^1/_4$ oz. maraschino liqueur

$^1/_4$ oz. curaçao

$^1/_4$ oz. green crème de menthe

$^1/_4$ oz. Parfait Amour

$^1/_4$ oz. cognac

Use a bar spoon to pour each layer into the serving glass, exactly in the order listed. One layer should float upon the other. *Do not stir!*

St. Moritz Pousse-Café

Serve in a 3 oz. pousse-café glass.

$^1/_4$ oz. raspberry syrup

$^1/_4$ oz. anisette

$^1/_4$ oz. Parfait Amour

$^1/_4$ oz. Yellow Chartreuse

$^1/_4$ oz. Green Chartreuse

$^1/_4$ oz. curaçao

$^1/_4$ oz. cognac

Use a bar spoon to pour each layer into the serving glass, exactly in the order listed. One layer should float upon the other. *Do not stir!*

This last drink includes a bright yellow layer. Some people like it. Some don't. Certainly, this is one pousse-café that will raise eyebrows.

Pousse L'Amour

Serve in a 3 oz. pousse-café glass.

$^1/_2$ oz. maraschino liqueur

1 unbroken egg yolk

$^1/_2$ oz. Benedictine

$^1/_2$ oz. Cognac

Pour the maraschino liqueur into the serving glass. Carefully float on the unbroken egg yolk, then use a bar spoon to pour the next two layers, one after the other. Add all ingredients exactly in the order listed. One layer should float upon the other. *Do not stir!*

Build Your Own Pousse-Café

As with a child and building blocks, there are few limits to the possible combinations of piling one liqueur upon another. To be exact, there are three limitations:

1. The relative weight of the liqueur

2. What tastes good—and does not taste good—to you

3. Your sense of color combination

The first limitation is rather easy to understand. The following is a list of popular pousse-café ingredients, from heaviest to lightest:

Anisette	Coffee brandy
Crème de noyaux	Peach brandy
Crème de menthe	Cherry brandy
Crème de banana	Blackberry brandy
Maraschino liqueur	Apricot brandy
Coffee liqueur	Rock and Rye
Cherry liqueur	Ginger brandy
Parfait Amour	Peppermint schnapps
Blue curaçao	Kummel
Blackberry liqueur	Peach liqueur
Apricot liqueur	Sloe gin
Orange curaçao	Cream
Triple sec	

Note that Anisette and crème de noyaux have almost identical specific gravities; it maybe difficult to layer these two together. The same is true for:

➤ cherry brandy and blackberry brandy

➤ blackberry brandy and apricot brandy

➤ apricot brandy and rock and rye

➤ peach liqueur and sloe gin

➤ cherry liqueur and Parfait Amour

➤ orange curaçao and triple sec

In general—subject to your taste, of course—you are best off layering liqueurs that are separated by at least three others (for example, put maraschino liqueur on top of anisette). This should ensure stable separation of layers.

How many liqueurs are you allowed to layer? As many as you want.

Do you really want to do this?

If you make a mistake, all of your work will be spoiled, and you'll be a laughingstock. The fact is that most pousse-cafés have three to five layers, with a few venturing to as many as seven. If you spend all of your time building pousse-cafés, you won't have much time left to *enjoy* the drink.

But experimenting can be fun—and the drinks still *taste* just as good—so practice before entertaining.

The Least You Need to Know

➤ Pousse-cafés require patience, a steady hand, and a relatively quiet place to build them. A busy bar setting is not conducive to creating a successful layered drink.

➤ Pousse-café recipes must be followed exactly, in order to ensure that the heaviest layer is poured first, the next heaviest next, the lighter layer after that, and so on.

➤ A twisted-handle bar spoon is an invaluable aid to pouring pousse-cafés.

➤ Small-diameter glassware is important in order to increase the surface tension that helps to separate each layer of liquid.

Part 6
A Fresh Round

Let's not lower an iron curtain between distilled spirits and fermented beverages. Brought together intelligently, "hard liquor" and wine, champagne, and even beer can create some lovely drinks. Many of these have been around for a very long time, but were only recently rediscovered. Others are quite new.

As the fermented spirits can be used to expand a mixed-drink vocabulary based on hard liquor, so thoughtful choice can be exercised to allow dieters to enjoy spirits without breaking the caloric bank. Here's a chapter full of delicious and varied recipes.

But mixing and enjoying adult beverages doesn't have to be all about liquor. A thoughtful host and bartender provides ample and tasty alternatives to alcohol, and this section closes with some of the most delightful adult drinks without spirits.

Chapter 19

More of a Good Thing: Wine, Champagne, and Beer Drinks

In This Chapter

➤ The emergence of wine as a mixer

➤ Ancient traditions of flavoring wine

➤ How wine, champagne, and beer can expand your mixed-drink repertoire

➤ Recipes with wine, champagne, and beer

Over the past two decades or so, wine has come to be regarded not just as the object of cultivated connoisseurship, to be consumed, discussed, and enjoyed for its own sake, but as an ingredient in mixed drinks. This new orientation may scandalize some wine snobs, but it has expanded the repertoire of bartenders as well as drinkers.

Less numerous, but also with a substantial history, are the ways of combining beer with spirits. If it does nothing else, this chapter will give you a fresh perspective on wine (including champagne) as well as beer.

Wine as a Mixer

Not long ago, in the United States, the world of alcohol was neatly divided into the realm of *distilled* spirits and *fermented* beverages, which includes wine and beer. The twain rarely met. More recently, however, the New World has been catching up with the Old, and wine is being combined routinely with distilled spirits to create a host of mixed drinks.

But we've got a lot of catching up to do, because, across the Atlantic, wine has been used as a mixed-drink ingredient since ancient times. The Greeks, Romans, and peoples of the Old Testament all routinely mixed wine with honey and spices. Many of today's *fortified wines* (wines to which a distilled spirit has been added), such as sherry, port, and Madeira, and *apéritifs* (spiritous beverages taken before meals) such as Dubonnet, developed directly out of the tradition of flavored wines.

Standard table wines as well as dessert wines, champagne and other sparkling wines, and apéritifs all figure in modern mixed drinks. Nothing is off-limits anymore.

> **Buzzed Words**
> A **fortified wine** is a fermented wine to which a distilled spirit, usually brandy, has been added. Brandy itself is often considered a fortified wine.
>
> An **apéritif** is a spiritous beverage taken before a meal as an appetizer. Its origin, in French, is hardly appetizing, however, originally denoting a purgative.

The Classics

> **Buzzed Words**
> A **spritzer** is a combination of wine—usually Rhine wine or other white wine—and club soda or seltzer. The word comes from the German for *spray*.

The recipes that follow are rediscovered classics. They've recently reemerged from the mixing glasses of American bartenders and hosts.

Kir, pronounced *keer*, is one of the best-known wine-based mixed drinks. It is named for Canon Félix Kir, the much-honored mayor of Dijon, France. It is a simple combination of a liqueur with dry white wine.

Every bartender and host should be familiar with the *spritzer*, a light drink for people who want a dash of summer refreshment without much alcohol. The spritzer is customarily made with white wine.

Kir

Serve in a large wine glass.

$1/2$ oz. crème de cassis

5 oz. dry white wine

The liqueur and the wine should be well chilled beforehand. Combine them in the serving glass.

Spritzer

Serve on the rocks in a highball glass.

1 part white wine

1 part club soda to fill

Lemon twist

Fill the serving glass with ice. Pour wine to fill half way. Add club soda to fill. Garnish with the twist.

Traditionalists insist on using Rhine wine for the spritzer. After all, the name of the drink is German.

Rhine Wine Spritzer

Serve on the rocks in a highball glass.

4 oz. Rhine wine

Club soda (may substitute sparkling mineral water) to fill

Lemon spiral

Pour wine into the serving glass filled with ice. Add club soda or sparkling mineral water to fill. Garnish with a long lemon peel curlicue; hang over the side of the glass.

Apéritif Assortments

The dry sophistication of the apéritif makes it a pleasure that can be enjoyed unmixed—or mixed.

Americano

Serve in an old-fashioned glass.

2 oz. sweet vermouth

2 oz. Campari

Club soda to fill

Orange twist

Combine vermouth and Campari in a mixing glass filled with ice. Stir, then strain into the serving glass one-third full of ice. Add club soda to fill and garnish with the twist.

When making an Appetizer, resist the easy out of using orange juice from a bottle or carton. Squeeze fresh oranges!

Appetizer

Serve in a chilled cocktail glass.

3 oz. Dubonnet rouge

Juice of 1 orange

Combine the Dubonnet and orange juice in a shaker with ice. Shake vigorously, then strain into the serving glass.

With a nod toward the maker of celebrated briefs, the initials of the next drink reflect the principal ingredients: *B*yrrh (an aromatic French aperitif redolent of orange and quinine) and *V*ermouth—*D*ry. The rum goes unrepresented in this monogram.

B.V.D.

Serve in a chilled cocktail glass.

1 oz. Byrrh (may substitute Dubonnet)   1 oz. light rum

1 oz. dry vermouth   Orange twist

Combine all ingredients except the twist in a mixing glass or small pitcher with ice. Stir, then strain into the serving glass. Garnish with the twist.

Finally, consider the Weep No More.

Weep No More

Serve in a chilled cocktail glass.

1½ oz. Dubonnet rouge   1½ oz. lime juice

1½ oz. cognac   Dash maraschino liqueur

Combine all ingredients in a shaker with ice. Shake vigorously, then strain into the serving glass.

Sherry Anyone? Port Perhaps?

Sherry is a fortified Spanish wine, with a nutlike flavor, that takes its name from an Anglicization of Jerez, a city in southwestern Spain, where sherry originated and from which the best sherry still comes. Port is also called *porto* and is named for the Portuguese town of Oporto, where true port is aged and bottled; however, other places also produce port wines. Like sherry, port is a fortified wine, but it is invariably sweet, whereas sherry ranges from dry to sweet.

Sherry, both in its dry and "cream" (sweet) incarnations, has enjoyed uninterrupted popularity. Port, in contrast, used to be a regular after-dinner or late evening tradition, then receded in popularity. During the last decade or two, however, it has been widely rediscovered. Both sherry and port make excellent mixers.

A *philomel* is a nightingale, and this cocktail may be served at about the time the nightingale sings. Since you won't find any nightingales here in North America, drink this any time.

Philomel Cocktail

Serve in a chilled wine goblet.

2¹/₂ oz. amontillado

1¹/₂ oz. St. Raphael (a French proprietary liqueur)

1 oz. light rum

1¹/₂ oz. orange juice

Pinch cayenne pepper

Combine all ingredients except cayenne pepper in a shaker with ice. Shake vigorously, then strain into the serving glass. Sprinkle with cayenne.

Amontillado takes well to sweetening, as in the Sherry Cobbler.

Sherry Cobbler

Serve in a chilled wine goblet.

Liberal dashes pineapple syrup

Liberal dashes curaçao

4 oz. amontillado

Lemon twist

Pineapple stick

Mint sprig

Fill the serving glass with crushed ice. Dash in pineapple syrup and curaçao, then stir with a bar spoon until the glass is well frosted. Add amontillado and continue stirring. Garnish with the twist, pineapple stick, and mint sprig.

Here is a trio of traditional sherry cocktails.

Straight Law Cocktail

Serve in a chilled cocktail glass.

2 oz. fino sherry

Lemon twist

1 oz. gin

Combine gin and sherry in a mixing glass or small pitcher with ice. Stir, then strain into the serving glass and garnish with the twist.

Tinton Cocktail

Serve in a chilled cocktail glass.

2 oz. port

2 oz. Calvados (may substitute applejack)

Combine in a mixing glass or small pitcher with ice. Stir, then strain into the serving glass.

Tuxedo Cocktail

Serve in a chilled cocktail glass.

3 oz. fino sherry

Liberal dashes maraschino liqueur

$^1/_2$ oz. anisette

Liberal dashes Angostura bitters

Combine all ingredients in a mixing glass or small pitcher with ice. Stir, then strain into the serving glass.

CLINK ∘ **Toast**

"There's many a toast I'd like to say, If only I could think it; So fill your glass to anything, And thank the Lord, I'll drink it!"

Vermouth Variations

Vermouth, in its sweet as well as dry forms, is a versatile mixer. It can carry a drink as the principal note, or it can serve in any number of supporting roles.

Achampañado

Serve in a chilled Collins glass.

3 oz. dry vermouth

1/2 tsp. sugar syrup

Juice of 1/4 lime

Club soda to fill

Fill serving glass to one third with ice cubes. Add vermouth, sugar syrup, and lime juice. Stir, then add club soda to fill.

Adonis Cocktail

Serve in a chilled cocktail glass.

3 oz. fino sherry

1 oz. sweet vermouth

Dash orange bitters

Orange twist

Combine sherry, vermouth, and bitters in a mixing glass or small pitcher with ice. Stir, then strain into the serving glass. Garnish with the twist.

One of the loveliest of vermouth cocktails—is the Chrysanthemum.

Chrysanthemum Cocktail

Serve in a chilled cocktail glass.

2 oz. dry vermouth

1 1/2 oz. Benedictine

Liberal dashes Pernod

Orange twist

Combine vermouth and Benedictine in a small pitcher or mixing glass with ice. Stir well, then strain into the serving glass. Garnish with the orange twist.

Even more interesting is the wicked Satan's Whiskers.

Satan's Whiskers

Serve in a chilled wine glass.

1½ oz. sweet vermouth   ½ oz. Grand Marnier
1½ oz. dry vermouth   3 oz. orange juice
1 oz. gin   Dash orange bitters

Combine all ingredients in a shaker with ice. Shake vigorously, then strain into the serving glass.

Third Rail? Shocking!

Third Rail

Serve in a chilled cocktail glass.

3 oz. dry vermouth   Liberal dashes peppermint schnapps
Liberal dashes curaçao   Lemon twist

Combine vermouth, curaçao, and schnapps in a small pitcher or mixing glass with ice. Stir well, then strain into the serving glass. Garnish with the twist.

The Vermouth Cassis is quiet and reserved, while the Victor Cocktail packs more "spiritual" authority.

Vermouth Cassis

Serve on the rocks in a highball glass.

3 oz. dry vermouth   Club soda to fill
1 oz. crème de cassis

Combine vermouth and crème de cassis in the serving glass over ice. Stir, then add club soda to fill.

Victor Cocktail

Serve in a chilled cocktail glass.

1^1/$_2$ oz. sweet vermouth	^{3}/$_4$ oz. gin
^{3}/$_4$ oz. brandy	Orange twist

Combine all ingredients except the twist in a shaker with ice. Shake vigorously, then strain into the serving glass. Garnish with the twist.

Zanzibar

Serve in a chilled cocktail glass.

3 oz. dry vermouth	1 tsp. sugar syrup
1 oz. gin	Liberal dashes orange bitters
^{3}/$_4$ oz. lemon juice	Lemon twist

Combine all ingredients except the twist in a shaker with ice. Shake vigorously, then strain into the serving glass. Garnish with the twist.

Bubbly Blends

Who hasn't seen *Casablanca* several dozen times? Well, maybe you've at least seen it enough to have noticed that the Champagne Cocktail is the drink ordered most—and seems to have been the particular favorite of the heroic freedom fighter Viktor Laszlo. Champagne, one of the greatest pleasures among fermented beverages, is a surprisingly versatile mixer.

Of course, champagne is pretty wonderful all by itself. The world's classic sparkling wine, it is named for its place of origin, the Champagne region of northeastern France, which still produces what most connoisseurs agree is the finest champagne on the planet, though other regions in other nations, including the United States, produce some very good sparkling wines that are called champagne. Champagne ranges from dry (*brut*) to sweet and fruity.

> **Buzzed Words**
> **Champagne** is *the* classic sparkling wine. Named for its place of origin, the Champagne region of northeastern France, champagne is also produced in other nations; however, most connoisseurs agree that the finest champagne is still produced in the Champagne of France. Champagne ranges from dry (**brut**) to sweet and fruity.

Every host who serves champagne should be familiar with the Champagne Cocktail and Mimosa.

Humphrey Bogart—beloved actor and Players member.

(Photo courtesy of the Everett Collection)

Champagne Cocktail

Serve in a champagne flute.

1 sugar cube

Liberal dashes Angostura bitters

Champagne to fill

Lemon twist

Drop cube in the serving glass and dash on the bitters. Add champagne to fill, stirring gently until the sugar dissolves. Garnish with the twist.

CLINK∘ Toast
"Here's looking at you, kid."—Humphrey Bogart to Ingrid Bergman in *Casablanca*, 1942

The refreshing Mimosa is probably the most frequently requested champagne cocktail. Use dry—brut—champagne and freshly squeezed orange juice.

Mimosa

Serve in a chilled wine goblet.

6 oz. brut champagne

3 oz. orange juice (freshly squeezed)

Orange slice

The champagne and orange juice should be thoroughly prechilled. Combine them in the serving glass. Garnish with the orange slice.

If you prefer a sweeter Mimosa, dash in some triple sec. And if you want something a little different, bring on the Midori melon liqueur.

Perfect Martini

Serve in a chilled cocktail glass.

$1^1/_2$ oz. gin

$^1/_2$ tsp. dry vermouth

$^1/_2$ tsp. sweet vermouth

Olive

Combine all ingredients except the olive in a mixing glass with ice. Stir well and strain into the serving glass. Garnish with the olive.

Midori Mimosa

Serve in a chilled wine goblet.

2 oz. Midori

2 tsp. lime juice

Champagne to fill

Lime wedge

The champagne and Midori should be thoroughly prechilled. Combine them in the serving glass. Add the lime juice, then garnish with the lime wedge.

Bellini

Serve in a chilled champagne flute.

3 oz. chilled peach nectar

Dash lemon juice

Dash grenadine

3 oz. chilled champagne

Combine the chilled peach nectar, lemon juice, and grenadine in the serving glass. Stir, then add the chilled champagne.

The Champagne Fizz features an innovative use for champagne: a stand-in for soda!

Champagne Fizz

Serve on the rocks in a highball glass.

2 oz. gin

1 oz. sour mix

Champagne to fill

Combine the gin and sour mix in a shaker with ice. Shake vigorously, then strain into the serving glass. Add champagne to fill.

Creative Coolers

Like a spritzer, a cooler is essentially a drink well diluted with sparkling water. All of these should be served on the rocks in tall glasses. If you have frosted glasses, use them.

Pineapple Wine Cooler

Serve on the rocks in a highball glass.

2^1/$_2$ oz. dry white wine

2^1/$_2$ oz. pineapple juice

1 oz. light rum

Club soda to fill

Lemon spiral

Orange spiral

Combine ingredients except club soda and fruit in the serving glass filled with ice. Stir. Add club soda to fill, and garnish with long lemon and orange curlicue spirals.

Red Wine Cooler

Serve on the rocks in a highball glass.

2 tsp. sugar syrup

1 oz. orange juice

Red wine to $^3/_4$ full

Club soda to fill

Combine ingredients except club soda in the serving glass filled with ice. Stir. Add club soda to fill.

White Wine Cooler

Serve on the rocks in a highball glass.

1 tsp. sugar syrup

White wine to $^3/_4$ full

Club soda to fill

Mint sprigs

Combine ingredients except club soda and mint sprigs in the serving glass filled with ice. Stir. Add club soda to fill. Garnish with mint sprigs.

The Champagne Cooler packs a punch.

Champagne Cooler

Serve on the rocks in a highball glass.

1 oz. brandy

1 oz. Cointreau

Champagne to fill

Mint sprigs

Combine ingredients except champagne and mint sprigs in the serving glass filled with ice. Stir. Add champagne to fill and garnish with the mint sprigs.

Beer—a Mixer?!

Maybe you're persuaded about the possibilities of wine as a mixer, but *beer*? It can be done. You can serve all of these drinks in a beer mug or a Pilsner glass, depending on your mood and inclination.

Most folks have heard of the Boilermaker, the classic drink of steel-mill hands and those who want you to think they're steel-mill hands.

Boilermaker

Serve in a beer mug (if you know what's good for you).

1¹/₂ oz. blended whiskey

12 oz. beer

Pour the beer into the mug. Add the whiskey.

You can transform the Boilermaker into a Depth Charge by dropping the whiskey—shot glass and all—into the beer.

What some folks call a Sneaky Pete is not the Sneaky Pete made with tequila, which we showed you in Chapter 14. This one is applejack and beer.

Sneaky Pete

Serve in beer mug.

1¹/₂ oz. applejack

12 oz. beer

Pour beer into a mug. Add applejack.

The Black Velvet is a layered drink, but it's no pousse-café.

Black Velvet

Serve in a tall Pilsner glass.

5–8 oz. porter or stout

Equal amount of extra brut champagne

Pour in the porter or stout, then *carefully* pour in the champagne, slowly, down the side of the glass in order to make two separate layers. Do not stir.

If you consume a drink like this immoderately, hopping, skipping, and going naked is the kindest fate you may expect.

Hop, Skip & Go Naked

Serve on the rocks in a beer mug or Pilsner glass.

1 oz. vodka   Juice of ½ lime

1 oz. gin   Beer to fill

Combine all ingredients except beer in the serving glass half filled with ice. Stir, then add beer to fill.

The Least You Need to Know

➤ The notion of combining wine with other flavorings and other spirits to create mixed drinks may be relatively new in the U.S., but it is rooted in ancient practices.

➤ Kir, spritzers, and coolers are all lightly alcoholic alternatives to the heavier and more potent mixed drinks.

➤ Beer can serve as a mixer in a variety of drinks, the simplest, best-known, and most potent of which is the Boilermaker.

Chapter 20

Lo Cal: Drinks for Dieters

In This Chapter
➤ Alcohol and calories
➤ How to cut calories without giving up spirits
➤ Quick and easy low-calorie alternatives
➤ Low-cal recipes

Every few years, some book or magazine article comes along to trumpet a miracle "alcohol" diet—a way that drinking spirits can actually help you lose weight. If you believe in these diets, we've got a little Three-Card Monte game we'd like to get you into.

Either way, you can't win.

While it is true that chronic abusers of alcohol sometimes become very thin indeed, liver disease and the loss of interest in food that accompanies it is not an attractive means of slimming down. The practical truth is that spirits will not help you lose weight. This chapter suggests ways to minimize, control, or at least be aware of your alcohol-related caloric intake.

The Truth about Alcohol and Calories

Here's the way it works. One gram of alcohol yields seven calories as it is metabolized by your body. This works out to some 200 calories per fluid ounce of absolute alcohol, but pure alcohol is something you wouldn't be drinking—so let's knock it down to a more realistic 100 calories per fluid ounce of 100-proof distilled spirits. Assuming proof and volume are constant, all distilled spirits—whiskey, rum, gin, vodka—contain the same number of calories. Beer contains a few more calories per ounce (about four), as do liqueurs.

Bar Tips

Liquor has as many calories *per ounce* as its proof; thus, 80-proof blended whiskey contains 80 calories per ounce. Just be aware that one drink is usually the equivalent of at least 1¹/₂ ounces of liquor.

Alcohol-related calories count just as much as food-related calories, except that (unfortunately) alcohol-related calories are "empty"—without nutritional value.

Counting Calories

If you're going to count calories, you'll need figures for the typical serving of an alcoholic beverage. Table 20.1 shows you the calorie counts of many liquors and mixers.

Table 20.1 Calorie Counts

Ingredient	Serving	Calories
Aperitif	2 ounces	80
Beer, lager	12 ounces	151
Beer, light	12 ounces	98
Bitters	Liberal dash (¹/₂ tsp.)	7
Champagne, 25-proof	3¹/₂ ounces	91 (approx.)
Club soda	10 ounces	0
Cola	12 ounces	144
Cola, diet	12 ounces	0
Cranberry juice cocktail	2 ounces	37
Ginger ale	12 ounces	113
Heavy cream	1 tbs.	53
Lemon juice, fresh	1 tbs.	4
Lime juice, fresh	1 tbs.	4
Liqueurs	1 fluid ounce	66-106
Liquor (gin, rum, tequila vodka, whiskey), 80-proof	1¹/₂ ounces	97
Liquor, 86-proof	1¹/₂ ounces	105
Liquor, 90-proof	1¹/₂ ounces	110

Ingredient	Serving	Calories
Liquor, 94-proof	1¹/₂ ounces	116
Liquor, 100-proof	1¹/₂ ounces	124
Orange juice, fresh	2 ounces	28
Pineapple juice (unsweetened)	2 ounces	34
Sherry	2 ounces	80
Tomato juice	2 ounces	12
Tonic water	12 ounces	113
Vermouth, dry	1 ounce	33
Vermouth, sweet	1 ounce	44
Wine, dessert	2 ounces	80
Wine, dry	3¹/₂ ounces	87
Wine, sweet	2 ounces	80

If that doesn't make it clear enough, here's a short list of popular drinks and their approximate calorie count:

Cocktail	Serving Size (ounces)	Approximate Calories
Bloody Mary	5	115
Daiquiri	4.5	250
Gin and Tonic	7.5	170
Martini	2.5	155
Piña Colada	4.5	260
Screwdriver	7	175
Tequila Sunrise	5.5	190
Tom Collins	7.5	120

Mixers/Juices	Serving	Cholesterol	Total fat	Saturated fat
Whole milk	1 cup	34 mg.	8.0 g.	4.9 g.
Apple	1 cup	0	0.3	0
Cranberry	1 cup	0	0.1	0
Lemon	1 cup	0	0	0
Lime	1 cup	0	0	0
Orange	1 cup	0	0.5	0.1
Pineapple	1 cup	0	0.2	0

continues

continued

Mixers/Juices	Serving	Cholesterol	Total fat	Saturated fat
Tomato	1 cup	0	0.2	0
Egg white	1 (large)	0	0	0
Egg yolk	1 (large)	213	5.6	1.6

Cutting Calories

The numbers are the numbers, and no amount of wishful thinking will make them smaller. But you can take steps to reduce your caloric intake:

➤ Don't drink.

➤ Reduce the amount of alcohol in simple mixed drinks. Make your Scotch and Soda with 1 ounce of scotch instead of 1¹/₂.

➤ Make smaller drinks. Instead of a Gin and Tonic consisting of 1¹/₂ ounces of gin and 6¹/₂ ounces of tonic (enough to fill a highball glass on the rocks), start out with an ounce of gin and add enough tonic to fill the glass to two thirds only.

➤ Enjoy spritzers (see Chapter 19) and some of the other drinks recommended in this chapter. The White Wine Spritzer—essentially white wine combined 50/50 with club soda—is an excellent low-calorie alternative.

Bar Tips
Low-alcohol drinks—even *very* low-alcohol drinks—are *not* no-alcohol drinks. Do not serve them to guests who want (or require) non-alcoholic beverages. See Chapter 21 for non-alcohol recipes.

➤ Reduce the amount of liquor in your highballs: one ounce instead of an ounce and a half. Use the pony jigger instead of the full jigger, pour to just below two fingers instead of at the two-finger mark, or count two instead of three when you use the speed pourer. (If none of this makes sense to you, reread—or read—Chapter 5.)

As with most other of life's pursuits and pleasures, the principle of the Golden Mean is a valuable guide. Enjoy your empty alcohol calories in moderation.

Ye Olde Standbys

You should be prepared to offer your guests a variety of low-calorie alcoholic beverages. Here are a few that have stood the test of time.

➤ Splash some Campari in a lowball glass half filled with ice, then add club soda to fill. Garnish with a lime wedge.

➤ Squeeze half a lemon into a lowball glass. Add ice and club soda to fill, then dash in two or three dollops of Angostura bitters.

➤ Start with half a lowball glass of ice. Add Perrier almost to the top. Squeeze in the juice of a quarter lemon or lime, then liberally dash in créme de cassis. Garnish with a fresh lemon or lime wedge.

➤ Take a four-ounce can of tomato juice and combine it in a lowball glass one-half full of ice with two ounces of dry vermouth. Stir, and garnish with a lime wedge.

Bar Tips
For extra zing, consider substituting V-8 Juice for ordinary tomato juice—and, if you want to reduce your sodium intake as well as your caloric intake, look for special Low-Sodium V-8.

Lightweights: Drinks Under 80 Calories

There is a surprising array of drink possibilities weighing in at under 80 calories.

Apéritif Drinks

Campari Special

Serve on the rocks in a lowball glass.

1¹/₂ oz. Campari	Dash orange bitters
Ginger ale to fill	Orange slice

Combine all ingredients except the orange slice in the serving glass filled with ice. Stir. Garnish with the orange slice.

Pansy

Serve on the rocks in a lowball glass.

¹/₂ oz. Pernod	Liberal dash Angostura bitters
Dash grenadine	Lemon twist

Combine all ingredients except the twist in the serving glass filled with ice. Stir. Garnish with the twist.

Lite Liquor Drinks

Versatile gin can be used—in relatively low volume—to make a raft of wonderful drinks for the calorie-conscious.

Biffy

Serve in a cocktail glass filled with crushed ice.

$^{1}/_{2}$ oz. gin   1 tbs. lemon juice

2 tbs. pineapple juice

Combine all ingredients in a shaker with ice. Shake well, then strain into the serving glass filled with crushed ice.

An alternative to the Bloody Mary is this gruesomely named 50-calorie libation.

Bloody Pick-Me-Up

Serve in a cocktail glass filled with crushed ice.

$^{1}/_{2}$ oz. gin.   1 tbs. lemon juice

1 tbs. ketchup   Dash Worcestershire sauce

Combine all ingredients in a blender. Blend at high speed for at least 15 seconds. Pour into the serving glass filled with crushed ice.

Tropical Sling

Serve on the rocks in a highball glass.

$^{1}/_{2}$ oz. gin $^{1}/_{2}$ tsp. maraschino bitters

$1^{1}/_{2}$ tsp. lime juice   Club soda to fill

1 tsp. grenadine   Mint sprigs

Combine all ingredients except the club soda and mint sprigs in a shaker with ice. Shake vigorously, then strain into the serving glass filled with ice. Add club soda to fill and garnish with the mint sprigs.

For those watching their calorie intake, rum may seem like an extra-high-calorie drink. In reality, it has no more (and no fewer) calories than any other distilled spirit. Use 86-proof rum rather than the 151-proof blockbusters for the following recipes.

Planter's Cocktail

Serve in a cocktail glass filled with crushed ice.

$^{1}/_{2}$ oz. light rum

1 tbs. orange juice

1 tsp. lemon juice

Mint sprig

Combine all ingredients except mint sprig in the serving glass over crushed ice. Garnish with the mint sprig.

Wine and Vermouth Drinks

Wine is probably the ideal foundation for low-cal drinks. The calories here aren't even entirely devoid of nutritional value. Fermenting does not strip away vitamins and minerals as distilling does.

Traditionally, a *posset* is served hot and contains sweetened milk curdled with wine or ale. The English Posset doesn't go quite that far.

Buzzed Words

A **posset** is a traditional English drink made with sweetened milk that has been curdled by the addition of wine or ale. It is usually served hot.

English Posset

Serve in a chilled sherry glass.

1 oz. dry sherry

$^{1}/_{2}$ oz. light cream

Pinch grated nutmeg

Combine the sherry and cream in a mixing glass with ice. Stir, then strain into the serving glass. Garnish with the nutmeg.

West Indian

Serve in a chilled sherry glass.

1 oz. dry sherry

1 tsp. limeade

1 tsp. guava nectar

2 oz. dark tea (cold)

Combine all ingredients in a shaker filled with ice. Shake vigorously, then strain into the serving glass.

The lordly Cardinal weighs in at a mere 45 calories.

Cardinal

Serve in a chilled cocktail or martini glass.

$^3/_4$ oz. dry vermouth

1 tbs. orange juice

1 tbs. tomato juice

Olive

Pre-chill the vermouth and juices. Combine in the serving glass and garnish with the olive.

The Country Club Cooler weighs in at only 50 calories.

Country Club Cooler

Serve in a chilled cocktail or martini glass.

$1^1/_2$ oz. dry vermouth

$^1/_4$ oz. grenadine

2 oz. club soda

Lime slice

Pre-chill the vermouth and juices. Combine in the serving glass and garnish with the lime slice.

Cynthia

Serve on the rocks in a lowball glass.

1 oz. dry vermouth

$^1/_2$ oz. sweet vermouth

1 tsp. gin

Mint sprigs

Combine the vermouths and gin in the serving glass filled with ice. Stir well, then garnish with mint sprigs.

Weighing In: 80–100 Calorie Drinks

Between 80 and 100 calories, the drinks get stronger and the options more varied.

Brandy Drinks

As a spirit for the calorie conscious, brandy hits its stride in drinks just under a hundred calories.

The Shriner is traditional, and relatively low in key and low in calories (90 of 'em).

Toast CLINK

"Here's to your health, and your family's good health, and may you all live long and prosper."

—Joseph Jefferson, 19th-century American matinee idol and member of The Players

Shriner

Serve in a chilled cocktail glass.

$^1/_2$ oz. brandy

$^1/_2$ oz. sloe gin

Dash Peychaud's bitters

1 tsp. grenadine

Combine all ingredients in a mixing glass with ice. Stir well, then strain into the serving glass.

The Northern Honey Bee weighs in just over the 100-calorie mark (103).

Northern Honey Bee

Serve in an eggnog-style mug.

1 oz. brandy

1 tsp. honey

$1/2$ oz. lemon juice

Warm the honey well in a ladle over a low gas flame. Combine in the mug with the juice and brandy. Serve warm.

Bar Tips

Lowering the calorie count of the drinks you make is only half the battle. Drinkers get the munchies, and alcohol tends to make us less conscious of how much we eat. Consider supplying your guests with some low-calorie snacks to go along with their low-calorie drinks.

Champagne Drinks

Feel deprived by having to count calories? These champagne drinks should banish all such negative emotions.

Alfonso Cocktail

Serve on the rocks in a lowball glass.

1 oz. champagne

Liberal dash Angostura bitters

2 oz. grape juice

Combine all ingredients in the serving glass filled with ice. Stir.

Champagne Cobbler

Serve in an American-style (saucer) champagne glass.

2 oz. champagne

1 oz. lemon sherbet

Fill glass with crushed ice. Combine champagne and sherbet in the serving glass.

Count Currey

Serve in a chilled cocktail glass.

2 oz. champagne

1/2 oz. gin

1 tsp. maple syrup

Mint sprig

Pre-chill the champagne and gin. Combine with the maple syrup in a shaker and shake vigorously. Pour into the serving glass and garnish with mint sprig.

The Hard Stuff

If you like gin, the Applejack Daisy is rich and sweet but still manages to slide in at under a hundred calories (99, to be exact).

Applejack Daisy

Serve in a cocktail glass filled with crushed ice.

1/2 oz. gin

1/2 oz. applejack

1 tbs. lemonade

Combine all ingredients in a mixing glass with ice. Stir well, then strain into the serving glass filled with crushed ice.

The Honolulu Sling and Lorenzo are both vodka drinks under a hundred calories.

Honolulu Sling

Serve in cocktail glass filled with crushed ice.

1 tbs. vodka

1 oz. sherry

1 oz. Hawaiian Punch (original flavor)

Combine all ingredients in a mixing glass filled with ice. Stir well, then strain into the serving glass filled with crushed ice.

Bar Tips

You may think that aromaless and flavorless vodka is a "dietetic" spirit, but don't kid yourself. An ounce of 80-proof vodka contains just as many calories as an ounce of 80-proof whiskey—namely, 80.

The Cherry Rum weighs in just over the 100-calorie mark (106).

Cherry Rum

Serve in a chilled cocktail glass.

$1/2$ oz. light rum

2 oz. canned sour cherries in syrup

1 tbs. light cream

3 oz. crushed ice

Combine all ingredients in a blender. Blend at low speed, then strain into the serving glass.

Light Liqueur Drinks

A delicious low-calorie liqueur cocktail is the Crème de Cacao Float.

Crème de Cacao Float

Serve in a chilled cocktail glass.

$1/2$ oz. crème de cacao

1 tsp. chocolate ice milk

Pour the liqueur into the serving glass first, then float the ice milk on top of it. Do not stir.

Fire and Ice

Serve in a cocktail glass.

$^1/_2$ oz. Cherry Heering   Orange slice
1 tbs. kirsch

Place a single large ice cube in the serving glass. Add liqueurs and stir until the ice cube is melted. Garnish with the orange slice.

The Least You Need to Know

➤ Although drinking will not help you lose weight, you can enjoy many relatively low-calorie alcoholic beverages.

➤ Counting alcoholic calories is easy: The caloric content is equal to the proof of the spirit (per ounce). An ounce of 100-proof vodka or whiskey contains 100 calories.

➤ Reducing the amount of alcohol in a drink or making smaller drinks are the easiest and surest ways of reducing the calorie count in a mixed drink.

➤ Remember that low-alcohol drinks are not *no*-alcohol drinks. Do not serve them to guests who do not want (or cannot have) alcohol-based beverages.

Chapter 21

Spiritless Yet Delicious: Drinks without Alcohol

Let's face it: This book exists because of alcohol. The drinks you've found here have spirits in their hearts. But not everyone likes to drink liquors, not everyone *should* drink them, not everyone *can* drink them, and even people who enjoy alcohol don't *always* feel like having a drink.

Your job as a host is to offer tempting and thoroughly satisfying alternatives to alcohol-based libations. The drinks should be delicious, and they should appeal to adults. That's what we've tried to supply in this chapter.

The Gracious Host

What does it mean to be a gracious host? It means, above all else, making your guests comfortable.

That last word deserves discussion. Of course, you want to see to your guests' physical comfort: pleasant places to sit, good food to eat, a temperate room. But "comfort" extends to the emotions as well—to providing a sense of well-being and ease, and at all times a feeling of welcome.

So far as drinks are concerned, this means providing alcoholic drinks for those who want them and nonalcoholic alternatives for those who don't. If you fail to provide attractive, appealing alternatives to beer, wine, and hard liquor, you fail to make all of your guests comfortable.

There are many reasons why people choose not to drink. They range from momentary preference, to taste, to upbringing, to social or religious conviction, to issues of health—issues that may be based on a general inclination not to drink or an acute condition: ulcer, diabetes, alcoholism, whatever. It is not your business to investigate the motives behind your guests' choices. It *is* your business to ensure that those choices can be made comfortably.

To Refresh and Satisfy Sans Spirits

Sure, you could discharge your "hostly" obligations by seeing to it that there are plenty of soft drinks available to your guests. And that *is* a good idea, as far as it goes. But does it go far enough?

Bar Tips
Use the same glassware and garnishes for nonalcohol drinks as you do for drinks with spirits. Doing so enhances the drinking experience, elevating it above the ordinary.

If you take the time and effort to prepare exciting mixed drinks for your alcohol-consuming guests, shouldn't you do the same for those who prefer drinks *without* spirits? You want to show everyone a good time, and that means ensuring that no one feels like a second-class guest.

Almost any soft drink will refresh. But, in a social setting, it takes something a little out of the ordinary to *satisfy*. That's why you should devote time and effort to making appealing non-spiritous drinks.

There's another reason to prepare exciting nonalcoholic drinks. People come to a party expecting a variety of spirits, wine, and beer to be served. Soft drinks, however, hardly get a second look. Come up with something more than the usual cola and fizzy drinks, and your guests will not only be grateful for your thoughtfulness, but will talk, long after the event, about the imagination that went into every detail.

Cider Surprises

Sweet apple cider has long been served as an alternative to booze. Really good cider tastes great on its own, but the following recipes make it even more tempting and delicious.

Aileen Peterson's Cider Cup

Serve in mugs.

1 cup fresh apple cider

1 cup hot tea

1 tsp. brown sugar

Dash orange juice

Dash lemon juice

Pinch powdered cinnamon

Pinch grated nutmeg

2 cinnamon sticks

Combine all ingredients except the cinnamon sticks in a saucepan over low heat. Let simmer, then pour into warmed mugs. Garnish with cinnamon sticks. *Recipe makes two drinks.*

Mulled cider, with or without alcohol, is a traditional token of hospitality. It's great for cold-weather get-togethers.

Mulled Cider

Serve in cups. Yield: 16 cups.

2 cinnamon sticks, broken

12 whole cloves

1 tsp. allspice berries

$^1/_2$ gallon apple cider

$^1/_2$ cup brown sugar

Dried apple rings

Whole cinnamon sticks

Place the broken cinnamon sticks, cloves, and allspice berries into a cheesecloth bag. Place the bag into a saucepan with the cider and brown sugar. Heat over a low flame, stirring constantly. Allow to simmer for several minutes, then remove the spice bag. Ladle the cider into cups.

Coffee Concoctions

Coffee makes a comfortable and appropriate alternative to spirits. You can dress it up in a number of ways to make it a very special alternative offering.

Bar Tips

Make sure that the glassware or mugs in which you serve hot drinks are heat-resistant.

Café Viennoise

Serve in a wine goblet.

1 cup strong, cold black coffee

1 oz. heavy cream

1 tsp. chocolate syrup

$^1/_2$ tsp. powdered cinnamon

Pinch grated nutmeg

Whipped cream

Combine all ingredients except nutmeg and whipped cream in a blender. Blend until smooth, then pour into the serving glass. Sprinkle with nutmeg and top with whipped cream.

Mocha Coffee

Serve in a coffee mug.

$^1/_2$ cup strong black coffee

$^1/_2$ cup hot chocolate

1 tbsp. whipped cream

Pinch powdered cinnamon

Pinch grated nutmeg

Pinch grated orange peel

Combine the coffee and hot chocolate in a mug. Stir, then top with whipped cream and add pinches of cinnamon, nutmeg, and grated orange peel.

Fruit Flavors

Fruit juice, of course, is frequently mixed with spirits because it tastes so good. Some drinkers think it's the best part of the drink! Why not showcase fruit juices in nonalcoholic drinks?

Beach Blanket Bingo

Serve on the rocks in a highball glass.

4 oz. cranberry juice

4 oz. grape juice

Lime wedge

Combine the cranberry and grape juices in the serving glass filled with ice. Garnish with the lime wedge.

With its battery of eight juices (plus a little something more), the Fruit Juice Combo is aptly named. Since it would require a set of laboratory glassware to measure out all the ingredients for a single small serving, this recipe makes enough to fill four highball glasses.

Toast

"May you live all the days of your life!"

—Jonathan Swift

Fruit Juice Combo

Serve on the rocks in highball glasses.

$^1/_2$ cup tomato juice

$^1/_2$ cup V-8 juice

$^1/_2$ cup apple juice

$^1/_2$ cup cranberry juice

$^1/_2$ cup grapefruit juice

$^1/_2$ cup lemonade

$^1/_2$ cup orange juice

$^1/_2$ cup pineapple juice

4 dashes Tabasco sauce

Pineapple slices

Orange slices

Apple slices

Combine all ingredients in a pitcher half full of ice. Prepare a skewer of the fruit slices. Use it to stir the pitcher and leave in as a garnish. Pour into serving glasses filled with ice. *Makes four drinks.*

If it's made with cranberry juice, it inevitably gets the sea in its name. Thank you, Ocean Spray!

Gentle Sea Breeze

Serve in a tall Collins glass or large tumbler.

$^1/_2$ cup cranberry juice

$^1/_2$ cup grapefruit juice

Combine juices in a blender until smooth and foamy. Pour into the serving glass one-third full of ice.

The Virgin Mary, a nonalcohol incarnation of the Bloody Mary, may well be the most frequently requested drink sans spirits. Every bartender and host should have a zesty, tempting recipe on hand—not just a can of tomato juice poured into a glass.

Virgin Mary

Serve in a chilled highball glass.

6 oz. V-8 Juice

1 tsp. chopped dill

1 tsp. lemon juice (freshly squeezed)

$^1/_4$ tsp. Worcestershire sauce

Few pinches celery salt

Pinch white pepper

Liberal dash or two Tabasco sauce

Combine all ingredients in a mixing glass with ice. Stir well, then pour into the serving glass. Add additional ice cubes, if necessary.

Bar Tips

Flavoring agents such as bitters and (usually) vanilla extract contain alcohol. Even a dash of these may be harmful to people who, for health reasons, must avoid alcohol. Make certain that dash of bitters is okay with your guest before serving the drink.

Hot Stuff

Hot stuff has nothing to do with thermal temperature. Drinks without alcohol often lack a certain zing, the bracing clash between spirit and palate. That's why the Indians called liquor "firewater."

Fortunately, there are plenty of fiery stand-ins for this aspect of the spiritous drink. Here are some suggestions.

Jones Beach Cocktail

Serve in a chilled highball glass.

5 oz. beef consommé or bouillon

3 oz. clam juice

Juice of $^1/_2$ lemon or lime

$^1/_2$ tsp. horseradish

Liberal dashes Worcestershire sauce

Pinch celery salt

Combine all ingredients in a shaker with cracked ice. Shake vigorously, then pour into the serving glass. Add additional ice, if necessary.

Sunset

Serve in lowball glasses.

3 cups V-8 juice
$^1/_2$ tsp. horseradish

$^1/_2$ tsp. Worcestershire sauce

Combine all ingredients in a pitcher half full of ice. Stir well and pour into serving glasses. Add additional ice, if necessary. *Makes four servings.*

Ice Cream, Milk Drinks, and Nogs

Some drinks fire up the palate, others caress it. And this is true for drinks with as well as without spirits. Here are some soothing nonalcohol alternatives.

Don't worry, the name of the Aryan has nothing to do with the Third Reich or skinheads. *Aryan* refers to the Indo-Iranian people who probably gave the world yogurt—the primary ingredient of this drink.

Aryan

Serve in a chilled wine goblet.

$^1/_2$ cup plain yogurt
$^1/_2$ cup cold spring water

2 tsp. mint, finely chopped
Pinch salt

Combine all ingredients in a blender. Blend until smooth, then pour into the serving glass. Add ice, if necessary.

You may remember the Black Cow as a childhood favorite—or maybe you called it a Brown Cow, or just a plain old root beer float. It's definitely retro, and it's definitely devoid of alcohol.

Black Cow

Serve in a well-chilled large root beer mug or other large tumbler.

2 scoops vanilla ice cream

Root beer to fill

Put the ice cream in the serving glass. Add root beer to fill. Stir a few times with a long-handled spoon. Serve with the spoon.

Breakfast Eggnog

Serve in a chilled wine goblet.

2 oz. frozen orange juice concentrate (unthawed)

3/4 cup whole milk

1 egg *

Grated nutmeg

Combine all ingredients except nutmeg in a blender. Blend until smooth and foamy. Pour into the serving glass and garnish with nutmeg.

Raw egg may be a source of salmonella bacteria. You may wish to avoid drinks calling for raw egg yolk or white.

Mickey Mouse

Serve in a Collins glass or other large tumbler.

1 scoop vanilla ice cream

Cola to fill

Whipped cream

2 maraschino cherries

Put the ice cream in the serving glass and add cola to fill. Stir a few times with a long-handled spoon, then top with whipped cream and add cherries. Serve with the spoon.

Anyone who doubts that chocolate is a mood-altering substance hasn't eaten enough of it. The Classic Malted dispenses much pleasure. Use no ice, but do make sure the milk is well chilled.

The Classic Malted

Serve in a tall tumbler with a straw.

1 cup whole milk

2 scoops chocolate ice cream

$^1/_4$ cup chocolate syrup

2 tbsp. malt powder

Combine all ingredients in a blender. Blend until smooth, then pour into the serving glass.

Embellished Soft Drinks

We observed at the outset of this chapter that too many hosts provide nothing more than a few soft drinks as the only alternatives to their spiritous offerings. Soft drinks *are* good options, but why not dress them up?

Faux Champagne

Serve in champagne glasses.

$^1/_2$ cup sugar

1 cup water

1 cup grapefruit juice

Juice of $^1/_2$ lemon

1 28-oz. bottle ginger ale

Dash grenadine

Combine all ingredients except ginger ale in a large pitcher with ice. Stir. Add ginger ale just before serving, and pour into champagne glasses. *Makes eight drinks.*

Pony's Neck

Serve in a highball glass or other tall glass.

1 lemon or orange zest in a long spiral

Ginger ale to fill

$^1/_2$ tsp. lime juice

Dash Angostura bitters

Maraschino cherry

Carefully cut away the zest (outer peel layer) of an orange or lemon in a long spiral. Place it in the serving glass, with one end draped over the rim. Fill glass to one third with ice cubes. Add chilled ginger ale to fill. Add lime juice and dash in bitters. Stir very gently, so that carbonation is not dissipated. Garnish with the cherry.

283

Here they are, two of the all-time classic drinks for kids to enjoy while Mom and Dad imbibe something stronger. You should learn them by heart. In an age before political correctness, Roy was for the boy, and Shirley for the girl.

Roy Rogers

Serve on the rocks in a highball glass.

Dash grenadine   Maraschino cherry
Cola to fill

Combine grenadine and cola in the serving glass filled with ice. Garnish with the cherry.

Shirley Temple

Serve in a chilled wine glass.

4 oz. ginger ale   Lemon twist
1 tsp. grenadine   Maraschino cherry
Orange slice

Combine ginger ale and grenadine in the serving glass with a single ice cube. Garnish with the orange slice, lemon twist, and maraschino cherry.

The Vanilla Cola uses vanilla extract, which often contains alcohol. Check the label. If alcohol is present, do not offer this drink to people who cannot drink any alcohol.

Vanilla Cola

Serve on the rocks in a highball glass.

Splash vanilla extract   Cola to fill
   (May contain alcohol! Check label.)

Combine vanilla and cola in the serving glass filled with ice.

Tropical Alternatives

Why should those who choose not to drink miss out on the kitschy revelry of elaborate tropical drinks? Bring on the little paper parasols!

Innocent Passion

Serve on the rocks in a highball glass.

4 oz. passion fruit juice

Splash cranberry juice

Splash orange juice

Juice of $1/2$ lemon

Club soda to fill

Pour the passion-fruit juice over ice in the serving glass. Add all other ingredients except the club soda. Stir, then add the club soda to fill.

Planter's Paunch

Serve in a chilled Collins glass.

2 oz. pineapple juice

2 oz. orange juice

1 oz. lime juice

1 oz. coconut syrup

1 oz. passion fruit juice

$1/2$ oz. grenadine

6 maraschino cherries

Club soda to fill

Pineapple slice

Orange slice

Combine all ingredients except club soda and fruit in a shaker with cracked ice. Shake vigorously, then pour into the serving glass. Add club soda to fill. Garnish with the fruit.

Behold another "virgin" version of a popular drink.

Virgin Colada

Serve in chilled highball glass.

4 oz. coconut cream

4 oz. pineapple juice

Maraschino cherry

Pineapple chunk

Combine all ingredients except the maraschino cherry and pineapple chunk in a blender with cracked ice. Blend until smooth, then pour into the serving glass.

Bar Tip
You'll find spirit-bearing punches in Chapter 23.

Party Punches

The punch bowl is a particularly welcoming and inviting way to serve any party drink, especially those without alcohol. The nonalcohol punch bowl offering says to your guests that they are special, but not unusual or weird for not choosing spirits.

Florida Punch

Serve in a large punch bowl.

2 qt. fresh orange juice

1 qt. fresh grapefruit juice

2 liter bottle ginger ale

1 cup lime juice (freshly squeezed)

1 cup orgeat syrup

¹/₂ cup grenadine

Prechill the punch bowl and all ingredients. Place a cake of ice in the punch bowl. Combine all ingredients and stir well. *Makes 46 servings.*

Red Rooster Punch

Serve in lowball glasses.

4 cups V-8 juice

10 oz. ginger ale

1 tbsp. lime juice

1 tsp. Worcestershire sauce

Dash Tabasco sauce

Combine all ingredients in a pitcher half full of ice. Stir well and pour into serving glasses. Add additional ice, if necessary. *Makes six servings.*

The Least You Need to Know

➤ Devote as much effort and imagination to preparing nonalcohol drinks as you devote to making spiritous beverages.

➤ Strive for variety in the nonalcohol beverage alternatives you provide.

➤ Present and garnish nonalcohol drinks the same way you would present alcoholic drinks.

➤ If you are making nonalcohol drinks for adults, make *adult* drinks—not too sweet, and with complex, rather than simple, flavors.

Part 7
Putting It All Together

If mixing one drink at a time is a challenge, what about laying out a spread for an entire party? Here's help with planning and logistics: how to figure out what to buy and how much to buy.

Many hosts have turned their backs on punch, which has acquired a reputation as a cheapskate substitute for individual drinks—a dull, flat, overly sweet disappointment in a bowl. But, traditionally, punch has served as the centerpiece of a party. Prepared with care, imagination, and knowledge, a great punch can fuel a party. You'll find here a chapter with the best traditional punch recipes.

The finale? How about an opportunity to turn pro? We end with a chapter on the bartender's vocation, everything you need to know if you want to tend bar and get paid for it. And even if a bartending career is not in your plans, this chapter will give you some tips to make your amateur *bartending a lot more professional.*

Chapter 22

It's My Party: Planning a Great Time

In This Chapter

➤ Setting up your bar

➤ What—and how much—liquor to buy

➤ How season influences your choice of liquor

➤ How to close the party

Just because a party should be fun doesn't mean you won't have to do plenty of work. Fortunately, most of your hard work comes *before* the party—in the planning. The time you spend planning will proportionately reduce the amount of work you have to do when you should be having fun with your guests. Panic? A little planning can reduce that to nil.

This book is about mixing drinks, not about the art of entertaining, so the emphasis in this chapter is on planning your guests' experience at the bar.

The Setup

Begin with the party space. Can you rearrange it to accommodate everyone? Do you have enough seating? If necessary, rent chairs—and think about renting some folding tables for setting out food and drink and even for setting up the bar. You can purchase inexpensive disposable table cloths, or you can rent more elegant linen at most party stores.

Bar Tips
You'll find great advice on all aspects of party-giving in *The Complete Idiot's Guide to Entertaining.*

Bar Tips
Consider compromising on the question of tending bar. While the party is just warming up, tend bar. Once you sense that it's rolling on its own, open up the bar to self-service.

Now let's begin to talk about the bar. You've got some basic decisions to make first:

➤ Do you want a self-service bar or a tended bar? For parties with fewer than 15 people, a self-service bar always works well. Parties with 20 or more benefit from the services of a bartender. With 100 or more guests, you'll need at least two barkeeps.

➤ Do you want to tend bar? A lot of hosts *really* enjoy tending bar. They feel that they are genuinely giving of themselves to their guests, and, since the guests come to the bartender, it offers an opportunity for the host to circulate without moving. On the other hand, some hosts find that tending bar keeps them too busy to entertain their guests adequately. In effect, the bartender host ends up missing the party!

➤ If you don't want to tend bar yourself or you are throwing a large party, consider hiring a professional bartender. Most party stores can help you find a good one, or you can consult your local Yellow Pages.

Give serious consideration to the placement of the bar:

➤ If it's a table—especially a folding table—make absolutely certain that it can support the weight of bottles and glassware, as well as the weight of guests leaning on it. It should also be stout enough to withstand the inevitable bumps to which people will subject it.

➤ If the table is a valued piece of furniture, be sure to protect it from spills by spreading a plastic table cloth over it. The setup will be more attractive if, over the plastic table cloth, you spread a table cloth of real linen.

➤ Avoid locating the bar close to a doorway. People sweeping in and out may cause spills or block access to the bar.

➤ If possible, shove the bar almost against the wall, with just enough room behind for the bartender. You want to discourage guests from sneaking around the bar to make their own drinks. This will quickly torpedo your bar setup.

➤ If you have a self-service bar in operation, push it all the way against the wall. Guests should prepare drinks from the front of the bar only; otherwise, any semblance of order in the setup of the bottles, glassware, and utensils will soon dissolve into an ugly mob scene.

For a party of fewer than 100 guests, one bar should be sufficient. If the party is larger, consider setting up an additional bar at the other side of the room.

Glassware: Real or Plastic?

We discussed glassware basics in Chapter 4, but you may have to recalculate your needs based on the size of the party. You have two decisions to make at the outset:

➤ Will you use real glass glassware or disposable plastic glassware?

➤ If you opt for real glass, should you buy or rent?

The first question depends in part on the feeling you wish to create at your party. While plastic is acceptable at all but the very highest-brow gatherings, genuine glass adds a substantial touch of elegance to the party and enhances the pleasure of drinking. Aside from expense, of course, the chief disadvantage of glass is the possibility of breakage, which may result in injury.

If you opt for plastic, you need to purchase only two types, which will be pressed into duty for all the drinks you serve. Get lowball glasses, which hold about nine ounces, and highball glasses, with a 12-ounce capacity. Figure that you will need two glasses per person for a four-hour party, and for every three highball glasses you buy, purchase one lowball glass.

If you opt for real glassware, decide whether you want to buy or rent. Most party stores—and many general rental agencies—have glassware available for rental and will even deliver and pick up.

> **Bar Tips**
> If you are serving drinks around a swimming pool, insist on plastic glassware. Broken glass is dangerous to barefoot guests!

> **Bar Tips**
> If you are throwing a dance party, increase the glassware-to-guest ratio from 2-to-1 to 3-to-1. Dancing guests typically set down their glasses, then forget them.

To calculate your needs, use the glass-to-guest ratios just given, and consider renting some specialty glassware in addition to the lowball and highball glasses. This depends on the size of the party, its level of formality, and the kinds of drinks you intend to serve.

Bar Basics

In addition to glassware, make sure you have all the bar utensils you'll need. (Review Chapter 4 for a list.) Unless your party is large enough to warrant two bartenders, the basics should be quite sufficient—with the addition of:

Bar Tips
Cocktail napkins are essential. Professional caterers deploy them in a stack at the bar and elsewhere. For an elegant touch, put down a stack of napkins, make a fist, press your knuckles into the napkins, then twist clockwise. The result will be an attractively fanned stack. Some folks use the bottom of a shot glass, rather than their knuckles, to fan the napkins.

➤ A large trash barrel

➤ A larger ice bucket than the one you probably already own

➤ An ice tub for keeping beer cold (if you don't buy a keg).

➤ A pitcher for water

➤ Two bar towels

➤ An ashtray or two at the bar

Some hosts fear that including an ashtray at the bar encourages smoking, but unless you prohibit smoking in your house, some of your guests *will* smoke, and you don't want them flicking (or just losing) ashes on your floor, rugs, or furniture while they wait in line at the bar.

Front Bar

In organizing a bar, professionals think in terms of a "front bar" and "back bar." They put the most frequently accessed items—and spirits—in the front bar and the less often used stuff in back. This concept may be adapted to the home party situation.

Set up your self-service bar like this.

 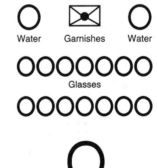

The self-service bar may be arranged in four tiers:

➤ Glasses and ice should be front and center, with bar towels and mixers available on either side of the glasses.

➤ Just behind this first tier, put garnishes and, on either side of them, pitchers of water.

➤ Along the third tier, array the liquor. A symmetrical arrangement is most effective, so that, facing the bar, your guests will see (from left to right) scotch, gin, bourbon, vodka, dry vermouth, sweet vermouth, vodka, bourbon, gin, and scotch.

➤ On either side of this array, place cocktail napkins and a couple of ashtrays.

➤ In the fourth tier, farthest from the guests, store extra mixers.

□ □   □ □   *If you or someone*
Ashtray Napkins   Napkins Ashtray   *else will be tending*
                                                                                    bar, set it up like
                                                                              ◯   *this.*
                                                                           Water

OOOOOOOO
Show Bottles

O O   OO   O O
Ginger Club   Sweet and Dry Vermouth   Tonic Cola
Ale   Soda

O O O   O O O
Bourbon Blended Scotch   Rum   Vodka   Gin
        Whiskey

⊠
Garnishes

OOOO   □□□O   OOOO
Lowball Glasses   Utensils Ice   Highball Glasses

BARTENDER

The setup for a one-bartender bar differs from the self-service bar:

➤ The bartender should be positioned behind the bar, facing the guests.

➤ Out of sight, on either side of the bartender, place receptacles for wet trash and dry trash.

293

➤ Directly in front of the bartender, position the utensils, a towel to the left of these, and the lowball glasses to the left of the towel.

➤ To the right of the utensils, place a bucket of ice, and to the right of that, the highball glasses.

➤ Garnishes can be positioned directly in front of the utensils.

➤ In the next tier away from the bartender and closer to the guests, arrange the spirits most often used (from the bartender's left to right): bourbon, blended whiskey, scotch, rum, vodka, and gin.

➤ In the next tier, arrange the mixers (from the bartender's left to right): ginger ale, club soda, sweet vermouth, dry vermouth, tonic, and cola.

Unlike table settings, which are governed by rules of etiquette, there's nothing hard and fast about setting up a bar. Create a layout that's convenient for you and your guests.

"Show" Bottles

In a saloon bar, "show" bottles—the less frequently used spirits, such as liqueurs, tequila, rye, and, often, the premium-label scotches and bourbons—are arranged up high and in the back, very much on display, but farthest from the bartender's reach. In the party bar, these show bottles are also arranged farthest from the bartender, but that means closest to the guests. It's an opportunity to display the best you have to offer.

Liquor Logistics

Unless you're springing for professional entertainment, spirits will be the most expensive ingredient in your party. You need to plan in order to ensure that you have enough on hand for your guests, but not a lot of surplus.

The Basic Cocktail Bar

There is no magic formula to put your buying decisions about type and quantity of liquor on automatic pilot. Review Chapter 4 and assess the contents of your current bar. Then consider the following rules of thumb:

➤ Stock a minimum of two kinds of light spirit—at least gin and vodka.

➤ Stock a minimum of two kinds of dark spirit—at least scotch and bourbon.

➤ Provide dry and sweet vermouths.

➤ Provide white and red wine.

➤ Provide beer.

➤ Always supply a variety of nonalcoholic drinks.

Be sure to break the seals on all bottles. If you don't, your guests may hesitate to help themselves and will, consciously or not, question your hospitality.

Party Time

The season influences what people drink. In warm weather, people will veer toward the light alcohols, so stock proportionately more gin, vodka, rum, and/or tequila. Cut back on bourbon and scotch. Beer and white wine are also favored in warm weather.

In winter, the dark spirits predominate, and you should add blended whiskey and Irish whiskey to your supply of scotch and bourbon. Coffee drinks and mulled drinks are welcome, as are red wine, sherry, and brandy.

Time of day is important, too. If you're giving a brunch party, expect to be making mimosas, screwdrivers, Bloody Marys, and the like, rather than Manhattans and Zombies. Drinks before dinner range from wine and aperitifs to the lighter cocktails. Later-evening parties require an even greater variety of drinks.

What's the Occasion?

The occasion or theme will provide a key to your selection of food and drink. You don't need to lay in a supply of Irish whiskey for a Mexican Fiesta, but you'd better have more than one kind of tequila available for such an occasion. On Valentine's Day, sweet drinks will probably be in order; at Christmas time, mulled wine or eggnog may set the tone.

Who Are Your Guests?

The average age of your guests may also influence your liquor-buying decisions. Younger guests generally prefer the light spirits, as well as wine and beer. Sweet drinks are also in order for this group. Older guests tend toward the darker spirits, often preferring them unmixed. If you are expecting an older, well-established, and more conservative crowd, invest less in mixers and more in premium-label scotch and bourbon.

There is no substitute for knowing what your friends like and don't like. To the degree that you are familiar with your guests' preferences, let this knowledge guide you.

Don't Ever Forget Soft Drinks

Whatever else you buy, never fail to supply ample quantities of soft drinks. You never want to make a guest feel coaxed or coerced into drinking spirits.

How Much Do You Need?

Assume a party duration of four hours. Purchase one 1-liter bottle of each "front bar" liquor for every six guests. Unless you are inviting substantially more

Bar Tips
Some liquor stores make it easy for you to match volume with number of guests. Ask the store if it will sell you the liquor on consignment. That way, you can return surplus, unopened, sealed bottles for a refund.

Bar Tips

If finances are a problem, consider giving a BYOB—Bring Your Own Bottle—party. You'll still want to prime the pump with a bottle of each of the basics and *all* the mixers. Work out with the core group of your closest friends just who will bring what. That way, you'll be certain to strike a balance between light and dark spirits, bourbon and scotch, gin and vodka, and so on.

than a hundred guests, one bottle each of sweet and dry vermouth is sufficient. These days, expect the demand for vodka to be heaviest—especially in warmer weather.

Still assuming the four-hour party, buy one case of beer (24 servings) for every 10 guests. Purchasing a keg becomes economical once your guest list hits 35 people or more. For 35 guests, a quarter-keg should suffice. A full keg serves 70.

Wine consumption varies widely, depending on the season and on the age of the group. Figure that a case of wine—12 bottles—contains 60 individual servings.

Order mixers on the assumption that you'll need two quarts of mixers for every liter of light alcohol you have. Buy extra.

Garnish needs can be calculated this way: you'll need one lime for every five guests, one orange for every 25, and one lemon for every 50. A full jar each of olives, cocktail onions, and maraschino cherries should be sufficient for most cocktail parties.

And don't forget the ice! For the four-hour party, you'll need one pound of ice per guest. If you're expecting a fair-sized crowd, consult your Yellow Pages to find a company that will deliver.

Food, Glorious Food

Bar Tips

Unless you have a huge, chest-type freezer, you'll be hard-pressed to store the ice, and in warm weather this can be a problem. Here's an idea: If you've got a washing machine, run it without clothes or detergent through two full cycles to rinse it out thoroughly. Then dump your ice into it (or leave the ice in the bags) and close the lid. This will retard melting. You can simply let any leftover ice melt away.

It is essential that you offer food at the party, not just because it is the hospitable thing to do, but because spirits should not be consumed, even moderately, on an empty stomach. A plentiful supply of food will help prevent your having a gang of tipsy guests on your hands. Check out *The Complete Idiot's Guide to Entertaining* and *The Complete Idiot's Guide to Cooking Basics* for party ideas.

➤ Offer peanuts or bar nuts, chips, pretzels, and other snack foods. This is the bare minimum.

➤ Dress up snack foods with easy-to-prepare dips.

➤ Take a significant—but still easy—step beyond snack food with crudités. These are nothing more than crisp raw vegetables, such as carrot sticks, celery sticks, small whole radishes, cauliflower, edible-pod peas, cucumber sticks, blanched fresh asparagus spears, and green onions.

➤ A tasty dip—or, better yet, assortment of dips—will make snack food more appealing and is absolutely essential to enjoying crudités. You can purchase ready-made dips, you can make a dip from onion soup mix and sour cream, or you can prepare something more ambitious.

➤ Tasty hors d'oeuvres elevate the party substantially above the level of chips-and-dip. Many cookbooks have excellent sections on hors d'oeuvres, and you will find a good many cookbooks solely devoted to the hors d'oeuvre.

> **Quick One**
> Overheard at a cannibal cocktail party—
> Guest: "Can this hors d'oeuvre be eaten with the fingers?"
> Host: "No. Eat the fingers separately."

The Party's Over

The final ingredient of a successful party is an end. There are times when, after everyone else has left, you enjoy the company of a few diehards. There are also parties that you wish would go on into the daylight hours. But, most of the time, there comes an hour to call it quits.

Signal the end of the party by packing up the bar. Begin with the extra liquor and mixers, then remove any speedpourers you may have in the active bottles, and put the caps back on. Your guests will soon decamp.

> **Bar Tips**
> Be sure to read or review Chapter 2 about responsible behavior. Never let a tipsy or drunk guest drive home! You'll find more advice on "shutting off" drunks in Chapter 24.

The Least You Need to Know

➤ Suit the bar setup to self-service or tended bar. In either case, try to put the bar against a wall and away from doorways.

➤ Offer spirits appropriate to the weather of the season and the time of day.

➤ Be sure to have enough spirits, mixers, ice, and nonalcoholic beverages on hand for the number of guests.

➤ Always offer food at any party where spirits are served. For cocktail parties and informal parties, a variety of finger foods is best.

Chapter 23

Packing a Punch: Festive Recipes by the Bowlful

In This Chapter

➤ Restoring the festive role of punch

➤ Learning from the "Rule of Five"

➤ Guidelines for making any punch

➤ Punch recipes

Alas, the poor punch. Once a source of festive delight, punch has degenerated into a sickly sweet money-saving substitute for "real" spirits. At their worst, many contemporary punches are just plain awful; at best, they're inoffensive and dull. Let's change that with this chapter.

There was a time—earlier in the 20th century and back into the 19th—when punch was a gracious expression of hospitality and festivity. The punch bowl was a place where guests could meet to partake communally of something delicious, and, while dipping into the bowl, could speak, arrange their dance cards, and flirt. They were never stuck for something to say, because the punch could always be depended on as the opening focus of a pleasant conversation.

The Rule of Five

Noted mixologist John J. Poister believes the word *punch* derived from *puncheon*, a small cask in which British Royal Navy crews stored their wines and spirits; however, Poister also alludes to another popular theory, which holds that *punch* comes from a Hindustani word, *panch*, meaning "five." A *panchamrit* is a mixture of five ingredients, and, according to certain mixologists, this is the origin of the Rule of Five. The rule holds that a successful punch should balance five elements:

1. One sour component.
2. Two sweet components.
3. Three strong components.
4. Four weak components.
5. A variety of spices.

Is it possible to obey the Rule of Five? Sometimes. Is it always desirable? Probably not. But the point of the rule is well taken: Create a punch in which no single component dominates to the point of becoming cloying or tiresome. If the punch bowl is a community cocktail, the punch itself should be a community of flavors, all living happily together.

New Life to a Festive Tradition

Your mission, should you choose to accept it, is to redeem the tradition of the punch. If you serve a punch at your party, decide that it will not be a mere shortcut, a labor-saving move, or a bid to save money. Treat the punch with care, and it will become one of the lively hubs around which your party forms.

Planning Your Attack

A successful punch takes planning and preparation. You have certain questions to answer and some choices to make.

➤ Who will drink the punch? If your guests will be of many age groups, go easy on the alcohol. If your guests are older and more experienced drinkers, a stronger punch is in order.

Bar Tips
If you provide an alcohol-based punch, offer a non-alcoholic alternative as well. See Chapter 21 for some tasty recipes.

➤ To calculate how much punch you'll need, assume that each quart of punch will yield eight four-ounce servings. In cool or cold weather, assume that each guest will consume three servings—then multiply the resulting number by two. In hot weather, multiply it by three.

➤ Let's talk about replenishing the punch bowl. Many a host has ruined a decent punch by repeatedly topping off the bowl as it gets lower. When the punch gets low in the bowl, remove it, take it into the kitchen, spill out the dregs, rinse the bowl, and either add a new batch that you have prepared or prepare a new batch.

➤ Do not let the bowl run dry before you replenish it. A dry bowl signals the end of the party.

Bar Tips

For larger parties, consider using two punch bowls, each filled, so that you can rotate one to the serving table while the other is getting refilled.

➤ For cold punches: Chill all ingredients in advance, and chill the bowl, too. Do not use ice cubes in punches! They will melt quickly, diluting the punch. Use blocks of ice.

➤ For hot punches, use a heat-resistant bowl. The punch should be *hot*, not warm, and you don't want to pour piping hot liquid into a glass or mug that will crack.

➤ Squeeze all fruit juices in advance, and strain them. Punch should be clear rather than murky.

➤ Sugar does not dissolve easily in alcohol. That is why drinks are usually sweetened with sugar syrup rather than dry sugar. When working with large quantities of spirits and sugar for a punch, dissolve sugar in the mixers first. Then add the spirits to this mixture.

➤ Try to hold off adding the spirits to the punch until about an hour before serving. Evaporation significantly reduces the refreshment's alcohol content.

Bar Tips

Prepare ice blocks or slabs for punches by freezing water in your freezer's ice trays *without* the cube dividers. Another method: Thoroughly rinse out milk cartons, pour in water, and put them in the freezer. Tear away the carton, and you'll have a block of ice. Be certain that the water you use is free from odor or taste.

➤ Carbonated mixers, champagne, and sparkling wines should be added to the punch *immediately* before serving. In a bowl, which has a large surface area, the bubbles will rapidly dissipate, and the punch will go flat quickly.

➤ An attractive and appropriate bowl will enhance enjoyment of the punch. If you rent a bowl for the occasion, choose carefully. For outdoor events, a rugged bowl—even a bucket or stock pot—is appropriate (and fun). Be certain to use a heat-resistant bowl for serving hot punch!

Brandy Based

Brandy makes a strong base for the more assertive punches.

Bombay Punch

Yields 50-60 servings.

12 lemons

Sugar to taste

1 750-ml. bottle cognac

1 750-ml. bottle medium-dry sherry

$^1/_2$ cup maraschino liqueur

$^1/_2$ cup curaçao

4 750-ml. bottles brut champagne, well chilled

2 1-liter bottles club soda

Place block of ice in a punch bowl, squeeze lemon juice over it, and sweeten to taste. Add everything except champagne and club soda. Stir. Add the champagne and club soda immediately before serving. You can decorate with festive fruits in season.

Brandy Punch

Yields 35-50 servings.

Juice of 12 lemons

Juice of 4 oranges

Sugar to taste

1 cup grenadine

1 cup triple sec

2 liters brandy

2 cups tea (optional)

1 quart club soda

Lemon slices

Orange slices

Combine the lemon and orange juice with the sugar, then combine with the other ingredients over an ice block in the punch bowl. Add the club soda immediately before serving. Garnish with the fruit slices.

Bar Tips

If practical, prepare champagne punches immediately before serving. At the very least, the champagne must be added only moments before serving. The bubbles dissipate rapidly in a bowl.

Champagne Punches

Champagne is a very popular festive base for punches. All too often, however, champagne punches are uninspired. This means that they are typically left out too long, so that the champagne bubbles dissipate, and the punch, dull from the get-go, becomes both flat and dull. The punches that follow are much better than the usual.

Champagne Punch

Yields 25-35 servings.

2–3 bottles champagne, well chilled

$^1/_2$ cup curaçao

$^1/_2$ cup lemon juice

1 quart club soda, well chilled

$^1/_2$ lb. confectioners' sugar

Prepare punch immediately before serving, combining all ingredients in a punch bowl. No ice is needed.

Bar Tip

Often, if the principal ingredients of champagne punches are well chilled—and the bowl is chilled as well—no ice is needed. This will prevent dilution and retard dissipation of bubbles. Some champagne punches are better with ice, however. Follow the suggestions in the recipes.

Champagne Punch (Version 2)

Yields 12-15 servings.

$^1/_2$ cup brandy

$^1/_2$ cup Cointreau or triple sec

2 bottles champagne, well chilled

Combine all ingredients in a small punch bowl, adding the champagne immediately before serving. No ice is needed.

Champagne Rum Punch

Yields approximately 40 servings.

2 liters rum

1 750-ml. bottle sweet vermouth

1 quart orange juice

1 bottle champagne, well chilled

Sliced bananas

Combine all ingredients except bananas in a punch bowl, adding champagne and ice block immediately before serving. Garnish with sliced bananas.

Holiday Punch

Yields approximately 30 servings.

1 8-oz. can crushed pineapple with juice

1 quart raspberry sherbet

1 bottle champagne, well chilled

2 quarts ginger ale, well chilled

Prepare immediately before serving. Put the pineapple and sherbet in a chilled punch bowl, then add the champagne and ginger ale. No ice is needed.

Players Script

Don Marquis, newspaperman, poet, and playwright, was one of The Players' fabled imbibers, celebrated for jumping on and falling off the wagon. After one protracted bout of abstinence, he tied one on at the Club, staggered to the top of the stairs, raised his right arm, grinned broadly, and declared to his fellow members: "Gentlemen, I wish you all to bear witness that, after a terrific struggle, I have conquered this goddamn willpower of mine."

Liqueur Punches

Liqueur-based punches are strongly flavored, sweet, and rich. They are not great thirst quenchers for sultry days, but are festive energizers that will please a crowd.

French Cream Punch

Yields 15-20 servings.

1 cup amaretto

1 cup Kahlúa

$1/4$ cup triple sec

$1/2$ gallon softened vanilla ice cream

Combine all ingredients in a punch bowl without ice. Stir well.

Southern Comfort Punch

Yields approximately 30 servings.

1 750-ml. bottle Southern Comfort

2 cups grapefruit juice

1 cup lemon juice

2 quarts 7-Up or Sprite (may substitute ginger ale)

Combine all ingredients in a punch bowl with a block of ice, adding the soda immediately before serving.

Rum Punches

Rum is the punch ingredient par excellence. It is naturally sweet without being cloying, and its heavy consistency holds its own among many other ingredients. For tropically accented drinks, it adds just the right touch of warm-weather exoticism.

Fish House Punch is a true classic. It is a very potent punch and should be served in gatherings of mature and responsible drinkers. This is not for a frat party.

Fish House Punch

Yields 25-35 servings.

1 liter rum

1 750 ml. bottle brandy

$^{1}/_{2}$ cup peach brandy

2–3 quarts cola (may substitute other flavored soda, lemonade, or strong tea)

Lemon slice

Lime slice

Orange slice

Combine all ingredients except fruit in a punch bowl with a block of ice. If you use cola or other soda, add this immediately before serving. Garnish with fruit slices.

Tropical Punch

Yields approximately 100 servings.

5 bottles white wine

1 lb. brown sugar

1 quart orange juice

1 pint lemon juice

5 sliced bananas

1 pineapple, cut or chopped

3 liters light rum

1 pint dark rum

2 cups crème de banane

Assorted fruit slices (banana, pineapple, orange, lime)

Combine the wine, brown sugar, juices, and fruit in a *large* mixing bowl, or perhaps more than one (store back-ups in the refrigerator). Stir very thoroughly, cover, and let stand overnight. Add the rums and liqueur, then strain into a large punch bowl containing a block or two of ice. Garnish with assorted fruit slices.

Vodka Punches

As many hosts see it, vodka, the great clean, neutral spirit, is the ideal vehicle to propel any punch to success. It goes especially well with any fruit you wish to add.

Fruit Punch

Yields approximately 40 servings.

1 liter vodka

1 bottle white wine

2 12-oz. cans frozen fruit juice concentrate (pineapple, grapefruit, or orange)

2 quarts club soda

Combine all ingredients except club soda in a punch bowl with a block of ice. Add the club soda immediately before serving.

Velvet Hammer Punch

Yields approximately 30 servings.

1 bottle sauterne

12 ounces apricot brandy

1 liter vodka

1 bottle champagne, well chilled

1 quart ginger ale

Combine all ingredients in a punch bowl with a block of ice, adding the champagne and ginger ale immediately before serving.

Wedding Punch

Yields approximately 35 servings.

1 liter vodka

3 cups orange juice

1 cup lemon juice

2 quarts ginger ale

Cherries

Lemons

Orange slices

Combine vodka and juices in a punch bowl. Add the ginger ale and a block of ice immediately before serving. Garnish with cherries, lemons, and orange slices.

Whiskey Punches

Whiskey punches mean business. They appeal to a more mature group.

Whiskey Punch

Yields 60-65 servings.

2 liters bourbon

$1/2$ cup curaçao

1 quart apple juice

Juice of 6 lemons

2 ounces grenadine

4 quarts ginger ale

Cherries

Combine all ingredients except cherries in a punch bowl, adding the ginger ale with a block of ice immediately before serving. Garnish with cherries.

Wine Punches

Wine punches appeal to a broad group of drinkers, of all ages and tastes. The degree of aggressiveness depends on the additional spiritous ingredients.

The Buddha Punch is refreshing without being overbearing. It is mild and as close to universally appealing as any punch can get.

Buddha Punch

Yields 25-30 servings.

1 bottle Rhine wine

$1/2$ cup curaçao

$1/2$ cup rum

1 cup orange juice

Orange slices

1 quart soda water

Angostura bitters to taste

1 bottle chilled champagne

Mint leaves

Combine all ingredients except champagne, mint, and orange slices in punch bowl. Add the champagne just before serving. Garnish with mint leaves and orange slices

A mulled wine punch is a classic for a party on a cold winter's eve. This one goes well at Christmastime.

Hot Mulled Wine

Yields 15-25 servings.

2 cups water

2 cinnamon sticks, whole

8 cloves

1 lemon peel cut into a long spiral

$1/2$ cup sugar syrup

2 bottles dry red wine

Cognac (see directions)

Lemon slices (see directions)

Combine all ingredients except wine, lemon slices, and cognac in a large saucepan. Allow to boil for 10 minutes. Add the wine, then resume heating, but do not bring to a boil. Serve hot in cups or glasses, garnishing each with a lemon slice and adding a splash of cognac.

The Wassail Bowl is a traditional Christmas punch and a treat that summons up visions of the brighter aspects of the world of Charles Dickens.

Wassail Bowl

Yields 25-30 servings.

1 cup brown sugar

2 tsp. grated nutmeg

2 tsp. powdered ginger

3 cinnamon sticks, broken

1/2 tsp. mace

6 whole cloves

6 allspice berries

3 750-ml. bottles Madeira, Marsala, sherry, or port

7 eggs*

1 cup cognac (may substitute gold rum)

4 baked apples

Preheat oven to 300°. Core apples and bake for 35 minutes or until they're soft inside, but still hold their shape. Set aside. Add sugar and spices to a saucepan over direct heat and add 1 to 2 cups of water. Bring to a boil, stirring until the sugar is dissolved. Add the wine and continue heating, but do not boil. Separate the eggs, and beat egg yolks and egg whites, then fold together and pour the folded eggs into a heat-resistant punch bowl. Slowly add the heated wine mixture to the bowl. Stir to blend wine with the eggs. Add cognac. Stir. Add the baked apples. Stir. To serve, add a bit of the baked apple to each cup of punch.

Raw egg may be a source of salmonella bacteria. You may wish to avoid drinks calling for raw egg yolk or white.

Great Eggnogs

Like punches, eggnogs have fallen on hard times. During the holiday season, supermarket shelves are lined with thick yellow nogs in cartons, loaded with sugar and much too much nutmeg. Do yourself and your guests a favor by reminding them—or revealing to them—what an eggnog is *supposed* to taste like.

Whiskey Eggnog

Serve in a chilled highball glass.

1 egg*

1 tsp. sugar

1 1/2 oz. blended whiskey

6 oz. milk

Grated nutmeg

Combine all ingredients except nutmeg in a shaker with ice. Shake vigorously, then strain into the serving glass. Sprinkle with nutmeg.

Raw egg may be a source of salmonella bacteria. You may wish to avoid drinks calling for raw egg yolk or white.

Your Basic Eggnog Punch

Yields 45-65 servings.

1 lb. confectioners' sugar

12 eggs, separated

1 pint brandy

1 pint light rum

1½ quarts milk

1 pint heavy cream

Grated or powdered nutmeg

In the punch bowl, beat confectioners' sugar in with egg yolks only, then slowly stir in the brandy, rum, milk, and cream. Chill. Fold in stiffly beaten egg whites immediately before serving. Punch must be well chilled. Do not serve with ice. Sprinkle nutmeg on top.

Planter's Punch (Times 2)

Bar Tips

You'll find Planter's Punch recipes for individual drinks in Chapter 13.

Planter's Punch is so popular that it merits its own section. The Myers's rum people popularized this drink, and you can't go wrong making it with their dark Jamaican rum.

Planter's Punch

Yields approximately 30 servings.

1 liter light rum

1 pint Myers's dark Jamaican rum

1 pint fresh lime juice

1 pint sugar syrup

1 quart club soda

Orange slices

Cherries

Combine all ingredients except club soda and fruit. Add the club soda immediately before serving and garnish with orange slices and cherries.

Variation on Planter's Punch

Yields approximately 20 servings.

1 liter light rum

1 cup Myers's dark Jamaican rum

1 cup curaçao

1 pint lemon juice

1 cup orange juice

1 cup pineapple juice

Orange slices

Cherries

Combine all ingredients except fruit in a punch bowl. Garnish with orange slices and cherries.

The Least You Need to Know

➤ Too many party punches are uninspired. Take the time and effort to create a special punch, and you will delight and surprise your guests.

➤ Do not view punch as a cheap, time-saving alternative to serving individual drinks. Use quality ingredients and take the time to prepare the punch from scratch.

➤ Cold punches should begin with chilled ingredients and should use block ice rather than cubes, which melt quickly and dilute the punch.

➤ Be careful with hot punches. They should be served piping hot, so make certain that the punch bowl you use is thoroughly heat resistant.

➤ Create a punch to suit your guests (in terms of their ages and preferences), the season (warm weather or cold), and the occasion (holiday, special celebration, whatever).

Chapter 24

Turning Pro: The Barkeep's Vocation

In This Chapter

➤ The challenge of professional bartending

➤ How much money do bartenders make?

➤ Breaking in as a bartender

➤ Dealing with customers

➤ The bartender's legal responsibilities

Amateur. Now there's a perfectly nice word that has gotten some very bad press. The word summons up images of bumbling, unprofessional incompetence. Actually, *amateur* comes from the Latin *amator*, which means lover. Nothing wrong with that, eh? An amateur is someone who does something not because it's a job, but because he or she *loves* it.

And so this book was written mainly with the *amateur* bartender in mind—the person who wants to mix drinks, not for cash, but for the pleasure of it.

But who says we can't do what we enjoy to make a living or supplement one? Here's a brief chapter on the *profession* of bartending.

Do You Really Want to Do This?

Ask us if the jigger is half empty or half full, and we'll give the pessimist's reply. Do you really want to spend hour after hour on your feet—pouring, measuring, and

pushing a damp towel into the wee hours? Do you want to endure the noise and inhale the smoke? Do you want to dwell perpetually in the company of those who "feel no pain"? And are you willing to listen to the same conversations over and over: spouse trouble, boyfriend trouble, girlfriend trouble, financial woes, and a blow-by-blow history of this lady's brand-new Beamer and that guy's cherished 'Vette?

Professional Bartending: What It Takes

If none of this daunts and discourages you, maybe you have what it takes to be a good—and happy—professional bartender. At the very least, you'll need:

➤ Manual dexterity

➤ Good eyesight

➤ Good hearing

➤ Good short-term memory—and long-term, in local spots.

➤ Good feet

➤ Stamina

➤ Excellent communication skills

➤ A pleasant manner—an enjoyment of talking to strangers

Bartending is a lot less about pouring and shaking than it is about people. If you don't have people skills, get them. And if you can't get them, don't even think about tending bar for a living. The well-worn cliché about the bartender being the poor-man's psychiatrist is well worn for a reason: it's true. You'll listen to hours of problems, both petty and profound. With some people you'll sympathize. You'll probably take a liking to many customers. But you can also count on running across a sizable number of jerks. To them you must also give attention and never let on what you may really feel.

This is not the only demand that will be placed on your people skills. What are you serving? A substance that affects the inhibitions. Usually, a bar is a happy and sociable place. But there will come times when you'll have to deal with drunks—some swaggering, some stubborn; others defiant, macho, obnoxious, pathetic, or downright scary. It is your responsibility keep an eye on your customers, to recognize when someone has had enough or more than enough, and it is your responsibility to refuse to give them more. If serving customers is demanding, *not* serving them can be even more challenging.

The Rewards—and Risks—of Bartending

Let's cut to the chase. What kind of money can a bartender expect? Despite what you may have heard about bartenders who really rake in the tips, pay often starts out at around $10,000 a year, with $14,000 the middle range, and the top level coming in at under $25,000 a year. Of course, in the right setting, with big tippers and heavy traffic, you *can* make much, much more.

According to Les Krantz's *Jobs Rated Almanac* (third edition, 1995), the average bartender works just under a 40-hour week. However, bartending is one of those jobs that usually can be worked part time or overtime.

While you'll probably never get rich as a full-time bartender—unless you use the job as a stepping stone to a management or ownership position—bartending can be an excellent part-time profession. Hours are often flexible, as are opportunities for mobility: few populated places on the globe are very distant from a bar. Nor are you restricted to working in a single type of environment. A bar may be set in the corner tavern; the local disco; the hottest, hardest-to-get-into nightclub; a motel off the Interstate; a hotel on the Grand Boulevard; a fine restaurant; an airport—you name it. You don't even have to work *in* a bar. Catering services set up bars in people's homes, in auditoriums and convention halls, at outdoor events, and so on.

Bartending's biggest challenge—dealing with a lot of people on an intimate level—is also, for most professionals, its greatest attraction. You'll meet a cross-section of humanity. You'll make friends. You'll make contacts you would not make in any other profession. You'll have the opportunity to watch people interact and be—*people*.

In most bars, bartending is not a particularly hazardous job. While it is true that the potential exists for unpleasant or even violent events, most larger bars employ some form of security personnel: a bouncer. In many popular and thickly populated clubs, off-duty police officers serve as the security staff.

Despite the presence of professional security personnel, a bartender can be at some personal risk. Women bartenders especially may find themselves fending off unwanted advances from customers. Such attention is often fairly benign, if annoying, but it can become intimidating and even threatening.

There are also the dangers associated with any late-night job, as you travel to and from work or even walk from the bar to your car at two in the morning (or even later in some locales).

Bar Tips
Beware of the attraction of cash income—tips. While tips leave no paper trail for the IRS to sniff at, the feds are quite sophisticated at calculating reasonable tip income, and they have their feelers out for waiters, bartenders, and others who may under-report tip income.

Bar Tips
The third edition (1995) of the *Jobs Rated Almanac* by Les Krantz rates the vocation of bartender as only moderately stressful: 68 jobs are less stressful, ranging from Medical Records Technician (the least stressful) to Physicist (only slightly less stressful than bartender). One hundred eighty-one jobs are more stressful, ranging from Antique Dealer and Philosopher (just a bit more stressful than bartender) all the way to President of the United States (the most stressful).

Bartending can be hazardous to your health in other ways. Possible assaults on your constitution include sleep deprivation, prolonged exposure to second-hand cigar and cigarette smoke, and hearing loss as a result of sustained bombardment by multidecibel music.

There is also a downside to being around so much liquor. A bartender who samples the wares rarely lasts long as a bartender. Not only are you drinking up profits, you simply cannot do your job well if you're chronically buzzed. Manual dexterity deteriorates, and short-term memory takes a vacation. But let's say you somehow get away with it. A bartender who drinks night after night is headed for all the ills alcohol can bring. Bartending is not a profession for people with addiction-prone personalities.

Breaking In to Bartending

The good news is that bartending is a high-turnover profession. Jobs open up all the time. The bad news is that bartending is a high-turnover profession. Plenty of bartenders burn out or get fired. Most just go on to something else, never having intended to make this job their life's work.

Starting at the Bottom

So bartending is hardly a closed-shop profession. You can break in fairly easily. You just can't expect to start at the top, which is probably exactly where you'd *like* to start.

But just where is the bottom? And how bad is it?

To answer the second question first, it's not that bad. In many professions, starting out at the bottom means doing all the dirty, disgusting, back-breaking, mind-numbing work nobody else wants to do. In bartending, it just means working in settings that don't pay much.

The easiest way to break into bartending is to apply to a catering service. The folks behind the portable bars set up at parties, cocktail receptions, and the like are usually not very experienced—and not very well paid. Tips at "catered affairs" are small or nonexistent. But you can use the experience to hone your craft, even as you find out, firsthand, whether or not bartending is really right for you.

A step up from catering work is a job with a hotel banquet facility. This is similar to tending bar for a catering service, but the work is usually more regular and frequent. The pay? Probably not much better than casual catering gigs.

Beyond the banquet bar are the cocktail lounges and bars found in airports and train stations. Here's a step up in salary, but tips in these way stations are usually dismal, and the customers are rarely jolly. They're tired, they're bored, they're numbing the pain, and just killing time. But at least you're working at a real bar.

Bars in hotels and restaurants offer more attractive salaries and a more varied work experience, but since you generally prepare drinks to be served by waiters and waitresses, you won't deal directly with the public. You may regard this as a minus or a plus, though on the minus side, without direct customer contact, you won't be pulling in the tips—but you will be "tipped out" by the servers.

You can experience "real" bartending—where you're dealing face to face with your customers—at local bars and neighborhood taverns. The crowds may be small, and the tip pool commensurately shallow, but the environment can be laid back and pleasant, and the experience valuable, enabling you, at some point, to make the leap into a major hot spot.

The crowds at large, popular bars create pressure and an unremitting pace, but they also tip well. The potential for making a decent living is greatest in such venues, and, if you're the type, the level of excitement, atmosphere, and activity can be highly energizing.

Players Script

Charlie Connolly gained nearly legendary status as The Players' bartender during much of the early 20th century.

"Don't you ever get tired of listening to some of these hard-luck stories?" a member once asked him.

"No, sir. I hear a lot of very interesting things from a lot of very interesting men."

"Well, I should think a lot of it would be pretty tedious."

"Oh, well, sir, if that's the way of it, you can just stop listening. They don't mind, and it just does them good to get it off their chests."

Getting In

The only way to get a job is to apply for one. In most bartending situations, this means talking to the manager. If you talk to a bartender—instead of the manager—he or she will almost certainly tell you that they aren't hiring. Don't waste your time. Go to the manager.

Present yourself and your skills to the manager. If the place isn't hiring at present, leave a résumé. Or if the place isn't hiring a *bartender* at present, see if you can get a job as a barback—an apprentice bartender and gofer—and work your way up from there.

Bar Tips
Don't ask to see the manager during peak business hours. Show savvy by dropping by between three and five in the afternoon, when most bars are pretty slow.

Buzzed Words

A **barback** is an assistant or apprentice bartender, who does the bartender's **scut work**, including tapping beer kegs, running ice, replacing glassware, preparing and stocking garnishes, restocking shelves, and so on.

Another way to ease yourself in is to offer to take the slow shift. Working the lunch crowd, Sunday brunches, and Monday and Tuesday evenings won't net you much in the way of tips, but it's a way to break in, since the more experienced bartenders don't want to put in hours during such slack time.

Conversely, you might look for work during peak periods. Bars in places that have a highly seasonal trade—summer and winter tourist resorts, for example—are likely to need extra help during the high season. But don't wait until then to start looking. Get the drop on the competition by applying early.

Looking the Part

As a customer-contact position, bartending demands a professional appearance. Present yourself as neat, clean, well-groomed, and attractively dressed. Most bar managers will tell you what constitutes appropriate dress for the bar, and some even supply clothes. "Appropriate" varies from bar to bar and depends on clientele; however, here's what to expect:

Bar Tips

Unless the bar promotes an "alternative" atmosphere, avoid any extremes in dress.

➤ For men: dark pants and shoes with a white shirt. If a tie is required, either wear a bow tie or a long tie "GI style"—that is, neatly tucked into your shirt just below the second button from the collar. A long tie dangling loose will inevitably end up in somebody's drink.

➤ For women: dark skirt or slacks with a white blouse. Avoid dangling jewelry.

➤ For men and women: Long hair is fine, but tie it back neatly.

Acting the Part

The successful bartender continuously broadcasts three messages:

➤ I am friendly and courteous and want to serve you.

➤ I am competent and efficient and will serve you well.

➤ I am supremely confident and will serve you with authority.

The last item is perhaps the most important. Act vague, confused, or tentative, and customers will question the quality of the drinks you mix (even if nothing is wrong with them). You will also find yourself in trouble when it comes time to refuse a drunk "one more for the road."

Project confidence in the way you move. Keep your bar well arranged, so that you can grab the right bottle in a single motion, quickly and firmly by the neck. Pour without hesitation, speak clearly, always express yourself positively.

None of this means that you have to be infallible. Obviously, the more you know about mixing drinks, the better, and you should certainly know the most frequently requested drinks by heart. But if you're stumped, boldly ask the customer: "You've got me there. What goes into a Sazerac?" Never reply that you don't know how to make such-and-such. Instead, ask the customer. If the customer doesn't know either, ask, "Well, do you mind if I look this one up?" Then consult this book!

Customer Relations

In most bars, your success—measured by customer satisfaction, which, you can measure by the quantity and magnitude of your tips—depends on how you treat your "guests."

A "Feel Good" Job

Your number-one customer-relations task is to make the patron feel good. This starts with a courteous, smiling greeting, and a "What can I get for you?" Did we say a bartender needs a good short-term memory? An accurate long-term memory is useful, too. Get to know the names of your repeat or regular customers, and get to know what they usually ask for: "Hi, Jill. Will it be the usual?"

Never intrude on customers' conversation. After serving the drink, step back. However, if you are actively sought in conversation, handle it as courteously and attentively as time and other customers permit. Remember, even customers who want to use you as their psychiatrist don't really need *answers* from you. They want a sympathetic ear—someone to whom they can vent.

Generally, to the degree that you do get involved in conversation, avoid expressing opinions on politics, religion, race, sex, and just about anything controversial or potentially offensive. Avoid giving advice, never talk disparagingly about another customer, and don't gossip.

If customers cause you grief, handle them with firm tact. Address the offensive behavior, remark, or action, not personality or character. If a customer hits on you, turn him or her off with cool thanks: "Thank you, but my boyfriend/girlfriend/husband/wife would not approve." Or: "I appreciate the compliment, but I don't socialize with my customers."

If a customer is rude to you, it is usually best to ignore it. If he or she persists, try something simple and neutral: "I'd appreciate it if you wouldn't talk to me that way." Make this even more effective by asking the customer his or her name, then use the name in your reply: "Mr. Johnson, I'd appreciate it if you wouldn't talk to me that way." Once the veil of anonymity is lifted, it's harder for a customer to persist in being abusive. Sometimes, obnoxious behavior is directed at other customers. Again, try to address behavior rather than personality: "Sir, I'm sorry, but language like that disturbs the other guests."

The bartender is an authority figure. Calm words directed toward correcting behavior are usually sufficient. Do not pick a fight. Do not hurl threats. If you cannot quickly and calmly deal with a bad seed, summon security. If necessary, tell the customer that you will call the police. If this warning fails to produce instant results, make the call.

Customer Service

Adopt a the-customer-is-always-right attitude, even if the customer is wrong. If a patron insists that you make a drink a certain way—even if it's the wrong way—don't argue. Just do it. If you are sure that the result will be absolutely awful, reply this way: "That's interesting. I've never made one that way. Have you ever tried it with...?" This will give the customer a chance to save face if he realizes he is wrong. If the customer still wants it *his* way, give it to him his way without another word.

Bar Tips
If a telephone call comes for a customer, *never* tell the caller that the customer is at the bar. Instead, tell the caller that you'll see if So-and-so is present. Then inform the customer of the call. Leave it up to the customer to take the call or not.

If you are asked to recommend a drink or a brand of liquor, do so, but never suggest to a customer that he or she has made a bad choice.

And accept that smoking and drinking go together. Never comment on smoking, pro or con. If a customer goes for a cigarette, light it, if you can. Keep the ashtrays clean, changing them by putting the clean ashtray over the dirty one, lifting both from the bar, putting the dirty one down behind the bar, and putting the clean one in its place. This is called *capping* the ashtray; it keeps ashes from fluttering out of the dirty one as you move it.

Handling Cash

In a busy bar, handling cash can be as tricky as making drinks. You'll need to polish your skills to do this smoothly, efficiently, and accurately. Unless the bar has a tab system, collect cash right after you serve the drink. Always announce the amount due, and announce it again when the customer hands you the money: "That's three-twenty-five out of five." This is not only for the customer's benefit, but for the benefit of your short-term memory. Put the bill on top of the cash register until you hand the customer change. Not only will this remind you of the amount from which you need to make change, it will settle any dispute if the customer claims to have handed you a larger bill. Count the change back to the customer.

Bar Tips
Accept tips graciously, thanking the customer as he or she gets up to leave. Never comment on the amount of the tip, great or small.

Dealing with Drunks

Review Chapter 2, which contains useful advice for dealing with people—whether guests or bar patrons—who've had too much to drink. It is best to "shut off" or "cut off" someone who's had enough matter-of-factly, with a light touch, and without moralizing. Offer a glass of water instead of a drink: "I can't serve you another martini this evening."

You probably won't get an argument, let alone a hostile reaction, but either one is *possible*. Don't argue, don't exchange threats, and don't get into a fight. Summon the bouncer, if necessary, before the situation gets out of hand. Or call the police.

Buzzed Words
Professional bartenders call refusing to serve an intoxicated patron **shutting off (or cutting off) a drunk.**

Bartending and the Law

While you're looking back at Chapter 2, review the discussion of the legal liability incurred by those who knowingly serve liquor to an intoxicated person. Bartending can be fun, but knowing when to "shut off a drunk" is serious business, with potentially life-saving benefits.

The Least You Need to Know

➤ Bartending is hard work and often pays modestly; however, it is a great job if you like to meet—and please—people.

➤ Prepare to break into bartending from the bottom up, beginning (perhaps) in a temp job with a caterer and working through the ranks to a job in a large public bar.

➤ Your number-one money-making responsibility is to satisfy the customer.

➤ Your number-one legal and moral responsibility is to ensure (kindly, gently, but firmly) that intoxicated customers get no more to drink at your bar.

Buzzed Word Glossary

absinthe   An aromatic, bitter, very strong (containing 68 percent alcohol) liqueur flavored chiefly with wormwood (*Artemisia absinthium*) and containing other botanicals— licorice, hyssop, fennel, angelica root, aniseed, and star aniseed. Famed as the favorite drink of Henri de Toulouse-Lautrec, absinthe was outlawed in many countries early in the 20th century because of its apparent toxicity.

aging   The storage of the distilled alcohol in wooden casks, most often oak. Over months or years, the wood reacts with the alcohol, imparting to it a distinctive color, aroma, and flavor.

alcoholism   The medical definition and the criteria of diagnosis of this condition vary, but, in general, this complex, chronic psychological and nutritional disorder may be defined as continued excessive or compulsive use of alcoholic drinks.

apéritif   A spiritous beverage taken before a meal as an appetizer. Its origin, in French, is hardly appetizing, however, originally denoting a purgative.

aquavit   Aqua vitae is not to be confused with *aquavit*, which is a very strong Scandinavian liquor distilled from potatoes and grain and flavored with caraway seeds.

arrack   A strong alcoholic beverage distilled from palm sap, rice, or molasses. It is popular in the Middle and Far East and is available in larger liquor stores.

Bacchanalia   The ancient Roman festival in honor of Bacchus. A drunken orgy with a specific religious purpose, it gave the literary English a word (spelled with a small *b*) to describe your everyday drunken orgies.

barback   An assistant or apprentice bartender, who does the bartender's scut work, including tapping beer kegs, running ice, replacing glassware, preparing and stocking garnishes, restocking shelves, and so on.

blackout Not a loss of consciousness, but an inability to remember, even after you are sober, what you did and said while intoxicated.

blended whiskey A blended whiskey may be a combination of *straight* whiskeys and neutral, flavorless whiskeys (this is true of Canadian whisky) or it may be a combination of similar whiskey products made by different distillers at different times (as in blended scotch).

blood-alcohol concentration (BAC) The concentration of alcohol in the blood, expressed as the weight of alcohol in a fixed volume of blood. Sometimes called *blood alcohol level* or BAL. It is used as an objective measure of intoxication.

bottled-in-bond Whiskey that, by federal law, must be a 100-proof, straight whiskey aged at least four years and stored in a federally bonded warehouse pending sale. Not until the whiskey is sold—withdrawn from the bonded warehouse—does the distiller have to pay the federal excise tax. Beyond these requirements, the "bottled-in-bond" designation says nothing about the quality or nature of the whiskey.

branch water Water withdrawn from the local "branch," or stream. Sadly, in most U.S. locations, this would be a risky undertaking these days, and "branch" or "branch water" is just a romantic appellation to describe what comes out of the faucet.

champagne As applied to cognac, champagne has nothing to do with the sparkling wine. The word is French for flat, open country, and its English-language equivalent is *plain.*

cobbler Traditionally, an iced drink made of wine or liqueur plus sugar and fruit juice.

Coffey still See *continuous still.*

congeners Acids, aldehydes, esters, ketones, phenols, and tannins that are byproducts of fermentation, distillation, and aging. These "impurities" may contribute to the character and flavor of the spirit, but they cause undesirable effects in some people, notably increasing the intensity of hangover.

continuous still Also called a Coffey still, after the inventor, Aeneas Coffey. A type of still for whiskey distillation that allows for continuous high-volume production, as opposed to the *pot still,* which must be emptied and "recharged" one batch at a time.

cordial In modern usage, a synonym for *liqueur;* however, the word originally designated only those liqueurs thought to have tonic or medicinal efficacy.

"cutting off (a drunk)" See *"shutting off (a drunk)."*

daiquiri A rum, lime juice, sugar drink named after the Cuban town near the original Bacardi rum distillery.

daisy A whiskey- or gin-based drink that includes some sweet syrup and a float of—usually golden—liqueur.

distilling   The process of evaporating the alcohol produced by fermentation, then condensing the evaporated fluid to concentrate and purify it. The increase in alcohol concentration is usually great.

dry martini   A martini with relatively little vermouth versus gin. Some drinkers prefer 12 parts gin to 1 part vermouth, while others insist on a 20-to-1 ratio. Extremists do away with the vermouth altogether and have a gin and olive on the rocks.

dry gin   You will often encounter the expression *dry gin* or *London dry gin* on bottle labels. These designations originated when gin was widely available in "sweet" (called *Old Tom*) as well as "dry" forms. Today, the distinction is mainly superfluous, because almost all English and American gin is now dry. Also note that a gin does not have to be made in London or even in England to bear the "London dry gin" designation on its label. This describes a manufacturing style, not a place of origin.

DUI or DWI   In some jurisdictions, drunk driving is called driving under the influence—*DUI*—in others, it's driving while intoxicated—*DWI*.

ethyl alcohol   The potable alcohol obtained from the fermentation of sugars and starches. For producing hard liquor, the ethyl alcohol is purified and concentrated by distillation.

fermenting   The chemical process whereby complex organic substances are split into relatively simple compounds. In the manufacture of alcohol, special yeasts are used to ferment—convert—the starches and sugars of grain (or some other organic substance) into alcohol.

fizz   Any drink made with soda and a sweetener.

flambé   As a verb, *flambé* means to drench with liquor and ignite. The word may also be used as a noun, synonymous with flaming drink.

flip   A drink containing liquor, sugar, spice, and egg. Often served hot. Flips were most popular in the 18th and 19th centuries.

fortified wine   A fermented wine to which a distilled spirit, usually brandy, has been added. Brandy itself is often considered a fortified wine.

freeze   A frozen drink.

garbage   A bit of fruit or vegetable added to a drink primarily for the sake of appearance. It does not significantly enhance the flavor of the drink.

garnish   A bit of fruit or vegetable added to a drink principally to enhance its flavor.

generic liqueurs   Liqueurs prepared according to standard formulas by a number of distillers.

grog   Originally, grog was nothing more than rum diluted with water and rationed to sailors of the 18th-century Royal Navy. Its namesake was Admiral Edward Vernon (1684–1757), who first ordered the ration: Vernon's nickname was Old Grogram, after his habit of wearing a grogram (coarse wool) cloak.

hard liquor   A beverage with a high alcoholic content. Gin, vodka, bourbon, sour mash whiskey, scotch, blended whiskey, rye, rum, and tequila are the most common "hard liquors."

hard cider   Fermented—and therefore alcoholic—apple cider.

jigger   The glass or the metal measuring cup used to measure drinks. It is also what you call the amount the jigger measures: $1^1/_2$ ounces.

light whiskey   Whiskey distilled at a high proof (in excess of 160 proof) and aged in used charred oak barrels. Light whiskey is more flavorful than neutral spirits, but not as strongly flavored as straight whiskey. It is an important component in blended whiskey.

liquor   Any alcoholic beverage made by fermentation *and* distillation rather than fermentation alone (as is the case with wine and beer).

London dry gin   See *dry gin*.

macerate   To make soft by soaking in liquid. Applied to the production of liqueurs, maceration is a process of soaking botanicals in the distilled alcohol to extract their flavor.

malt   Grain (usually barley) that has been allowed to sprout. Used as material for fermentation to produce beer or certain distilled spirits.

malting   The practice of allowing the grain (usually barley) to sprout before fermentation. In whiskey production, this produces a variety of characteristic flavors in the finished product.

mash   The fermentable starchy mixture from which an alcoholic beverage is produced.

master blender   The craftsperson in charge of selecting and proportioning the component whiskies that make up a blended whiskey.

mixed-grain whiskey   Whiskey distilled from a mash in which no single type of grain predominates. Contrast straight whiskey, which is made from mash containing at least 51 percent of a certain grain.

muddle   To mash and stir. One muddles such things as mint leaves and other solids in order to make a suspension or a paste with fluid. A special pestle-like wooden *muddler* can be used, but any spoon will do.

muddler   See *muddle*.

mull   To heat and spice a drink. Traditionally, the heating was done by inserting a hot poker into the drink; today, *mulled* drinks are usually heated on a stove.

Old Tom   A special form of gin, slightly sweetened. It is not widely enjoyed today and may be quite hard to find.

pick-me-up Many spiritous drinks advertise themselves as a *pick-me-up*. Typically acting first to suppress inhibitions, alcohol can, indeed, make you feel energized. Just be aware, however, that alcohol is ultimately a sedative or depressant.

pony Strictly speaking, a 1-ounce measure; however, pony glasses range in capacity from 1 to 2 ounces.

port (also called *porto*) Named after the Portuguese town of Oporto, birthplace of this fortified wine and the origin of "true" port today—though other regions also produce port wines. Port is sweet, whereas sherry ranges from dry to sweet.

posset A traditional English drink made with sweetened milk that has been curdled by the addition of wine or ale. It is usually served hot.

pot still See *continuous still.*

pousse-café A drink made with two or more liqueurs and, sometimes, cream. The different spirits vary in specific gravity, so float in discrete layers if carefully combined. The layered effect is novel and pretty.

proof The alcoholic content of a spirit. It is determined by multiplying the percentage of alcoholic content by two, so that liquor that is 40 percent alcohol is 80 proof.

proprietary liqueurs "Brand-name" products prepared according to closely guarded trade-secret formulas that are the property of specific distillers.

rickey Any alcohol-based drink with soda water and lime—and sometimes sugar.

sangria A cold drink made with red (sometimes white) wine mixed with brandy, sugar, fruit juice, and soda. Its blood-red color and red-blooded robustness are underscored by the meaning of the word in Spanish: the act of bleeding.

schnapps A word used to describe any number of strong, dry liquors, but, recently, has been applied to a variety of flavored liqueurs. The word derives from the German original, spelled with one *p* and meaning "mouthful."

scut work The menial chores behind the bar, such as tapping beer kegs, running ice, stocking shelves, and so on; often performed by a *barback.*

sherry A fortified Spanish wine with a nutlike flavor. Its name is an Anglicization of Jerez, a city in southwestern Spain, where sherry was first produced and from which region the most highly respected sherry still comes.

shooter A drink meant to be downed in a single shot, often accompanied by table banging and gasps of pleasurable pain.

"shutting off (a drunk)" Professional bartenders call refusing to serve an intoxicated patron "shutting him off." Also called "cutting off."

sling Any brandy, whiskey, or gin drink that is sweetened and flavored with lemon.

327

sloe gin   Despite the name, *sloe gin* is not a gin at all, but a sweet liqueur. Its principal flavoring is the sloe berry, the small, sour fruit of the blackthorn.

specific gravity   Applied to liquids, *specific gravity* is the ratio of the mass of the liquid to the mass of an equal volume of distilled water at 39 degrees Fahrenheit.

spirits (or *spirit*)   A generic term for an alcoholic beverage based on distilled *liquor*.

spritzer   A combination of wine—usually Rhine wine or other white wine—and club soda or seltzer. The word comes from the German for *spray*.

still   A device for distilling liquids (including alcohol) to concentrate and purify them. In its simplest form, it consists of a vessel in which the liquid is heated to vapor, a coil (or other apparatus) to cool and condense the vapor, and a vessel to collect the condensed vapor (called the distillate). Stills are made in a great many varieties, ranging from small batch stills to huge industrial continuous stills, capable of producing large volumes of distillate.

straight whiskey   The term *straight whiskey* is not to be confused with ordering "whiskey, straight" (that is, "neat," with neither ice, water, nor a mixer). The mash for straight whiskey contains at least 51 percent of a certain grain: straight malt whiskey mash contains 51 percent barley; straight rye, 51 percent rye; and straight bourbon, 51 percent corn; however, straight corn whiskey is made from mash that contains 80 percent corn.

surface tension   A molecular property of liquids by which the surface of the liquid tends to contract, taking on the characteristics of a stretched elastic membrane.

sweet cider   Nonalcoholic apple cider.

tequila añejo   Tequila that has been aged in oak casks. It acquires a deep gold coloring and is therefore often called gold tequila; however, not all gold tequila is aged. Unaged tequila is clear and called *white* tequila.

toddy   A hot drink consisting of liquor—often rum—water, sugar, and spices.

whiskey versus whisky   American and Irish distillers spell the word with an *e*, while Scotch and Canadian distillers jump right from the *k* to the *y*.

wort   A soluble starch in the form of an infusion of malt. It is used in the fermentation processes of making whiskey and beer.

Last Call

The recipes presented in the main body of this book are all tried and all true. For the more adventurous bartender and drinker, however, we have collected some very intriguing new or out-of-the-ordinary drinks.

This is the place to come when you're stumped behind the bar, or just looking for something unusual to knock the socks of your guests. You've become familiar with most of the recipes commonly associated with each spirit. Now explore some variations on the original recipe—or stroll down entirely new avenues with intoxicating combinations like Between the Sheets, the Woo Woo, or the impressive Ramos Gin Fizz.

Walk on the Wild Side

Some of the following are new, some not so new, but all are—shall we say—highly stimulating. They are not for the scotch-and-water or Whiskey Sour crowd.

B-52

Serve straight-up in a shot glass.

$1/2$ oz. Grand Marnier

$1/2$ oz. Bailey's Irish Cream

$1/2$ oz. Kahlúa

Combine ingredients in a mixing glass, stir, then pour into the shot glass.

Kamikaze

Serve in a chilled cocktail glass.

1 oz. triple sec

1 oz. vodka

1 oz. lime juice

Combine all ingredients in a shaker with ice. Shake vigorously, then strain into the serving glass.

Bahama Mama

Serve in a chilled Collins glass.

Dash grenadine	1 oz. pineapple juice
$1^{1}/2$ oz. light rum	$2^{1}/2$ oz. orange juice
$1^{1}/2$ oz. gold rum	Maraschino cherry
$1^{1}/2$ oz. dark rum	Orange slice
2 oz. sour mix	

Put a dash of grenadine in the bottom of the serving glass and set aside. Combine all other ingredients except the cherry and orange slice in a shaker filled with ice. Shake vigorously, then pour into the serving glass. Garnish with the cherry and orange slice.

Long Island Iced Tea

Serve in a chilled Collins glass.

$1/2$ oz. gin	3 oz. sour mix
$1/2$ oz. vodka	Cola
$1/2$ oz. white tequila	Lemon wedge
$1/2$ oz. light rum	Mint sprigs
$1/4$ oz. white crème de menthe	

Combine all ingredients except the cola, lemon wedge, and mint sprig with cracked ice in a blender. Blend well, then pour into the serving glass. Add cola to fill, and garnish with the lemon wedge and mint sprig.

Brain

Serve straight-up in a shot glass.

$3/4$ oz. Kahlúa

$3/4$ oz. vodka

Splash Bailey's Irish Cream

Combine the Kahlúa and vodka in the shot glass, then splash in the Bailey's. Do not stir. The swirling of the Bailey's creates the texture that suggests a brain.

Melon Ball Sunrise

Serve on the rocks in a highball glass.

1 oz. vodka	Orange juice to fill
$1/2$ oz. Midori melon liqueur	Drop grenadine

Combine vodka and Midori in the serving glass filled with ice. Add orange juice to fill. Stir well. Insert bar spoon into drink and slide a drop of grenadine down it. Allow the grenadine to rise from the bottom of the drink for the sunrise effect. Do not stir.

Jell-O Shots

Serve solid and eat with a spoon, or serve semigelatinous in shot glasses.

12 oz. vodka	12 oz. water

6 oz. Jell-O gelatin mix (choose flavor)

Combine 6 oz. vodka with 6 oz. water in a saucepan. Bring to a boil and stir in Jell-O gelatin mix. Remove from stove and add remaining 6 oz. of water and 6 oz. of vodka. Let set in the refrigerator overnight.

Note: Whether in fully gelled or in semiliquid/ semigelatinous form, this drink tends to retard the body's absorption of the alcohol, making it more difficult to tell when you have had "enough."

Midori Sour

Serve in a chilled whiskey sour glass.

2 oz. Midori

1 oz. lemon juice

1 tsp. sugar syrup

Combine all ingredients in a shaker with ice. Shake vigorously, then strain into the serving glass.

Sex on the Beach

Serve on the rocks in a highball glass.

1¹/₂ oz. vodka   Cranberry juice to ³/₄ full

1 oz. peach schnapps   Orange juice to fill

Combine all ingredients in the serving glass full of ice. Stir.

Woo Woo

Serve on the rocks in a highball glass.

³/₄ oz. vodka

³/₄ oz. peach schnapps

3 oz. cranberry juice cocktail

Combine the ingredients over ice in the serving glass. Stir well.

Toasted Almond

Serve in a chilled highball glass.

¹/₂ oz. Kahlúa

¹/₂ oz. amaretto

2 oz. cream

Combine all ingredients in a shaker filled with ice. Shake vigorously, then strain into the serving glass. Add more ice, if you wish.

Worth Mixing

The following drinks are less in demand than those in the main body of the book, and some take a bit of effort to make, but they are well worth mixing, drinking, and enjoying.

More Joys of Gin

Alexander II

Serve straight-up in a chilled cocktail glass.

1 oz. gin   1 oz. heavy cream

1 oz. crème de cacao

Vigorously shake all ingredients with ice in a shaker or blend; strain into the serving glass.

Bermuda Highball

Serve on the rocks in a chilled highball glass.

1 oz. gin   1 oz. dry vermouth

1 oz. brandy   Club soda or ginger ale to fill

Stir the ingredients, except for the club soda/ginger ale, with ice in the serving glass. Pour in the club soda or ginger ale to fill.

Alexander III

Serve straight-up in a chilled cocktail glass.

1 ¹/₂ oz. gin   ³/₄ oz. heavy cream

¹/₂ oz. white or green crème de menthe

Vigorously shake all ingredients with ice in a shaker or blend; strain into the serving glass.

Dubonnet Cocktail

Serve straight-up or on the rocks in a chilled old-fashioned or lowball glass.

1¹/₂ oz. gin   Lemon twist

1¹/₂ oz. Dubonnet rouge

Vigorously shake the gin and Dubonnet, with ice, in a shaker or blend; pour into the serving glass. Garnish with a lemon twist.

Gin Cobbler

Serve in an old-fashioned or lowball glass.

2 oz. gin	Club soda to fill
1 tsp. orgeat syrup	Orange slice

Stir the gin and orgeat in the serving glass with ice; cracked ice works best. Fill with club soda. Garnish with an orange slice.

Red Lion Cocktail

Serve in a chilled cocktail glass.

1 oz. gin	$^1/_2$ oz. orange juice
1 oz. Grand Marnier	$^1/_2$ oz. lemon juice

Combine all ingredients in a shaker or blender with cracked ice. Shake or blend vigorously. Strain into the serving glass.

Ramos Gin Fizz

Serve in a Collins or highball glass.

4 oz. gin	2 tsp. heavy cream
1 oz. lime juice	Several dashes orange flower water
1 oz. lemon juice	1 egg white *
2 tsp. sugar syrup	Club soda to fill

In a shaker or blender with cracked ice combine all ingredients except for the club soda. Shake or blend vigorously. Pour into the serving glasses. Add club soda to fill. Recipe makes two drinks. (Orange flower water is an extract of orange blossom and is available at gourmet stores.)

* Raw egg may be a source of salmonella bacteria. You may wish to avoid drinks calling for raw egg yolk or white.

The Vider Vorld of Vodka

Coffee Cooler

Serve in a large old-fashioned glass.

$1^1/_2$ oz. vodka	4 oz. iced coffee
1 oz. Kahlúa	Scoop of coffee ice cream
1 oz. heavy cream	

Combine all ingredients except the ice cream in a shaker. Shake vigorously and pour into the serving glass. Top with the ice cream.

Dubonnet Fizz

Serve on the rocks in a highball glass.

1 oz. vodka	Club soda to fill
3 oz. Dubonnet rouge	Lemon peel

Combine the vodka and Dubonnet in the serving glass one-third full of ice. Add the club soda to fill and garnish with the lemon twist.

Cosmopolitan

Serve in a cocktail glass.

$^3/_4$ oz. vodka	1 oz. cranberry juice
$^1/_2$ oz. triple sec	$^1/_2$ oz. lime juice

Shake with ice; serve up in a cocktail glass. Garnish with a lemon twist.

Russian Cocktail

Serve in a chilled cocktail glass.

1 oz. vodka	1 oz. white crème de cacao
1 oz. gin	

Combine the ingredients with cracked ice in a shaker. Shake vigorously, then strain into the serving glass.

Russian Bear

Serve in a chilled cocktail glass.

1 oz. vodka

1 oz. heavy cream

1 oz. dark crème de cacao

Combine all the ingredients with cracked ice in a shaker. Shake vigorously, then strain into the serving glass.

Sea Breeze with Cranberry Liqueur

Serve in a chilled highball glass.

1 1/2 oz. vodka

1 oz. cranberry liqueur

4 oz. grapefruit juice

Orange slice

Combine all ingredients except the orange slice in a shaker with cracked ice. Shake vigorously. Pour into the serving glass, and garnish with the orange slice.

Russian Rose

Serve straight-up in a chilled cocktail glass.

2 oz. vodka

Dash of orange bitters

1/2 oz. grenadine

Combine all ingredients in a shaker with cracked ice. Shake vigorously. Strain into the serving glass.

Vodka Grand Marnier

Serve in a chilled cocktail glass.

1 1/2 oz. vodka

1/2 oz. lime juice

1/2 oz. Grand Marnier

Orange slice

Combine all ingredients except the orange slice in a shaker with cracked ice. Shake vigorously and pour into the serving glass. Garnish with the orange slice.

More Produce from Kentucky and Tennessee

Bourbon Cooler

Serve in a chilled Collins glass.

3 oz. bourbon

Club soda to fill

1/2 oz. grenadine

Pineapple stick

1 tsp. sugar syrup

Orange slice

Few dashes peppermint schnapps

Maraschino cherry

Few dashes orange bitters (optional)

Combine all ingredients except the fruit and club soda in a shaker with cracked ice. Shake vigorously, then pour into the serving glass. Fill with club soda. Garnish with the fruit.

Champagne Julep

Serve in a Collins glass.

6 mint leaves

Mint sprig

1 tsp. sugar syrup

3 oz. bourbon

Brut champagne

In the bottom of the serving glass, *muddle* (stir and mash) six mint leaves in the sugar syrup. Fill glass two-thirds with cracked ice. Add bourbon. Stir vigorously. Add champagne to fill. Garnish with a mint sprig.

Bourbon Milk Punch

Serve in a chilled old-fashioned glass.

1 1/2 oz. bourbon

Dash vanilla extract

3 oz. half-and-half

Grated nutmeg

1 tsp. honey

Combine all ingredients except the nutmeg in a shaker with cracked ice. Shake vigorously, then pour into the serving glass and sprinkle with nutmeg.

Commodore Cocktail

Serve in a chilled cocktail glass.

1 1/2 oz. bourbon

1/2 oz. lemon juice

3/4 oz. white crème de cacao

Combine all ingredients in a shaker with cracked ice. Shake vigorously and strain into the serving glass.

333

Southside

Serve in a lowball glass.

6 mint leaves	2 oz. bourbon
1 tsp. sugar syrup	Plain water
Juice of 1/2 lemon	Mint sprig

In the serving glass, muddle the mint leaves together with the lemon juice and sugar syrup. Add bourbon and a splash of water. Add crushed ice to fill. Muddle again. Garnish with a mint sprig.

Waldorf Cocktail

Serve in a chilled cocktail glass.

1 1/2 oz. bourbon	1/2 oz. sweet vermouth
3/4 oz. Pernod	Dash of Angostura bitters

Combine all ingredients in a mixing glass with ice. Stir well and strain into the serving glass.

Whirlaway

Serve in a chilled old-fashioned glass.

2 oz. bourbon	Few dashes Angostura bitters
1 oz. curaçao	Club soda to fill

Combine all ingredients except soda in a shaker with ice. Shake vigorously and strain into the serving glass. Add club soda to fill.

Whiskey Cobbler

Serve in a goblet or large snifter.

1 tsp. sugar syrup	2 oz. blended whiskey
1 tsp. orgeat syrup or amaretto liqueur	Dash curaçao
Mint sprig	

Fill the goblet or snifter with crushed ice. Add the sugar and orgeat (or amaretto). Stir well. Add whiskey. Stir again, so that frost forms on the outside of the serving glass. Dash on curaçao and garnish with the mint sprig.

'Round the Blend—Again

Frisco Sour

Serve in a sour glass.

1 1/2 oz. blended whiskey	1 tsp. lime juice
3/4 oz. Benedictine	Dash grenadine
1 tsp. lemon juice	Orange slice

Combine all ingredients except orange slice in a shaker with ice. Shake vigorously, then strain into the serving glass. Garnish with the orange slice.

Horse's Neck

Serve in a Collins glass.

1 lemon

3 oz. blended whiskey

Ginger ale to fill

Peel the lemon in one continuous strip and place it in the serving glass. Fill the glass one-third with ice cubes. Add whiskey. Squeeze a few drops of lemon juice over the whiskey, then add ginger ale to fill.

Los Angeles Cocktail

Serve in chilled old-fashioned glasses.

4 oz. blended whiskey	Few dashes sweet vermouth
1 oz. lemon juice	1 egg
2 oz. sugar syrup	

Combine all ingredients in a shaker with cracked ice. Shake vigorously and pour into the serving glasses.

New Orleans Old-Fashioned

Serve in a chilled old-fashioned glass.

1/2 tsp. sugar syrup	2 oz. blended whiskey
Few dashes Angostura bitters	Few dashes Peychaud's bitters
2 tsp. water	Lemon twist

Combine the sugar syrup, Angostura bitters, and water in a mixing glass and stir until the sugar is dissolved. Add the whiskey and one-third glass of ice cubes. Stir well, then dash on the Peychaud's and garnish with the lemon twist.

New York Sour

Serve in a sour glass.

2 oz. blended whiskey	1/2 oz. dry red wine
1/2 oz. lemon juice	1/2 slice lemon
1 tsp. sugar syrup	

Combine all ingredients except the lemon slice and red wine in a shaker with cracked ice. Shake vigorously, then pour into the serving glass. Add the wine and garnish with the lemon slice.

Temptation Cocktail

Serve in a chilled cocktail glass.

1 1/2 oz. blended whiskey	Few dashes Pernod
1/2 oz. Dubonnet rouge	Orange twist
Few dashes curaçao	Lemon twist

Combine all ingredients except twists in a shaker with ice. Shake vigorously and strain into the serving glass. Garnish with the twists.

Scotland and Ireland Revisited

Affinity Cocktail

Serve in a chilled cocktail glass.

1 oz. scotch	Liberal dashes Angostura bitters
1 oz. dry sherry	Lemon twist
1 oz. port	Maraschino cherry

Combine all ingredients except fruit in a mixing glass with ice. Stir well, then strain into the serving glass and garnish with the twist and cherry.

Royal Rob Roy

Serve in a chilled cocktail glass.

1 1/2 oz. scotch	1/4 oz. sweet vermouth
1 1/2 oz. Drambuie	Maraschino cherry
1/4 oz. dry vermouth	

Combine all ingredients except the cherry in a shaker with cracked ice. Shake vigorously, then strain into the serving glass and garnish with the cherry.

Flying Scot

Serve in a chilled old-fashioned glass.

1 1/2 oz. scotch	Few dashes sugar syrup
1 oz. sweet vermouth	Few dashes Angostura bitters

Combine all ingredients in a shaker with cracked ice. Pour into the serving glass.

Scottish Horse's Neck

Serve on the rocks in a Collins glass.

Lemon peel curlicue	1/2 oz. sweet vermouth
3 oz. scotch	1/2 oz. dry vermouth

Arrange the long lemon peel curlicue so that it hangs off the rim of the serving glass. Fill with ice, then pour in the scotch and vermouths. Stir well.

Kinsale Cooler

Serve in a chilled Collins glass.

1 1/2 oz. Irish whiskey	Equal portions club soda and ginger ale to fill
1 oz. Irish Mist	
1 oz. lemon juice	Lemon twist

Combine all ingredients except the sodas and the twist in a shaker with cracked ice. Shake vigorously, then pour into the serving glass and add equal portions of club soda and ginger ale to fill. Garnish with the twist.

Scotch Julep

Serve in a chilled large (double) old-fashioned glass.

6 mint leaves	2 oz. scotch
Splash water	Mint sprig
1 oz. Drambuie	

Muddle (mash and stir) the mint leaves, Drambuie, and a splash of water in the bottom of the serving glass. Fill glass with *finely* crushed ice. Add the scotch, then muddle again to work the scotch and Drambuie through the ice. If you want a stronger drink, add as much as another ounce of scotch. Garnish with the mint sprig.

Scotch Mist

Serve in an old-fashioned glass filled with finely crushed ice.

2 oz. scotch

Lemon twist

Pour the whiskey into the serving glass filled with finely crushed ice. Garnish with the twist.

Scotch Sour

Serve in a chilled sour glass.

1½ oz. scotch	Orange slice
½ oz. lemon juice	Maraschino cherry
1 tsp. sugar syrup	

Combine all ingredients except fruit in a shaker with ice. Shake vigorously, then strain into the serving glass. Garnish with the orange slice and cherry.

Rum Round Two

Cocoa-Colada

Serve in a chilled Collins glass.

1½ oz. Myers's rum	1 oz. cream of coconut
1 oz. Kahlúa	Orange slice
2 oz. pineapple juice	

Combine all ingredients except the orange slice in a blender with a scoop of crushed ice. Blend until smooth, then pour into the serving glass and garnish with the orange slice.

Nutty Colada

Serve in a chilled Collins glass.

2 oz. amaretto	2 oz. pineapple juice
1 oz. gold rum	Pineapple slice
1½ oz. cream of coconut	

Combine all ingredients except the pineapple slice in a blender with a scoop of crushed ice. Blend until smooth, then pour into the serving glass and garnish with the pineapple slice.

Frozen Daiquiri

Serve in a chilled cocktail glass or in an American-style (saucer) champagne glass.

2 oz. light rum	1 tsp. sugar
½ oz. lime juice	

Combine all ingredients in a blender with at least 4 oz. of crushed ice. Blend at low speed until snowy, then pour into the serving glass.

Pineapple Daiquiri

Serve in a chilled cocktail glass or wine glass.

2 oz. light rum	3 oz. pineapple juice
½ oz. Cointreau	¼ oz. lime juice

Combine all ingredients in a blender with at least 3 oz. of cracked ice. Blend with ice on frappé. Pour into the serving glass.

Frozen Peach Daiquiri

Serve in a chilled cocktail glass or in an American-style (saucer) champagne glass.

1½ oz. light rum	1 tbsp. diced peaches (fresh, canned, or frozen)
½ oz. lime juice	1 tsp. lemon juice

Combine all ingredients in a blender with at least 4 oz. of crushed ice. Blend at low speed until snowy, then pour into the serving glass.

Rum Collins

Serve in a chilled Collins glass.

2 oz. light rum	½ lime
1 oz. sugar syrup	Club soda to fill

Combine the rum and sugar syrup in the serving glass. Stir. Squeeze in lime juice, then drop in peel as garnish. Add a few ice cubes and club soda to fill.

Rum Old-Fashioned

Serve in a chilled old-fashioned glass.

1 tsp. sugar syrup	3 oz. gold rum
Splash water	Lime twist
Liberal dashes Angostura bitters	Orange twist

Combine sugar syrup and water in the serving glass. Stir. Add bitters and rum. Stir, then add several ice cubes. Garnish with the twists.

Rum Screwdriver

Serve in a chilled Collins glass.

2 oz. light rum	Orange slice
5 oz. orange juice	

Combine rum and juice in a blender with cracked ice. Blend until smooth, then pour into the serving glass. Garnish with orange slice.

Rum Sour

Serve in a chilled sour glass.

2 oz. light or dark rum	1 tsp orange juice
Juice of $1/2$ lime	Orange slice
1 tsp. sugar syrup	Maraschino cherry

Combine all ingredients except fruit in a shaker with ice. Shake vigorously, then strain into the serving glass and garnish with the orange slice and cherry.

Scorpion

Serve in a chilled wine goblet.

2 oz. light rum	$1^1/2$ oz. lemon juice
1 oz. brandy	$1/2$ oz. orgeat syrup
2 oz. orange juice	Gardenia (if available)

Combine all ingredients except the gardenia in a blender with 3 oz. of shaved ice. Blend until smooth, then pour into the serving glass. Garnish with the gardenia.

Strawberry Colada

Serve in a chilled pilsner glass.

3 oz. gold rum	1 oz. strawberry liqueur or strawberry schnapps
4 oz. commercial Piña Colada mix	Whole strawberry
1 oz. strawberries (fresh or frozen)	

Combine all ingredients except liqueur or schnapps and whole strawberry in a blender with cracked ice. Blend until smooth, then pour into the serving glass, top with the liqueur or schnapps, and garnish with the whole strawberry.

Return to the Halls of Montezuma

Golden Margarita

Serve in a chilled lowball glass rimmed with salt.

2 oz. gold tequila	Coarse salt
1 oz. curaçao	Lime slice
$3/4$ oz. lime juice	

Combine all ingredients except salt and lime slice in a shaker with cracked ice. Shake vigorously, then pour into the serving glass. Garnish with the lime slice.

Tequila Collins

Serve on the rocks in a tall Collins glass.

$1^1/2$ oz. white tequila	Club soda to fill
1 oz. lemon juice	Maraschino cherry
Sugar syrup to taste	

Pour tequila, lemon juice, and sugar syrup over ice in the serving glass. Stir, then add club soda to fill. Garnish with the cherry.

Tequila Gimlet

Serve on the rocks in an old-fashioned glass.

1½ oz. white or gold tequila   Lime wedge

1 oz. Rose's lime juice

Combine the tequila and lime juice over ice in the serving glass. Stir, then garnish with the lime wedge.

Tequila Sour

Serve in a chilled cocktail glass.

1½ oz. tequila   1 tsp. confectioner's sugar

1 oz. lime or lemon juice

Combine all ingredients in a shaker with ice. Shake vigorously, then strain into the serving glass.

Tequila Manhattan

1½ oz. gold tequila   Lime slice

Dash or two sweet vermouth

Combine tequila and vermouth in a shaker with ice. Shake vigorously, then strain into the serving glass. Garnish with the lime slice.

Tequila Stinger

Serve in a chilled cocktail glass.

1½ oz. gold tequila

¾ oz. white crème de menthe

Combine all ingredients in a shaker with cracked ice. Shake vigorously, then pour into the serving glass.

Tequila Maria

Serve in a chilled large (double) old-fashioned glass.

1½ oz. white or gold   Liberal dashes Tabasco
tequila   sauce

4 oz. tomato juice   Pinch white pepper

Juice of ¼ lime   Pinch celery salt

½ tsp. fresh grated horseradish Pinch oregano

Liberal dashes Worcestershire
sauce

Combine all ingredients in a mixing glass half filled with cracked ice. Stir, then pour into the serving glass.

Another Snifter

Between the Sheets

Serve in a chilled cocktail glass.

1½ oz. cognac   ¾ oz. curaçao (may substitute triple sec)

1 oz. light rum   ½ oz. lemon juice

Combine all ingredients in a shaker with ice. Shake vigorously, then strain into the serving glass.

Bombay

Serve in a chilled old-fashioned glass.

1 oz. brandy   ½ tsp. curaçao

1 oz. dry vermouth   Dash Pernod

½ oz. sweet vermouth   Orange slice

Combine all ingredients except orange slice in a shaker with cracked ice. Shake vigorously, then pour into the serving glass. Garnish with the orange slice.

Brandy Fizz

Serve in a chilled highball glass.

3 oz. brandy	1/2 oz. sugar syrup
1 1/2 oz. lemon juice	Club soda to fill

Combine all ingredients except soda in a shaker with cracked ice. Shake vigorously, then pour into the serving glass. Add club soda to fill. Additional ice cubes are optional. Omit the club soda, and you have a Brandy Fix.

Brandy Julep

Serve in a chilled large (double) old-fashioned glass.

6 mint leaves	Brandy to fill
1 tsp. honey	Mint sprig
Splash water	Powdered sugar

Combine the mint leaves, honey, and a splash of water in the serving glass. Muddle (mash and stir) until the leaves are well bruised. Fill serving glass with shaved ice. Add brandy to fill. Stir well so that glass frosts. Add additional brandy and ice as necessary to fill. *Glass should be full and thoroughly frosted.* Garnish with sprigs, then dust with powdered sugar.

Brandy Manhattan

Serve in a chilled cocktail glass.

2 oz. brandy	Dash Angostura bitters
1/2 oz. sweet or dry vermouth	Maraschino cherry

Combine all ingredients except cherry in a mixing glass one-third full of ice. Stir well, then strain into the serving glass. Garnish with the cherry.

Brandy Milk Punch

Serve in a chilled large (double) old-fashioned glass.

2 oz. brandy	1 tsp. sugar syrup
8 oz. milk	Pinch ground nutmeg

Combine all ingredients except nutmeg in a shaker with cracked ice. Shake vigorously, then pour into the serving glass. Sprinkle with nutmeg.

Brandy Old-Fashioned

Serve in a chilled old-fashioned glass.

1 sugar cube	3 oz. brandy
Liberal dashes Angostura bitters	Lemon twist
Splash water	

Put sugar cube in the serving glass, dash on bitters, and add a splash of water. Muddle (mash and stir) until the sugar cube is dissolved. Half fill glass with ice cubes and add brandy. Garnish with twist.

Index

345

S

X - Y - Z